Mastering JavaScript Single Page Application Development

An in-depth guide to exploring the design, architecture, and techniques behind building sophisticated, scalable, and maintainable single-page applications in JavaScript

Philip Klauzinski
John Moore

BIRMINGHAM - MUMBAI

Mastering JavaScript Single Page Application Development

First published: October 2016

Production reference: 1241016

Published by Packt Publishing Ltd.
Livery Place
35 Livery Street
Birmingham
B3 2PB, UK.

ISBN 978-1-78588-164-0

www.packtpub.com

Credits

Authors

Philip Klauzinski
John Moore

Copy Editor

Safis Editing

Reviewers

Ciro Artigot

Project Coordinator

Ritika Manoj

Commissioning Editor

Wilson D'souza

Proofreader

Safis Editing

Acquisition Editor

Reshma Raman

Indexer

Rekha Nair

Content Development Editor

Divij Kotian

Graphics

Jason Monteiro

Technical Editor

Sachit Bedi

Production Coordinator

Aparna Bhagat

About the Authors

Philip Klauzinski is a senior frontend developer specializing in JavaScript Single Page Application (SPA) development. He has over 20 years of experience in web design and web development and is a leading expert in web application development, client-side JavaScript, and Search Engine Optimization (SEO). Philip has worked as a frontend developer across multiple industries, including consumer e-commerce, business-to-business e-commerce, big data, Web hosting, direct marketing, domain name services (DNS), and manufacturing.

> *I would like to thank my Mom and Dad for always stressing the importance of education in my life, not just institutional education, but more importantly, the pursuance of self-education. My own interest in technology and software from a young age has driven my subsequent, self-taught approach to my career. As a result, I love what I do for a living, and I have been able to shape my professional life around the things in which I am truly interested. I am inherently driven to learn more every day, and I believe that is what has led to my success. Thank you, Mom and Dad!*

John Moore has been working in web development for 20 years. He is an industry expert in JavaScript and HTML5. He has developed award-winning web applications and worked and consulted for Digital Equipment Corporation, Ernst & Young, Wachovia Bank, and Fidelity Investments. Having focused his early career on frontend web development, he helped usher in responsive web design and Single Page Applications in his roles in development and architecture. Most recently, he led Full Stack development in JavaScript, serving as CTO of a Maine-based startup company.

> *I would like to thank my wife, Dr. Myra Salapare, and daughters, Mila Moore and Sophia Moore, for all of their support. I would also like to thank Andrea Shiflet, Erin Benner, and Lauren Grousd for their tremendous help.*

About the Reviewer

Ciro Artigot is currently working as an IT manager at ECODES, an Spanish foundation that works for the welfare of all people within the limits of our planet.

He has developed websites for over 15 years. He is a Full Stack developer and CMS expert and is addicted to Joomla, He has worked for 10 years in open source GNU projects, mainly in LAMP .

For the last few years, he has been investigating and working with SPA in MEAN environments.

I would like to thank Pampa, Diego,and Hugo, for giving me the time to review this book, and my parents and brothers, for making it possible for me to devote myself to what I like best—develop

www.PacktPub.com

For support files and downloads related to your book, please visit www.PacktPub.com.

Did you know that Packt offers eBook versions of every book published, with PDF and ePub files available? You can upgrade to the eBook version at www.PacktPub.com and as a print book customer, you are entitled to a discount on the eBook copy. Get in touch with us at service@packtpub.com for more details.

At www.PacktPub.com, you can also read a collection of free technical articles, sign up for a range of free newsletters and receive exclusive discounts and offers on Packt books and eBooks.

https://www.packtpub.com/mapt

Get the most in-demand software skills with Mapt. Mapt gives you full access to all Packt books and video courses, as well as industry-leading tools to help you plan your personal development and advance your career.

Why subscribe?

- Fully searchable across every book published by Packt
- Copy and paste, print, and bookmark content
- On demand and accessible via a web browser

Table of Contents

Preface

Created in 1995 by Brendan Eich of Netscape, JavaScript has gone from being a toy scripting language used only in browsers to being one of the most popular languages in the world for full-stack development. With the introduction of Node.js, built on top of Chrome's V8 JavaScript Engine, developers are now able to build powerful and performant applications using JavaScript. With the addition of MongoDB, a modern NoSQL database, applications can utilize JavaScript at every tier.

Many popular web applications are implemented, partially or in whole, as single-page applications, or SPAs. With SPAs, users load a single web page, and that page is updated dynamically in response to user interaction or incoming server data. The advantage is an application experience that is smoother, replicates native application interaction, and may require less network traffic and server load.

The MEAN stack is a set of JavaScript tools representing a full stack, from database to runtime environment, application framework, and frontend. This book provides a thorough background in building SPAs using the MEAN stack and other tools in the JavaScript ecosystem. It covers the basics of SPA architecture and JavaScript tools. The book then expands to more advanced topics, such as building, securing, and deploying an SPA built with the MEAN stack.

What this book covers

Chapter 1, *Getting Organized NPM*, Bower, and Grunt, introduces JavaScript frontend package-management, build, and task-running tools. These tools form the foundation for you to set up an ideal development environment.

Chapter 2, *Model-View-Whatever*, goes beyond the original MVC design pattern and explores its translation into frontend frameworks and its evolution into Model-View-*, or Model-View-Whatever (MVW), in which the Controller layer is more open ended and often abstracted into other layers more suited to an SPA environment.

Chapter 3, *SPA Essentials - Creating the Ideal Application Environment*, introduces you to the common components/layers of an SPA, the best practices and variations around these components, and how to put them together and lay the groundwork for a modern SPA.

Chapter 4, *REST is Best - Interacting with the Server Side of Your Application*, goes into further detail about the server side of SPA architecture—in particular, with regard to the REST (representational state transfer) architectural pattern. You'll become familiar with different methods to interact with a REST API using JavaScript and AJAX, with practical examples.

Chapter 5, *Its All About the View*, focuses on the concept of views in the SPA architecture and how views can be initialized in a single-page container. It discusses JavaScript templates and provides examples from different libraries, going deeper into how AngularJS views are implemented.

Chapter 6, *Data Binding, and Why You Should Embrace It*, teaches you about data binding, describes one-way versus two-way data binding, and discusses the practicality of data binding in an SPA and why you should use it. You will also cover the continual evolution of the ECMAScript/JavaScript standard and how it now supports native data binding in some clients.

Chapter 7, *Leveraging the MEAN Stack*, introduces you to the MEAN stack (MongoDB, Express, AngularJS, and Node.js) and how they work together. You will install and configure MongoDB and Node.js and explore working with each on the command line. You'll create a database for a new SPA and learn about AngularJS and Express, the two other pieces of the stack.

Chapter 8, *Manage Data Using MongoDB*, teaches you how to create and manage databases in MongoDB. Using the command line, you will execute CRUD (create, read, update, and delete) functions.

Chapter 9, *Handling Web Requests with Express*, familiarizes you with the Express routing middleware and handling requests from and responses to the browser. After configuring the Express router, you'll create a number of routes, which return dynamically generated data to the web browser when requested, organize your routes logically, and handle POST requests from forms.

Chapter 10, *Displaying Views*, explores combining dynamic view rendering in Express along with AngularJS. You will configure the Express application to use EJS (Embedded JavaScript) templates and use Bootstrap for basic styling.

Chapter 11, *Adding Security and Authentication*, teaches you how to secure the Express-based SPA by preventing common exploits such as cross-site request forgery (CSRF). You will install passport-authentication middleware for Node.js and configure it for local authentication and set up session management.

Chapter 12, *Connecting the App to Social Media*, extends the SPA by connecting it to multiple social media platforms. You will set up passport authentication using Facebook and Twitter strategies and share data from the SPA.

Chapter 13, *Testing with Mocha, Karma, and More*, teaches you testing, both on the server side and in the view.

Chapter 14, *Deploying and Scaling the SPA*, walks you through setting up a production database on MongoLab and deploying your SPA to Heroku. Finally, you will explore scaling your SPA in the cloud.

What you need for this book

The book requires very few pieces of software besides your web browser and your operating system's command line or terminal. You will need an editor for writing code. Any text editor will do, from Notepad to an IDE such as Jetbrains WebStorm.

Who this book is for

This book is ideal for JavaScript developers who want to build complex SPAs in JavaScript. Some basic understanding of SPA concepts will be helpful but are not essential.

Conventions

In this book, you will find a number of text styles that distinguish between different kinds of information. Here are some examples of these styles and an explanation of their meaning.

Code words in text, database table names, folder names, filenames, file extensions, path names, dummy URLs, user input, and Twitter handles are shown as follows: "We can include other contexts through the use of the include directive."

A block of code is set as follows:

```
module.exports = function(grunt) {

    grunt.initConfig({
        pkg: grunt.file.readJSON('package.json'),
```

When we wish to draw your attention to a particular part of a code block, the relevant lines or items are set in bold:

```
grunt.initConfig({
    pkg: grunt.file.readJSON('package.json'),
    clean: ['dist/**'],
    copy: {
        main: {
        files: [
```

Any command-line input or output is written as follows:

```
$ npm install -g grunt-cli
grunt-cli@0.1.13 /usr/local/lib/node_modules/grunt-cli
├── resolve@0.3.1
├── nopt@1.0.10 (abbrev@1.0.7)
└── findup-sync@0.1.3 (lodash@2.4.2, glob@3.2.11)
```

New terms and important words are shown in bold. Words that you see on the screen, for example, in menus or dialog boxes, appear in the text like this: "Clicking the **Next** button moves you to the next screen."

Warnings or important notes appear in a box like this.

Tips and tricks appear like this.

Reader feedback

Feedback from our readers is always welcome. Let us know what you think about this book-what you liked or disliked. Reader feedback is important for us as it helps us develop titles that you will really get the most out of. To send us general feedback, simply e-mail feedback@packtpub.com, and mention the book's title in the subject of your message. If there is a topic that you have expertise in and you are interested in either writing or contributing to a book, see our author guide at www.packtpub.com/authors.

Customer support

Now that you are the proud owner of a Packt book, we have a number of things to help you to get the most from your purchase.

Downloading the example code

You can download the example code files for this book from your account at `http://www.packtpub.com`. If you purchased this book elsewhere, you can visit `http://www.packtpub.com/support` and register to have the files e-mailed directly to you.

You can download the code files by following these steps:

1. Log in or register to our website using your e-mail address and password.
2. Hover the mouse pointer on the **SUPPORT** tab at the top.
3. Click on **Code Downloads & Errata**.
4. Enter the name of the book in the **Search** box.
5. Select the book for which you're looking to download the code files.
6. Choose from the drop-down menu where you purchased this book from.
7. Click on **Code Download**.

Once the file is downloaded, please make sure that you unzip or extract the folder using the latest version of:

- WinRAR / 7-Zip for Windows
- Zipeg / iZip / UnRarX for Mac
- 7-Zip / PeaZip for Linux

The code bundle for the book is also hosted on GitHub at `https://github.com/PacktPublishing/Mastering-JavaScript-Single-Page-Application-Development`. We also have other code bundles from our rich catalog of books and videos available at `https://github.com/PacktPublishing/`. Check them out!

Errata

Although we have taken every care to ensure the accuracy of our content, mistakes do happen. If you find a mistake in one of our books-maybe a mistake in the text or the code-we would be grateful if you could report this to us. By doing so, you can save other readers from frustration and help us improve subsequent versions of this book. If you find any errata, please report them by visiting http://www.packtpub.com/submit-errata, selecting your book, clicking on the **Errata Submission Form** link, and entering the details of your errata. Once your errata are verified, your submission will be accepted and the errata will be uploaded to our website or added to any list of existing errata under the Errata section of that title.

To view the previously submitted errata, go to https://www.packtpub.com/books/content/support and enter the name of the book in the search field. The required information will appear under the **Errata** section.

Piracy

Piracy of copyrighted material on the Internet is an ongoing problem across all media. At Packt, we take the protection of our copyright and licenses very seriously. If you come across any illegal copies of our works in any form on the Internet, please provide us with the location address or website name immediately so that we can pursue a remedy.

Please contact us at copyright@packtpub.com with a link to the suspected pirated material.

We appreciate your help in protecting our authors and our ability to bring you valuable content.

Questions

If you have a problem with any aspect of this book, you can contact us at questions@packtpub.com, and we will do our best to address the problem.

1
Getting Organized with NPM, Bower, and Grunt

JavaScript was the bane of the web development industry during the early days of the browser-rendered Internet. It now powers hugely impactful libraries such as jQuery, and JavaScript-rendered (as opposed to server-side-rendered) content is even indexed by many search engines. What was once largely considered an annoying language used primarily to generate pop-up windows and alert boxes, has now become arguably the most popular programming language in the world.

Not only is JavaScript now more prevalent than ever in frontend architecture, but it has become a server-side language as well, thanks to the *Node.js* runtime. We have also seen the proliferation of document-oriented databases, such as MongoDB, which store and return JSON data. With JavaScript present throughout the development stack, the door is now open for JavaScript developers to become full-stack developers without the need to learn a traditional server-side language. Given the right tools and know-how, any JavaScript developer can create *single page applications* comprised entirely of the language they know best, and they can do so using an architecture like *MEAN* (MongoDB, Express, AngularJS, and Node.js).

Organization is key to the development of any complex **Single Page Application** (**SPA**). If you don't get organized from the beginning, you are sure to introduce an inordinate number of regressions to your app. The Node.js ecosystem will help you to do this with a full suite of indispensable and open-source tools, three of which we will discuss here.

In this chapter, you will learn about:

- **Node Package Manager** (**NPM**)
- Bower frontend package manager
- **Grunt** JavaScript task runner

- How these three tools can be used together to create an organized development environment that is ideal for creating an SPA and is essential to the MEAN stack architecture.

What is Node Package Manager?

Within any full-stack JavaScript environment, **Node Package Manager** will be your *go-to* tool for setting up your development environment and for managing server-side libraries. NPM can be used within both global and isolated environment contexts. We will first explore the use of NPM globally.

Installing Node.js and NPM

NPM is a component of *Node.js*, so before you can use it you must first install Node.js. You can find installers for both Mac and Windows at nodejs.org. Once you have Node.js installed, using NPM is incredibly easy and is done from the **Command Line Interface** (**CLI**). Start by ensuring you have the latest version of NPM installed, as it is updated more often than Node.js itself:

```
$ npm install -g npm
```

When using NPM, the -g option will apply your changes to your global environment. In this case, you want your version of NPM to apply globally. As stated previously, NPM can be used to manage packages both globally and within isolated environments. In the following, we want essential development tools to be applied globally so that you can use them in multiple projects on the same system.

With Mac and some Unix-based systems, you may have to run the npm command as the superuser (prefix the command with sudo) in order to install packages globally, depending on how NPM was installed. If you run into this issue and wish to remove the need to prefix npm with sudo, see docs.npmjs.com/getting-started/fixing-npm-permissions.

Configuring your package.json file

For any project you develop, you will keep a local `package.json` file to manage your Node.js dependencies. This file should be stored at the root of your project directory and it will only pertain to that isolated environment. This allows you to have multiple Node.js projects with different dependency chains on the same system.

When beginning a new project, you can automate the creation of the `package.json` file from the command line:

```
$ npm init
```

Running `npm init` will take you through a series of JSON property names to define through command line prompts, including your app's `name`, `version` number, `description`, and more. The `name` and `version` properties are required, and your Node.js package will not install without them defined. Several of the properties will have a default value given within parentheses in the prompt so that you may simply hit *Enter* to continue. Other properties will simply allow you to hit *Enter* with a blank entry and will not be saved to the `package.json` file, or will be saved with a blank value:

```
name: (my-app)
version: (1.0.0)
description:
entry point: (index.js)
```

The `entry point` prompt will be defined as the `main` property in `package.json` and is not necessary unless you are developing a Node.js application. In our case, we can forgo this field. The `npm init` command may in fact force you to save the `main` property, so you will have to edit `package.json` afterward to remove it; however, that field will have no effect on your web app.

You may also choose to create the `package.json` file manually using a text editor, if you know the appropriate structure to employ. Whichever method you choose, your initial version of the `package.json` file should look similar to the following example:

```
{
    "name": "my-app",
    "version": "1.0.0",
    "author": "Philip Klauzinski",
    "license": "MIT",
    "description": "My JavaScript single page application."
}
```

If you want your project to be private and want to ensure that it does not accidently get published to the NPM registry, you may want to add the `private` property to your `package.json` file, and set it to `true`. Additionally, you may remove some properties that only apply to a registered package:

```
{
    "name": "my-app",
    "author": "Philip Klauzinski",
    "description": "My JavaScript single page application.",
    "private": true
}
```

Once you have your `package.json` file set up the way you like it, you can begin installing Node.js packages locally for your app. This is where the importance of dependencies begins to surface.

NPM dependencies

There are three types of dependencies that can be defined for any Node.js project in your `package.json` file: dependencies, devDependencies, and peerDependencies. For the purpose of building a web-based SPA, you will only need to use the devDependencies declaration.

devDependencies are those which are required for developing your application, but not required for its production environment or for simply running it. If other developers want to contribute to your Node.js application, they will need to run `npm install` from the command line to set up the proper development environment. For information on the other types of dependencies, see docs.npmjs.com.

When adding devDependencies to your `package.json file`, the command line again comes to the rescue. Let's use the installation of Browserify as an example:

```
$ npm install browserify --save-dev
```

This will install Browserify locally and save it along with its version range to the devDependencies object in your `package.json` file. Once installed, your `package.json` file should look similar to the following example:

```
{
    "name": "my-app",
    "version": "1.0.0",
    "author": "Philip Klauzinski",
    "license": "MIT",
    "devDependencies": {
```

```
    "browserify": "^12.0.1"
  }
}
```

The `devDependencies` object will store each package as a key-value pair in which the key is the *package name* and the value is the *version number* or *version range*. Node.js uses semantic versioning, where the three digits of the version number represent `MAJOR.MINOR.PATCH`. For more information on semantic version formatting, see `semver.org`.

Updating your development dependencies

You will notice that the version number of the installed package is preceded by a **caret** (^) symbol by default. This means that package updates will only allow *patch* and *minor* updates for versions above 1.0.0. This is meant to prevent major version changes from breaking your dependency chain when updating your packages to the latest versions.

To update your `devDependencies` and save the new version numbers, you can enter the following from the command line:

```
$ npm update --save-dev
```

Alternatively, you can use the `-D` option as a shortcut for `--save-dev`:

```
$ npm update -D
```

To update all globally installed NPM packages to their latest versions, run `npm update` with the `-g` option:

```
$ npm update -g
```

For more information on semantic versioning within NPM, see `docs.npmjs.com/misc/semver`.

Now that you have NPM set up and you know how to install your development dependencies, you can move on to installing Bower.

Bower

Bower is a package manager for frontend web assets and libraries. You will use it to maintain your frontend stack and control version chains for libraries such as jQuery, AngularJS, and any other components necessary to your app's web interface.

Installing Bower

Bower is also a Node.js package, so you will install it using NPM, much like you did with the Browserify example installation in the previous section, but this time you will be installing the package globally. This will allow you to run bower from the command line anywhere on your system without having to install it locally for each project:

```
$ npm install -g bower
```

You can alternatively install Bower locally as a development dependency so that you may maintain different versions of it for different projects on the same system, but this is generally not necessary:

```
$ npm install bower --save-dev
```

Next, check that Bower is properly installed by querying the version from the command line:

```
$ bower -v
```

Bower also requires a *Git* version control system, or *VCS*, to be installed on your system in order to work with packages. This is because Bower communicates directly with GitHub for package management data. If you do not have Git installed on your system, you can find instructions for Linux, Mac, and Windows at git-scm.com.

Configuring your bower.json file

The process of setting up your bower.json file is comparable to that of the package.json file for NPM. It uses the same JSON format, has both dependencies and devDependencies, and can also be automatically created:

```
$ bower init
```

Once you type bower init from the command line, you will be prompted to define several properties with some defaults given within parentheses:

```
? name: my-app
? version: 0.0.0
? description: My app description.
? main file: index.html
? what types of modules does this package expose? (Press <space> to? what
types of modules does this package expose? globals
? keywords: my, app, keywords
? authors: Philip Klauzinski
```

```
? license: MIT
? homepage: http://gui.ninja
? set currently installed components as dependencies? No
? add commonly ignored files to ignore list? Yes
? would you like to mark this package as private which prevents it from
being accidentally published to the registry? Yes
```

These questions may vary, depending on the version of Bower you install.

Most properties in the bower.json file are not necessary unless you are publishing your project to the Bower registry, indicated in the final prompt. You will most likely want to mark your package as private, unless you plan to register it and allow others to download it as a Bower package.

Once you have created the bower.json file, you can open it in a text editor and change or remove any properties you wish. It should look something like the following example:

```json
{
  "name": "my-app",
  "version": "0.0.0",
  "authors": [
    "Philip Klauzinski"
  ],
  "description": "My app description.",
  "main": "index.html",
  "moduleType": [
    "globals"
  ],
  "keywords": [
    "my",
    "app",
    "keywords"
  ],
  "license": "MIT",
  "homepage": "http://gui.ninja",
  "ignore": [
    "**/.*",
    "node_modules",
    "bower_components",
    "test",
    "tests"
  ],
  "private": true
}
```

If you wish to keep your project private, you can reduce your `bower.json` file to two properties before continuing:

```
{
  "name": "my-app",
  "private": true
}
```

Once you have the initial version of your `bower.json` file set up the way you like it, you can begin installing components for your app.

Bower components location and the .bowerrc file

Bower will install components into a directory named `bower_components` by default. This directory will be located directly under the root of your project. If you wish to install your Bower components under a different directory name, you must create a local system file named `.bowerrc` and define the custom directory name there:

```
{
  "directory": "path/to/my_components"
}
```

An object with only a single `directory` property name is all that is necessary to define a custom location for your Bower components. There are many other properties that can be configured within a `.bowerrc` file. For more information on configuring Bower, see bower.io/docs/config/.

Bower dependencies

Bower also allows you to define both the `dependencies` and `devDependencies` objects like NPM. The distinction with Bower, however, is that the `dependencies` object will contain the components necessary for running your app, while the `devDependencies` object is reserved for components that you might use for testing, transpiling, or anything that does not need to be included in your frontend stack.

Bower packages are managed using the `bower` command from the CLI. This is a user command, so it does not require super user (sudo) permissions. Let's begin by installing jQuery as a frontend dependency for your app:

```
$ bower install jquery --save
```

The `--save` option on the command line will save the package and version number to the `dependencies` object in `bower.json`. Alternatively, you can use the `-S` option as a shortcut for `--save`:

```
$ bower install jquery -S
```

Next, let's install the Mocha JavaScript testing framework as a development dependency:

```
$ bower install mocha --save-dev
```

In this case, we will use `--save-dev` on the command line to save the package to the `devDependencies` object instead. Your `bower.json` file should now look similar to the following example:

```
{
  "name": "my-app",
  "private": true,
  "dependencies": {
    "jquery": "~2.1.4"
  },
  "devDependencies": {
    "mocha": "~2.3.4"
  }
}
```

Alternatively, you can use the `-D` option as a shortcut for `--save-dev`:

```
$ bower install mocha -D
```

You will notice that the package version numbers are preceded by the **tilde** (~) symbol by default, in contrast to the caret (^) symbol as is the case with NPM. The tilde serves as a more stringent guard against package version updates. With a `MAJOR.MINOR.PATCH` version number, running `bower update` will only update to the latest patch version. If a version number is composed of only the major and minor versions, `bower update` will update the package to the latest minor version.

Searching the Bower registry

All registered Bower components are indexed and searchable through the command line. If you don't know the exact package name of a component you wish to install, you can perform a search to retrieve a list of matching names.

Most components will have a list of keywords in their `bower.json` file so that you can more easily find the package without knowing the exact name. For example, you may want to install PhantomJS for headless browser testing:

```
$ bower search phantomjs
```

The list returned will include any package with `phantomjs` in the package name or within its keywords list:

```
phantom git://github.com/ariya/phantomjs.git
dt-phantomjs git://github.com/keesey/dt-phantomjs
qunit-phantomjs-runner git://github.com/jonkemp/...
parse-cookie-phantomjs git://github.com/sindresorhus/...
highcharts-phantomjs git://github.com/pesla/highcharts-
phantomjs.git
mocha-phantomjs git://github.com/metaskills/mocha-phantomjs.git
purescript-phantomjs git://github.com/cxfreeio/purescript-
phantomjs.git
```

You can see from the returned list that the correct package name for PhantomJS is in fact `phantom` and not `phantomjs`. You can then proceed to install the package now that you know the correct name:

```
$ bower install phantom --save-dev
```

Now you have Bower installed and know how to manage your frontend web components and development tools, but how do you integrate them into your SPA? This is where Grunt comes in.

Grunt

Grunt is a *JavaScript task runner* for Node.js, and if you haven't used it before, it is perhaps the best tool you never knew you needed. You will find it useful for a myriad of tasks including CSS and JavaScript linting and minification, JavaScript template pre-compilation, LESS and SASS pre-processing, and so much more. There are indeed alternatives to Grunt, but none with as large an ecosystem of plugins (at the time of writing).

There are two components to Grunt: the *Grunt CLI*, and the *Grunt task runner* itself. The Grunt CLI allows you to run the Grunt task runner command from the command line within a directory that has Grunt installed. This allows you to have a different version of Grunt running for each project on your machine, making each app more maintainable. For more information, see `gruntjs.com`.

Installing the Grunt CLI

You will want to install the Grunt CLI globally, just as you did with Bower:

```
$ npm install -g grunt-cli
```

Remember that the Grunt CLI is not the Grunt task runner. It simply makes the grunt command available to you from the command line. This distinction is important, because while the grunt command will be globally available from the command line, it will always look for a local installation in the directory from which you run it.

Installing the Grunt task runner

You will install the Grunt task runner locally from the root of your app where your package.json file is located. Grunt is installed as a Node.js package:

```
$ npm install grunt --save-dev
```

Once you have Grunt installed locally, your package.json file should look like the following example:

```
{
  "name": "my-app",
  "version": "1.0.0",
  "author": "Philip Klauzinski",
  "license": "MIT",
  "devDependencies": {
    "grunt": "^0.4.5"
  }
}
```

You will notice a devDependencies object has been added to your package.json file, if it was not already there from a previous install.

Now that you have Grunt installed locally, let's begin installing some plugins to work with.

Installing Grunt plugins

All Grunt task plugins are Node.js packages, so they will be installed using NPM as well. There are thousands of Grunt plugins written by a multitude of authors, as Grunt is an open-source project. Every Node.js package for Grunt is prefixed with grunt in the name. The Grunt team, however, does maintain many plugins themselves. The officially maintained Grunt plugins are all prefixed with grunt-contrib, so this is how you can differentiate them if you wish to stick with only officially maintained Grunt plugins. To view and search all registered Grunt plugins, see gruntjs.com/plugins.

Since you will be writing a JavaScript SPA, let's begin by installing a JavaScript *linting* plugin for Grunt. Linting refers to running a program against your code to analyze it for errors and, in some cases, proper formatting. It is always a good idea to have a linting utility running to test your JavaScript code for valid syntax and formatting:

```
$ npm install grunt-contrib-jshint --save-dev
```

This will install the officially maintained Grunt plugin for JSHint and add it to the devDependencies object in your package.json file as shown in the following example:

```
{
    "name": "my-app",
    "version": "1.0.0",
    "author": "Philip Klauzinski",
    "license": "MIT",
    "devDependencies": {
        "grunt": "^0.4.5",
        "grunt-contrib-jshint": "^0.11.3"
    }
}
```

JSHint is a popular tool for detecting errors and potential problems in your JavaScript code. The Grunt plugin itself will allow you to automate that process so that you can easily check your code as you develop.

Another invaluable Grunt plugin is grunt-contrib-watch. This plugin allows you to run a task which will automatically run other Grunt tasks when you add, delete, or edit files in your project that match a predefined set of rules.

```
$ npm install grunt-contrib-watch --save-dev
```

After installing the grunt-contrib-watch plugin, the devDependencies object in your package.json file should look like this:

```
"devDependencies": {
    "grunt": "^0.4.5",
    "grunt-contrib-jshint": "^0.11.3",
    "grunt-contrib-watch": "^0.6.1"
}
```

Now that you have a couple of Grunt plugins installed, let's begin writing some tasks for them. In order to do that, you will first need to create a local configuration file for Grunt.

Configuring Grunt

Unlike NPM and Bower, Grunt does not provide an init command for initializing its configuration file. Instead, *scaffolding* tools can be used for this. Project scaffolding tools are designed to set up some basic directory structure and configuration files for a development project. Grunt maintains an official scaffolding tool called grunt-init, which is referenced on their website. The grunt-init tool must be installed separately from the grunt-cli global package and the local grunt package for any particular project. It is most useful if installed globally, so it can be used with any project.

```
$ npm install -g grunt-init
```

We will not go into further detail on grunt-init here, but if you would like to learn more, you can visit gruntjs.com/project-scaffolding.

The best way to learn about configuring Grunt is to write its configuration file by hand. The configuration for Grunt is maintained in a file called Gruntfile.js, referred to as a Gruntfile, located in the root directory of your project, along with package.json and bower.json. If you are not familiar with Node.js and its concept of modules and exports, the syntax for a Gruntfile may be a bit confusing at first. Since Node.js files run on the server and not in a browser, they do not interact in the same way that files loaded in a browser do, with respect to browser globals.

Understanding Node.js modules

In Node.js, a module is a JavaScript object defined within a file. The module name is the name of the file. For instance, if you want to declare a module named foo, you will create a file named foo.js. In order for the foo module to be accessible to another module, it must be exported. In its most basic form, a module looks something like the following example:

```
module.exports = {
    // Object properties here
};
```

Every module has a local exports variable that allows you to make the module accessible to others. In other words, the object module within a file refers to the current module itself, and the exports property of module makes that module available to any other module (or file).

Another way of defining a module is by exporting a function, which is of course a JavaScript object itself:

```
module.exports = function() {
    // Code for the module here
};
```

When you call for a Node.js module from within a file, it will first look for a core module, all of which are compiled into Node.js itself. If the name does not match a core module, it will then look for a directory named node_modules beginning from the current or root directory of your project. This directory is where all of your local NPM packages, including Grunt plugins, will be stored. If you performed the installs of grunt-contrib-jshint and grunt-contrib-watch from earlier, you will see that this directory now exists within your project.

Now that you understand a bit more about how Node.js modules work, let's create a Gruntfile.

Creating a Gruntfile

A Gruntfile uses the function form of module.exports as shown previously. This is referred to as a *wrapper function*. The grunt module itself is passed to the wrapper function. The grunt module will be available to your Gruntfile because you installed the grunt NPM package locally:

```
module.exports = function(grunt) {
    // Grunt code here
};
```

This example shows what your initial Gruntfile should look like. Now let's flesh it out some more. In order to configure Grunt and run tasks with it, you will need to access the grunt module that is passed in to your Gruntfile.

```
module.exports = function(grunt) {
    'use strict';
    grunt.initConfig({
        pkg: grunt.file.readJSON('package.json')
    });
};
```

This basic format is what you will be working with the rest of the way. You can see here that the grunt.initConfig method is called and passed a single configuration object as a parameter. This configuration object is where all of your Grunt task code will go. The pkg property shown in this example, which is assigned the value of grunt.file.readJSON('package.json'), allows you to pass in information about your project directly from your package.json file. The use of this property will be shown in later examples.

Defining Grunt task configuration

Most Grunt tasks expect their configuration to be defined within a property of the same name as the task, which is the suffix of the package name. For example, jshint is the Grunt task name for the grunt-contrib-jshint package we previously installed:

```
module.exports = function(grunt) {
    'use strict';
    grunt.initConfig({
        pkg: grunt.file.readJSON('package.json'),
        jshint: {
            options: {
                curly: true,
                eqeqeq: true,
                eqnull: true,
                browser: true,
                newcap: false,
                es3: true,
                forin: true,
                indent: 4,
                unused: 'vars',
                strict: true,
                trailing: true,
                quotmark: 'single',
                latedef: true,
                globals: {
                    jQuery: true
                }
            },
            files: {
                src: ['Gruntfile.js', 'js/src/*.js']
            }
        }
    });
};
```

Here you can see that the `jshint` property of the configuration object is defined and is assigned its own properties which apply to the `jshint` Grunt task itself. The `options` property defined within `jshint` holds the settings you wish to validate against when linting your JavaScript files. The `files` property defines a list of the files you wish to validate. For more information on the supported options for JSHint and what they mean, see jshint.com/docs/.

Let's now add an additional configuration for the `grunt-contrib-watch` plugin `watch` task below the `jshint` task configuration:

```
watch: {
    jshint: {
        files: ['js/src/*.js'],
        tasks: ['jshint']
    }
}
```

Here we add an additional namespace of `jshint` underneath the `watch` task, which allows for other *targets* to be defined within the same configuration property and run separately if needs be. This is what is known as a *multitask*. Targets within a multitask can be named arbitrarily and will simply be run in the order which they are defined if the multitask is called alone. A target can be called directly as well, and doing so will ignore any of the other targets defined within the multitask's configuration:

```
$ grunt watch:jshint
```

This particular configuration for the target `jshint` tells the `watch` task that if any files matching `js/src/*.js` are changed, then to run the `jshint` task.

Now you have your first two Grunt task configurations defined within your `Gruntfile`, but in order to use them, we must load the Grunt tasks themselves.

Loading Grunt plugins

You have already installed the `grunt-contrib-jshint` plugin as a Node.js module, but in order to execute the `jshint` task, you must load the plugin within your `Gruntfile`. This is done after the `grunt.initConfig` call:

```
grunt.loadNpmTasks('grunt-contrib-jshint');
```

This is the same method call you will use to load all Grunt tasks within your `Gruntfile`, and any Grunt task will not be accessible without doing so. Let's do the same for `grunt-contrib-watch`:

```
grunt.loadNpmTasks('grunt-contrib-watch');
```

Your full `Gruntfile` should now look like this:

```
module.exports = function(grunt) {
    'use strict';
    grunt.initConfig({
        pkg: grunt.file.readJSON('package.json'),
        jshint: {
            options: {
                curly: true,
                eqeqeq: true,
                eqnull: true,
                browser: true,
                newcap: false,
                es3: true,
                forin: true,
                indent: 4,
                unused: 'vars',
                strict: true,
                trailing: true,
                quotmark: 'single',
                latedef: true,
                globals: {
                    jQuery: true
                }
            },
            files: {
                src: ['Gruntfile.js', 'js/src/*.js']
            }
        },
        watch: {
            jshint: {
                files: ['js/src/*.js'],
                tasks: ['jshint']
            }
        }
    });
    grunt.loadNpmTasks('grunt-contrib-jshint');
    grunt.loadNpmTasks('grunt-contrib-watch');
};
```

Running the jshint Grunt task

Now that you have the plugin loaded, you can simply run `grunt jshint` from the command line to execute the task with its defined configuration. You should see the following output:

```
$ grunt jshint
Running "jshint:files" (jshint) task
>> 1 file lint free.
Done, without errors
```

This will run your JSHint linting options against the defined files, which as of now consist of only `Gruntfile.js`. If it looks like the example file shown and includes the call to `grunt.loadNpmTasks('grunt-contrib-jshint')`, then it should pass without errors.

Now let's create a new JavaScript file and intentionally include some code which will not pass the JSHint configuration so we can see how the errors are reported. First, create the `js/src` directory, which is defined in the `files` property of the `jshint` task:

```
$ mkdir -p js/src
```

Then create a file named `app.js` within this directory and place the following code in it:

```
var test = function() {
    console.log('test');
};
```

Now run `grunt jshint` again from the command line. You should see the following output:

```
$ grunt jshint
Running "jshint:files" (jshint) task
   js/src/app.js
      2 |    console.log('test');
                ^ Missing "use strict" statement.
      1 |var test = function() {
              ^ 'test' is defined but never used.
>> 2 errors in 2 files
Warning: Task "jshint:files" failed. Use --force to continue.
Aborted due to warnings.
```

You will notice that two errors are reported for `js/src/app.js` based on the `jshint` task configuration options. Let's fix the errors by changing the code in `app.js` to the following:

```
var test = function() {
    'use strict';
    console.log('test');
};
test();
```

Now if you run `grunt jshint` from the command line again, it will report that the files are lint free and have no errors:

```
$ grunt jshint
Running "jshint:files" (jshint) task
>> 2 files lint free.
Done, without errors.
```

Running the watch Grunt task

As mentioned earlier, when the `watch` task is run it will wait for changes that match the file patterns defined in its configuration and run any corresponding tasks. In this case, we configured it to run `jshint` when any files matching `js/src/*.js` are changed. Since we defined a target within the `watch` task called `jshint`, the `watch` task can be run in two different ways:

```
$ grunt watch
```

Running `grunt watch` will watch for changes matching all target configurations defined within the `watch` task:

```
$ grunt watch:jshint
```

Running `grunt watch:jshint` with the colon (`:`) syntax runs `watch` for just the file patterns matching that target configuration. In our case, only one target is defined, so let's just run `grunt watch` and see what happens in the console:

```
$ grunt watch
Running "watch" task
Waiting...
```

You will see that the task now shows a status of `Waiting...` on the command line. This indicates that the task is running to watch for matching changes within its configuration, and if any of those changes are made, it will automatically run the corresponding tasks. In our example with the `jshint` task, it will allow your code to automatically be linted every time you make changes to your JavaScript files and save them. If a `JSHint` error occurs, the console will alert you and display the error.

Let's test this by opening a text editor and changing `js/src/app.js` again:

```
var test = function() {
    console.log('test');
};
test()
```

Here, we removed the opening `use strict` statement and the semicolon after the call to `test()` at the end of the file. This should raise two `JSHint` errors:

```
>> File "js/src/app.js" changed.
Running "jshint:files" (jshint) task
   js/src/app.js
      2 |     console.log('test');
              ^ Missing "use strict" statement.
      4 |test()
                ^ Missing semicolon.
>> 2 errors in 2 files
Warning: Task "jshint:files" failed. Use --force to continue.
Aborted due to warnings.
```

Now let's correct these errors and return the file to the way it was before:

```
var test = function() {
    'use strict';
    console.log('test');
};
test();
```

Press *Ctrl* + *C* from the command line at any time to abort the `watch` task, or any Grunt task, while it is running.

Defining the default Grunt task

Grunt allows you to define a `default` task which will run when you simply type `grunt` on the command line with no parameters. To do this, you will use the `grunt.registerTask()` method:

```
grunt.registerTask('default', ['jshint', 'watch:jshint']);
```

This example sets the default Grunt task to run the defined `jshint` task first and then the `watch:jshint` multitask target. You can see that the tasks passed to the `default` task are in an array, so you can set the `default` task for Grunt to run any number of tasks by simply typing `grunt` on the command line:

```
$ grunt
Running "jshint:files" (jshint) task
>> 2 files lint free.
Running "watch:jshint" (watch) task
Waiting...
```

From looking at the output, you can see that the `jshint` task was run once initially, and then `watch:jshint` was run to wait for additional changes to the configured file patterns.

Defining custom tasks

Grunt allows you to define your own custom tasks, in the same way that you defined the default task. In this way, you can actually write your own custom tasks directly within the `Gruntfile`, or you can load them from an external file, just as you did with `grunt-contrib-jshint` and `grunt-contrib-watch`.

Alias tasks

One way of defining a custom task is to simply call one or more existing tasks in the order you want them to be run:

```
grunt.registerTask('my-task', 'My custom task.', ['jshint']);
```

In this example, we have simply defined a task named `my-task` to serve as a proxy for `jshint`. The second parameter is an optional description of the task, which must be a string. The third parameter, which passes an array, including only `jshint` in this example, must always be an array. You can also forgo the second parameter with the description and pass in your array of tasks there instead. This way of defining a task is known as an *alias task*.

Basic tasks

When you define custom Grunt tasks, you are not limited to only calling other tasks that exist within your configuration, but you can write JavaScript code to be called directly as a function. This is called a *basic task*:

```
grunt.registerTask('my-task', 'My custom task.', function() {
    grunt.log.writeln('This is my custom task.');
});
```

In this example, we simply write a string to the command line output for the task. The output should look like this:

```
$ grunt my-task
Running "my-task" task
This is my custom task.
```

Let's expand upon this example and pass in some arguments to our basic task function, as well as access the arguments from within the function:

```
grunt.registerTask('my-task', 'My custom task.', function(arg1, arg2) {
    grunt.log.writeln(this.name + ' output...');
    grunt.log.writeln('arg1: ' + arg1 + ', arg2: ' + arg2);
});
```

You will notice that there is a property available to the basic task, `this.name`, which is simply a reference to the name of the task. In order to call a basic task from the command line and pass arguments in, you will use a colon after the task name to define each argument in succession. This syntax is just like the syntax for running a multitask target; however, in this case you are passing in arbitrary arguments:

```
$ grunt my-task:1:2
```

Running this will output the following:

```
Running "my-task:1:2" (my-task) task
my-task output...
arg1: 1, arg2: 2
```

If you do not pass in the arguments to a task that is expecting them, it will simply resolve them as undefined:

```
$ grunt my-task
Running "my-task" task
my-task output...
arg1: undefined, arg2: undefined
Done, without errors.
```

You can also call other tasks from within a custom task:

```
grunt.registerTask('foo', 'My custom task.', function() {
    grunt.log.writeln('Now calling the jshint and watch tasks...');
    grunt.task.run('jshint', 'watch');
});
```

In this example, we have created a task, foo, that defines a custom function that calls the existing jshint and watch tasks:

```
$ grunt foo
Running "foo" task
Now calling the jshint and watch tasks...
Running "jshint:files" (jshint) task
>> 2 files lint free.
Running "watch" task
Waiting...
```

For more information on creating custom tasks with Grunt, see gruntjs.com/creating-tasks.

These examples of tasks only scratch the surface of what is capable with Grunt, but you should be able to glean from them the power of it and begin to think about what might be possible with Grunt tasks when building your own SPA.

Summary

Now that you have learned to set up an optimal development environment with NPM, supply it with frontend dependencies using Bower, and automate development tasks using Grunt, it's time to start learning more about building a real app. In the next chapter, we will dive into common SPA architecture design patterns, what they mean, and what is the best design pattern to choose based on the type of SPA you are building.

2
Model-View-Whatever

If you are a frontend developer, you may not be familiar with the traditional software architectural pattern referred to as **Model-View-Controller** (**MVC**). Variations of this pattern have found their way into frontend software architectural patterns in recent years through such frameworks as *Backbone.js*, *Ember.js*, and AngularJS. Regardless of your experience in these areas, this chapter will discuss the evolution of the so-called **Model-View-Whatever** (**MVW**) pattern and its relevance to SPA development through the following topic areas:

- The original MVC pattern
- **Model-View-Presentation** (**MVP**)/**Model-View-ViewModel** (**MVVM**) explained
- **View-Interactor-Presenter-Entity-Router** (**VIPER**) and other variations of MVW
- AngularJS and MVW
- Using the MVW pattern in a SPA

The original MVC pattern

The MVC software architectural pattern has existed in one form or another since the 1970s, but it became more popular and generally accepted with its use in web application frameworks such as Ruby on Rails, CakePHP, and Django. MVC frameworks like these brought a higher level of organization and sophistication to web application development than had been previously conceived, and in doing so, paved the way for modern SPA development.

To understand the relevance of MVC to modern SPA development, let's first break down the components and ideology of MVC.

The Model

The *Model* component of MVC deals with an application's data. This includes data that is displayed to the user, received from the user, and stored in the database. Additionally, the Model handles all **Create, Read, Update, Delete (CRUD)** operations with the database. Many frameworks also use the Model to handle an application's *business logic*, or how the data should be manipulated before being saved or viewed, but this is not necessarily a standard.

In the simplest terms, the Model in an MVC web application is a representation of the application's data. That data may include anything relevant to the application, such as the current user's information. Traditional web application frameworks use relational databases, such as MySQL, to store data. Modern SPA architectures, however, are now gravitating more and more toward document-oriented databases, or what is commonly referred to as *NoSQL*. MongoDB and many other NoSQL databases use JSON documents to store records. This is great for frontend architectures because JavaScript can directly parse JSON, and in the case of the MEAN stack, JSON data is native to every tier of the architecture.

Let's take a current web application's user information as an example. We will refer to this as the *User Model*:

```
{
    "id": 1,
    "name": {
        "first": "Philip",
        "last": "Klauzinski"
    },
    "title": "Sr. UI Engineer",
    "website": "http://webtopian.com"
}
```

A simple JSON document like this will be returned from the database to your app for direct parsing by JavaScript. There is no need for any **Structured Query Language (SQL)** with a document-oriented database, hence the term *NoSQL*.

The View

The core component of MVC is the *View*, and it is likely the one you are most familiar with if you are a frontend developer. The View embodies everything that the user interacts with, and in the case of a web application, what the browser consumes. Traditional MVC frameworks serve Views from the server, but in the case of a JavaScript SPA and using an architecture like the MEAN stack, the View is contained entirely in the frontend. From a development and asset management standpoint, this makes things a lot easier to maintain because the dual aspect of dealing with Views both on the server side and the frontend does not exist.

The templates for Views in a JavaScript SPA are written using HTML mixed with some type of web template system such as Underscore, Handlebars, or Jade, as only a few examples. A web template system allows your HTML markup to be parsed by JavaScript and evaluated for expressions that place dynamic data and content within your Views. For example, let's look at a simple Handlebars template using the User Model from earlier:

```
<h1>User Information</h1>
<dl>
    <dt>Name</dt>
    <dd>{{name.first}} {{name.last}}</dd>
    <dt>Title</dt>
    <dd>{{title}}</dd>
    <dt>Website</dt>
    <dd>{{website}}</dd>
</dl>
```

Imagine an AJAX request is made for the currently logged-in user's data, and the SPA returns the User Model JSON document from a `GET` request. The properties from that JSON document can be directly inserted into the View for that request. In the case of Handlebars, a set of two opening and closing curly braces (`{{` ... `}}`), or double curly brace notation, is used to identify expressions to be parsed within the template. In this case, those expressions are simply the user's first name, last name, and title. For more information on Handlebars templates, see `handlebarsjs.com`.

The Controller

The *Controller* component in the MVC pattern is the most variable between different frameworks, and thus the most difficult to define with true clarity as a general concept. In a traditional web application MVC framework such as Ruby on Rails or CakePHP, the Controller takes input from the user in the form of web requests, or *actions*, and makes changes to the Model before rendering a new response in the View. The following diagram shows the flow of the Controller within the MVC paradigm:

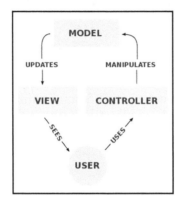

(Diagram from Wikipedia – https://en.wikipedia.org/wiki/Model%E2%80%93view%E2%80%93control ler#Components)

With this representation of the Controller, it is easy to see how it could encapsulate a great deal of application code, and in fact when working with some MVC web frameworks, it is often difficult to know where to draw the line between Controller logic, business rules for the Model, validation rules for the View, and many other common components of a web application. This nebulous nature of the Controller has led to the decision of the authors of many modern web frameworks to move away from the term *Controller* entirely and adapt a new concept in its place.

The Model and the View components of MVC are easy to understand and to differentiate their purposes within a web application, but the Controller is not so clear-cut. Let's now explore some of the concepts that have replaced the Controller in more recent web application architectural patterns.

MVP and MVVM

The term *Model-View-Whatever* came about amid the rise of many architectural patterns that included a Model and a View, but replaced the Controller with a different concept for a core component, or even with a number of them.

MVP

MVP is a variation on the MVC architectural pattern in which the *Presenter* component replaces the Controller. The Presenter also acts as the Controller in this pattern, but it takes on additional responsibility in that it serves to handle presentation logic for the View. The reasoning behind this paradigm is to enhance the testability of an application by having the View itself contain little to no presentation logic.

Another key difference between MVP and MVC is that a Presenter in MVP has a one-to-one relationship with a View, meaning there is a unique Presenter defined for every View, whereas MVC allows the Controller to have a one-to-many relationship with the View. In other words, MVC allows there to be any number of Views defined for a Controller and each View is mapped to an *action* of that Controller. MVP maps only one View to a Presenter. Additionally, MVP prohibits a direct relationship between the View and the Model, which is again for enhancing testability by keeping business logic out of the View:

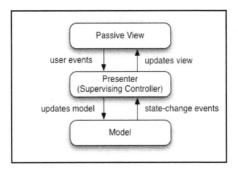

(Diagram from Wikipedia– `https://en.wikipedia.org/wiki/Model%E2%80%93view%E2%80%93present` `er)`

MVVM

MVVM is yet another variation on the MVC architectural pattern. The *ViewModel* in this paradigm is a representation of the Model data for the current user's session. Changes to the ViewModel are always made before any changes are made to the Model.

MVVM is like MVP in that the View has no knowledge of the Model, but in contrast, the View has a many-to-one relationship with the ViewModel. This means that multiple Views can be mapped to one ViewModel. The ViewModel component also contrasts with the Presenter in MVP in that it has no knowledge of the View. Instead, the View has a reference to the ViewModel, which allows it to be updated based on changes to the ViewModel.

The primary distinction of MVVM from the other architectural patterns in regard to SPA development, however, is the support of *two-way data binding*. This means that changes to the ViewModel are automatically reflected in the View, and changes to data in the View by the user are automatically updated in the ViewModel. This makes MVVM a more viable pattern for modern SPA development because the View can be updated and stays in sync with the ViewModel without the need for a new page request, which is what would be required in a traditional MVC or MVP architecture:

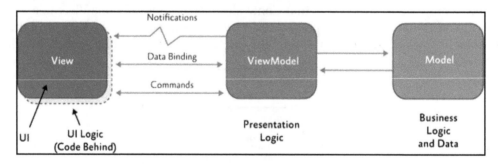

(Diagram from http://social.technet.microsoft.com/wiki/contents/articles/13347.mvvm-model-view-viewmodel-part-1.aspx)

Data binding will be discussed further in Chapter 6, *Data Binding, and Why You Should Embrace It.*

Summarizing the differences between MVC, MVP, and MVVM

Now you should have a basic understanding of the MVC architectural pattern and the MVP and MVVM variations of it. A full understanding of these concepts is not necessary to move forward with learning JavaScript SPA development, but it is important to have some knowledge of the types of components that can comprise a multitier stack. Shown here is a diagram highlighting the key differences between the three architectural patterns discussed in this section:

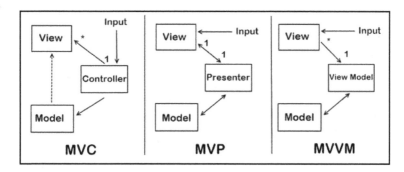

(Diagram from `http://geekswithblogs.net/dlussier/archive/2009/11/21/136454.aspx`)

VIPER and other variations of MVW

The primary reason that modern architectural patterns have moved away from MVC is that the Controller in MVC generally embodies too much application code and becomes unwieldy, thereby being difficult to test. This has led to patterns that not only replace the Controller with something else, but that add multiple layers in its place to further establish a separation of concerns within an application.

VIPER

In the world of *iOS*, Apple's mobile operating system, MVC was long encouraged as the pattern to follow. More recently, however, many iOS developers have moved away from pure MVC and have adopted patterns that establish more than just three layers within an application's architecture. One of these patterns is *VIPER*, which stands for **View, Interactor, Presenter, Entity, and Routing** (or Router).

Let's briefly cover what each of these components is:

- **View**: Just as with MVC, the View represents the user interface.
- **Interactor**: Contains the business logic for a particular behavior and corresponding View within the app. An Interactor is similar to a Controller in MVC, but it may interact with multiple Models and is not constrained to only one Model.
- **Presenter**: Contains logic for the View, just as with MVP.
- **Entity**: Another word for *Model*, simply used to achieve the *E* in the **VIPER** acronym.
- **Routing**: Each request in an app is made using a unique call, and in the case of a web application, a URL or *route* from the browser is used to make an application request. This layer may also be called the Router.

It is evident from the description of the components in VIPER that they do not actually flow in the order of the acronym itself, but rather are ordered as such for aesthetic purposes. The diagram below shows the true flow of the VIPER pattern, along with representations of the browser and the database to supplement the understanding of this flow:

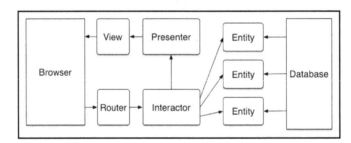

(Diagram from http://khanlou.com/2014/03/model-view-whatever/)

Other variations of MVW

So far, we have covered the traditional MVC architectural pattern, MVP, MVVM, and the more recently contrived VIPER pattern. What should be clear is the patterns that have followed MVC do not represent a full paradigm shift, but rather a restructuring of the traditional Controller component to embody more clarity, and in the case of VIPER, to be divided into a further separation of concerns. The general paradigm is not lost in these other patterns because the concept of the Model and the View remain intact. This trend is what has led to the generalized paradigmatic term *Model-View-Whatever* or MVW.

What we are left with is a multitude of architectural patterns that have been conceived as abstractions of MVC. So, what pattern should you choose for a JavaScript SPA? This is a highly subjective topic, so the best answer is that you should choose a pattern based on the type of app you are building, and also based on what makes the most sense to you and what you are most comfortable with.

The software libraries and frameworks you choose to work with should also factor into what pattern you use. In that regard, let's take a look at how AngularJS has adapted MVC for its own version of MVW.

AngularJS and MVW

AngularJS is a frontend JavaScript framework for building web applications, and it is a core component of the MEAN stack. It provides developers with the ability to use custom HTML attributes and elements to drive behavior within an app. It also provides some handy features such as two-way data binding and dependency injection.

A brief history of AngularJS

AngularJS began as a side project of two Google developers, but eventually became an official Google open source project. Since its inception, it has undergone many changes in its methodology, including a transition away from touting MVC as its pattern of choice. Instead, the AngularJS team now labels it as *a JavaScript MVW framework* (at the time of writing).

The reason for the declaration of AngularJS to be MVW was in response to extensive debate and confusion from the developer community over what pattern AngularJS follows. The label itself may not be important to some developers, but it is important in highlighting the fact that the architectural pattern AngularJS uses is more complex than traditional MVC. AngularJS does, however, include a Controller component, among others. Let's take a closer look at what those components are.

AngularJS components

AngularJS is designed for creating web applications, and as such, it includes conceptual components that do not exist in traditional MVC. Also keep in mind that AngularJS is a frontend framework only, so it is agnostic of what server-side framework and database solution is used.

Template

A **Template** in AngularJS is an HTML document that contains special markup allowing it to be parsed to handle dynamic data, as with any web template system. AngularJS uses its own proprietary web template system as opposed to a third-party one, such as **Handlebars**. Just like Handlebars, however, AngularJS uses double curly brace notation to identify expressions within the HTML markup:

```
<html ng-app="myApp">
<head>
    <script src="angular.js"></script>
    <script src="app.js"></script>
</head>
<body ng-controller="UsersController">

    <ul>
        <li ng-repeat="user in users">
            {{user.first_name}} {{user.last_name}}
        </li>
    </ul>

</body>
</html>
```

This is an example of a simple AngularJS template. You can see that it is constructed like a normal HTML document, but it also includes AngularJS expressions. You will also notice that there are special HTML attributes prefixed by ng-, which convey different types of application information to the AngularJS framework.

Directives

Directives are special HTML markup that AngularJS uses to drive behaviors within the DOM. A directive can be driven by a custom HTML attribute prefixed with ng, a custom HTML element name such as `<my-element></my-element>`, a comment, or a CSS class.

You can define your own directives for your application, but AngularJS also includes some predefined directives for common use cases. For example, the `ng-repeat` attribute shown in the previous example uses the built-in `ngRepeat` directive, which is used to render template markup once per item while iterating over a collection:

```
<ul>
    <li ng-repeat="user in users">
        {{user.first_name}} {{user.last_name}}
    </li>
</ul>
```

In the example, the `users` object is iterated over and properties of each `user` are rendered from the template.

Model

The *Model* is a representation of the variable data available for use within expressions in the current View. The Model available to a View is confined to a particular **Scope**, or context:

```
$scope.users = [
    {
        id: 1,
        first_name: 'Peebo',
        last_name: 'Sanderson'
    },
    {
        id: 2,
        first_name: 'Udis',
        last_name: 'Petroyka'
    }
];
```

In this example, an array of `users` is registered on the `$scope` object. This exposes the `users` variable to a template that has access to this particular scope.

Scope

The Scope is a JavaScript object that defines the Model context for variables within the View. As shown in the previous example, `$scope.users` would be accessed in the View for that Scope as `{{users}}`.

Expressions

An **Expression** in AngularJS is just like an expression in any web template system, as explained earlier. Double curly brace notation is used to identify expressions in AngularJS:

```
<ul>
    <li ng-repeat="user in users">
        {{user.first_name}} {{user.last_name}}
    </li>
</ul>
```

In this example, `{{user.first_name}}` and `{{user.last_name}}` are AngularJS expressions.

Compiler

The **Compiler** parses Template markup and evaluates it for Directives and Expressions to drive the behavior and data within the View. The AngularJS compiler is internal to the framework and not something that you will often access or interact with directly.

Filter

A **Filter** is used to format an Expression in the View to be presented in a particular way. For example, the View may be passed a currency amount from the Model in the form of a number. A Filter can be added to the Expression in order to format what the user sees as a monetary value with a currency symbol. The pipe | symbol is used within the double curly brace notation to append a filter:

```
<p><strong>Cost:</strong> {{ total | currency }}
```

In this example, `total` represents the Expression and `currency` represents the Filter.

View

Just as with traditional MVC, the View in AngularJS is the user interface. Views are composed of Templates, and the terms are largely interchangeable in the context of an AngularJS application.

Data binding

Data binding in AngularJS is *bidirectional*, or two-way, so data changed in the View is updated in the Model, and data changed in the Model is updated in the View. This is done automatically, without the need for any additional business logic to handle the changes.

Controller

A Controller is really a *View Controller* in AngularJS, since it is a purely frontend framework. Like traditional MVC, the Controller contains business logic, but that business logic only pertains to the View:

```
var myApp = angular.module('myApp', []);
myApp.controller('UsersController', function($scope) {
    $scope.users = [
        {
            id: 1,
            first_name: 'Peebo',
            last_name: 'Sanderson'
        },
        {
            id: 2,
            first_name: 'Udis',
            last_name: 'Petroyka'
        }
    ];
});
```

A `UsersController` could be created, for example, that contains the `users` Model shown previously and exposes it in the View through its `$scope` object.

Dependency injection

The term *dependency injection* is commonly used with respect to JavaScript as the ability to asynchronously add resources to the current web page. In AngularJS, the concept is similar, but only with regard to other AngularJS components. For example, Directives, Filters, and Controllers are all injectable.

Injector

The **Injector** is the container for dependencies and is responsible for finding them and adding them when needed. It is decoupled from the application code using declarative syntax within the View and is typically not accessed directly.

Module

The **Module** is a container for all the main components of an app. It gives the app a main namespace reference to all associated Directives, Services, Controllers, Filters, and any additional configuration information:

```
Var myAppModule = angular.module('myApp', []);
```

If your Module depends on any other Modules, you can add them to the empty array parameter shown in the previous example.

To apply a Module to an SPA using AngularJS, you can simply declare the name of the module within your main page's HTML using the custom `ng-app` attribute on your app container element:

```
<body ng-app="myApp">
```

Service

The **Service** is a component that differentiates AngularJS from traditional MVC in that it is used to contain reusable business logic that you may want to share across different Controllers within your app. This helps to keep Controllers from becoming too large and complicated, and also allows different parts of the app to share some commonly used business logic. Currency conversion, for example, is something that could be written as a Service because you may want to use it in multiple Controllers.

The following diagram illustrates how the components of AngularJS interact with each other:

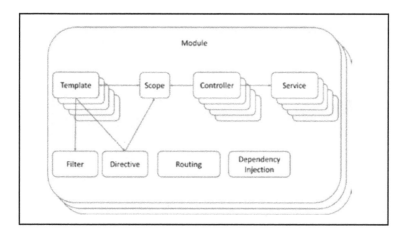

(Diagram from https://dzone.com/refcardz/angularjs-essentials)

AngularJS 2.x (in beta at the time of writing) differs in its architectural pattern from v1.x, which is the version represented here.

Now that you have a better understanding of the components that comprise the AngularJS MVW architectural pattern and how those components pertain to a frontend SPA architecture, let's apply some of these MVW principles to a simple JavaScript SPA example.

Using the MVW pattern in an SPA

It should now be clear to you that MVW is not a precise architectural pattern, but rather a paradigm in which you have a Model, a View, and a nebulous third component, or more components, depending on how fine-grained you decide to break down your separation of concerns. Everything falling within that gray area is based on what type of application you are building, what architectural components you are comfortable with as a developer, and what frameworks and libraries you are working with.

Building a simple JavaScript SPA

The complexity of your SPA should always be a factor in what technologies you use to build it. More to the point, you should not go into every project assuming you will always use a certain technology stack or framework. This rule goes for the MEAN stack as well.

Let's take the User Model example from earlier, and the accompanying Handlebars template View, and actually build it out as an SPA, complete with the AJAX request to retrieve the User Model data. For something simple like this, using AngularJS and the MEAN stack would definitely be overkill. Let's begin by using the NPM, Bower, and Grunt environment you set up in *Chapter 1 Getting Organized NPM, Bower, and Grunt*. So how do we proceed?

Creating the Model

The Model is the simple JSON object of user data we defined earlier. Rather than setting up a database for this, let's simply place it in a text file and name it `user.json`:

```
{
    "id": 1,
    "name": {
        "first": "Philip",
        "last": "Klauzinski"
    },
    "title": "Sr. UI Engineer",
    "website": "http://webtopian.com"
}
```

Save the file to the same directory as your `package.json`, `bower.json`, and `Gruntfile.js`. Feel free to replace the user information with your own for this example.

Creating the View

The View for this example will be the web template document we defined earlier with a definition list containing user information:

```
<h1>User Information</h1>
<dl>
    <dt>Name</dt>
    <dd>{{name.first}} {{name.last}}</dd>
    <dt>Title</dt>
    <dd>{{title}}</dd>
    <dt>Website</dt>
    <dd>{{website}}</dd>
</dl>
```

Save this file to the root directory of your project as well and name it `user.handlebars`.

Setting up frontend assets

We are not creating a complex SPA in this case, so we will not use any frontend frameworks, but we do want to install a few libraries to make development easier.

If you followed the examples in *Chapter 1, Getting Organized with NPM, Bower,* and Grunt you should already have jQuery installed via Bower. If you have not yet installed it, go ahead and do so now:

```
$ bower install jquery --save
```

We will use jQuery for handling AJAX requests and DOM manipulation within the SPA.

Now let's install the Handlebars library for parsing our web template View:

```
$ bower install handlebars --save
```

Compiling web templates

A web template has to be compiled to JavaScript before it can be parsed for expressions. This can be done in the browser using the Handlebars frontend library, but it means longer execution times when loading templates, and it also means loading a larger library asset file on the initial page load. The initial page load is critical for a SPA because you do not want the user waiting a long time for your app to download assets and prepare the page for the initial View. Additionally, if you want to separate your Views into separate files, as we did with user.handlebars, then those View files have to be loaded asynchronously at some point to hand over to the compiler.

Precompiling web templates

To circumvent large asset payloads and extraneous round trips to the server to fetch Views, Handlebars allows you to *precompile* web templates to JavaScript so that they can be used immediately within your app. This gives you the ability to separate your Views into different files and keep things organized and still maintain a lower initial page load.

For this example, let's install the Handlebars Node.js package globally so that it can be used from the command line in any directory:

```
$ npm install handlebars -g
```

This will now allow you to compile your templates on the command line to create a precompiled JavaScript template file you can use in your SPA. From the root of your project directory, enter the following:

```
$ handlebars *.handlebars -f templates.js
```

This command is telling the Handlebars compiler to take all files with the extension .handlebars (in this case only user.handlebars) and compile them to a single file named templates.js. This could allow to you have 100 separate web template View files and precompile them to one JavaScript file, for example. This is a good practice because it allows you to map each View file to a REST API endpoint on your server side. In the case of our SPA example, our endpoint will be requesting the user.json file through AJAX.

Handling server HTTP requests

Now we will install the *PayloadJS* library for handling REST requests within the SPA:

```
$ bower install payloadjs --save
```

PayloadJS will allow us to easily make AJAX requests triggered from our SPA markup by using custom data- HTML attributes to define behaviors and parameters in the DOM.

Creating the SPA layout

One of the most important pieces of a SPA is the *single page* itself, or the *layout* for your app. This is the one and only server-side HTML page that you will load in order to initialize and display your app.

Create a file in the root of your directory named index.html, and enter the following code into it:

```html
<!doctype html>
<html>
    <head>
        <title>My Application</title>
    </head>
    <body>
        <p><a href="#" data-url="/user.json" data-template="user" data-selector=".results">Load user data</a></p>
        <div class="results"></div>
        <script src="/bower_components/jquery/dist/jquery.min.js"></script>
        <script
src="/bower_components/handlebars/handlebars.runtime.min.js"></script>
        <script src="/bower_components/payloadjs/payload.js"></script>
```

```
        <script src="/templates.js"></script>
        <script>
            Payload.deliver({
                templates: Handlebars.templates
            });
        </script>
    </body>
</html>
```

This will be the main layout page for your SPA. You will notice that `script` tag references have been added that point to jQuery, Handlebars, PayloadJS, and the `templates.js` file we created. These are all of the assets you will need loaded in order to run this SPA. Additionally, the `Payload.deliver()` command is run at the bottom of the page and passed an object to overwrite any of its default initialization options. This method simply initializes PayloadJS to drive the behavior within the DOM indicated in the `data-` attributes on the link with the text **Load user data**. In this case, we are setting the `templates` property that is passed in to `Handlebars.templates`, since that is the namespace containing our Handlebars template.

For more information on using PayloadJS, please see payloadjs.com.

Serving the SPA

Now you have all of the necessary files in place to run this simple SPA. The only thing left is a local server to run and load the `index.html` file for testing. Let's install a simple HTTP server with NPM for this purpose:

```
$ npm install http-server -g
```

Install this package globally so that it can be run from the command line. This simple Node.js HTTP server can be run specifying any local directory as your server. In this case, we want to run the server for the current project directory:

```
$ http-server ./
```

After running this command, you should see something similar to the following output in your console:

```
Starting up http-server, serving ./
Available on:
  http:127.0.0.1:8080
  http:192.168.0.2:8080
Hit CTRL-C to stop the server
```

This indicates that the HTTP server is running and available locally.

Now you should be able to go to a browser and load the URL `localhost:8080` and you will see the contents of the `index.html` page you created. The only visible content of the page is the link with the text **Load user data**. If everything is set up properly and you click on that link, you should notice a **Loading...** indicator below it for a brief moment, followed by the contents of the `user.handlebars` template file populated with the data from the `user.json` file loaded into the page:

Load user data

User Information

Name
    Philip Klauzinski
Title
    Sr. UI Engineer
Website
    http://webtopian.com

The full page with the response after clicking on the link should look similar to the preceding screenshot.

Overview of a simple JavaScript SPA

So we have created a simple JavaScript SPA using a general MVW pattern with the following components:

- Model: `user.json`
- View: `user.handlebars`
- Precompiled templates file: `templates.js`
- SPA layout page: `index.html`
- HTTP server: Node.js *http-server* package

This is about as simple as it gets, but you have created an SPA nonetheless. This example should give you an idea of how powerful JavaScript can be for creating a single page application. Feel free to extend this simple SPA with more Model data files, additional web template Views, some CSS, and a bit of your own creativity.

Summary

You should now have an understanding of the traditional MVC pattern, MVP, MVVM, VIPER, and the reasons for the transition away from traditional MVC and conventions leading to the more generalized MVW pattern. The should also understand that the term *Model-View-Whatever*, or *MVW*, was largely popularized by the AngularJS team, and that this was done in regard to the modern SPA requiring a new and more complex set of components that were non-existent when the original MVC pattern was conceived of.

You also should now have the ability to build a simple JavaScript SPA with just a few Node.js and Bower packages. Now it's on to bigger and better things. In the next chapter, we will discuss how to create the ideal application development environment for a SPA by expanding on the Node.js environment we have been working with so far.

3
SPA Essentials – Creating the Ideal Application Environment

You should now be fairly comfortable working within the Node.js ecosystem of modules, tasks, and package management. In this chapter, we will dive a bit deeper into the intricacies of a JavaScript SPA and its dependencies. We will explore various data formats and database types, SPA encapsulation architectural patterns, and more through the following topics:

- JSON and other data formats
- The differences between SQL and NoSQL databases
- When to use SQL versus NoSQL databases
- Methods of presenting a single page application container
- Serving and managing layouts

The JSON data format

JavaScript Object Notation (**JSON**) is something that most JavaScript developers today are quite familiar with. Despite its name, JSON is a language-independent standard that is really just a text document, and it must first be parsed by JavaScript, or any language interpreter, before it can be used as data representing objects with name-value pairs, or as simple sequences of values.

The reason the JSON acronym includes the word *JavaScript* is because its formatting is based on the structure of JavaScript objects and arrays. This is why working with JSON data and JavaScript is so straightforward, and why it makes a lot of sense to consume JSON data from within JavaScript applications.

The contents of the `user.json` file we created in `Chapter 2`, *Model-View-Whatever* is an example of the JSON data interchange format:

```
{
    "id": 1,
    "name": {
        "first": "Philip",
        "last": "Klauzinski"
    },
    "title": "Sr. UI Engineer",
    "website": "http://webtopian.com"
}
```

JSON follows the format of standard JavaScript objects, but must also adhere to a few important rules to be valid:

- Property names must be formatted as strings in double quotes
- A value can be a string in double quotes, a number, `true` or `false`, an object, or an array
- Objects and arrays can be nested
- Double quotes contained within a string must be escaped using backslashes

These rules allow the JSON format to be parsed directly to native JavaScript while still being strict enough to make it an easily interchangeable format across languages. Although native JavaScript object notation does not enforce the use of double quotes around property names, it is required for JSON in order to prevent JavaScript reserved word exceptions from occurring.

Reserved words in JavaScript are not allowed to be used as variable or function names because they represent some current or potential future construct of the language. For example, the reserved word `class` is often misused by inexperienced developers as a variable name for holding a CSS class:

```
Var class = 'myClass';
```

This example would throw an exception because `class` is a reserved word. Additionally, using it as a straight property name in a JavaScript object would throw an exception:

```
{
    class: 'myClass'
}
```

An experienced JavaScript developer would know not to use this word as a property name due to it being a reserved word, but if your application is consuming JSON data from an external source, you have no control over the property names that may be pulled in with an object. For example, you may retrieve data from an application running on another server that is not JavaScript and has no awareness of the reserved word restrictions of any other application that may consume it. If this application wants to convey CSS class information, it is likely that it may use the word `"class"` to do so:

```
{
    "class": "myClass"
}
```

In this example, the property name is valid because it is in double quotes and thereby parsed as a string instead of as a reserved word. For this reason, the rule requiring double quotes around property names is strictly enforced, and no JSON parser will allow property names without them.

Other data formats

JSON was first conceived of in 2001 by Douglas Crockford. Before then, data interchange had long been a practice using established formats that were already integrated with many programming languages.

XML

Long before JSON was commonly known, **Extensible Markup Language** (**XML**) was one of the most widely used web application data interchange formats. XML was first introduced in 1996 and would become an international standard. It is a form of **Standard Generalized Markup Language** (**SGML**) and was created by the **World Wide Web Consortium** (**W3C**):

```
<?xml version="1.0" encoding="UTF-8"?>
<note>
    <to>Tobums Kindermeyer</to>
    <from>Jarmond Dittlemore</from>
    <heading>A Message</heading>
    <body>Hello world!</body>
</note>
```

This is a simple example of a XML document. If you haven't worked with XML before, you most likely have at least heard of it. XML was a precursor to many other data formats, including SOAP, RSS, Atom, and XHTML. XHTML is also well known to many web developers, and it was the recommended standard for serving web pages before the HTML5 specification was introduced. Notice that the formatting of the preceding example is similar to HTML.

YAML

YAML is a recursive acronym, meaning it refers to itself, for *YAML Ain't Markup Language*. What makes YAML interesting, aside from its silly name, is that its syntax for hierarchy requires the use of lines and indentation as delimiters, rather than structured enclosures such as curly braces and brackets, which are used in JSON:

```
item-key-one:
  - list item 1
  - list item 2
item-key-two:
  nested_key_one: this is an associative array
  nested_key_two: end the associative array
```

The syntax for YAML was designed to make the hierarchy structure of data more easily human-readable by requiring the lines and spaces for explicit delineation of its structure. In contrast, other data formats that use characters such as brackets for defining structure can find it difficult to convey hierarchy to the human eye, especially when in compressed format.

YAML was first created around the same time as JSON, but it has not received nearly the amount of notoriety that JSON has in the web development community. YAML is arguably more flexible than JSON in that it allows for more features, such as comments and relational anchors, but it is likely the simplicity of JSON that makes it a more popular data format for consumption within web applications and beyond.

BSON

Binary JSON (BSON) is a binary form of JSON that is used primarily as the data storage format for the MongoDB document-oriented database system. BSON is just like JSON, with the main difference being that BSON supports more complex data types such as Date, Timestamp, and `ObjectId`. An `ObjectId` in BSON and MongoDB is a 12-byte unique identifier for a stored object. MongoDB requires that every object has a unique identifier field named `_id` and an `ObjectId` is the default mechanism for assigning this field a value. This concept is much like a *primary key* in a relational database system.

A BSON document that uses the `ObjectId` and `Timestamp` data types might look something like this:

```
{
    "_id": ObjectId("542c2b97bac0595474108b48"),
    "timestamp": Timestamp(1412180887, 1)
}
```

When we discuss MongoDB and document-oriented databases in this text, the term JSON may be used interchangeably for BSON with the implication that this distinction is understood. You can learn more about the BSON specification at bsonspec.org.

Why does JSON reign supreme?

JSON is simple, easy to read, and structured in a way that is easily understood by just about any programming language in existence. Lists (or arrays) and name-value pairs (or associative arrays) are a fundamental concept and common implementation in computer languages. The simpler a format is, the easier it is to parse, and thus more platforms will develop a way to inherently consume that data format. Such has been the case with JSON.

Additionally, the JSON specification was only changed a few times after it was first developed. Its creator, Douglas Crockford, intentionally gave no version number to the specification so that it would be set in stone and could not change over time. This may likely be the biggest factor in JSON's dominance over other data formats. Since it does not change over time, the parsers built to consume it across myriad programming languages and platforms don't have to change either. This has created an ecosystem in which JSON exists with only one version in every place, making it entirely predictable, widely understandable, and virtually unbreakable.

The differences between SQL and NoSQL databases

In *Chapter 2*, *Model-View-Whatever*, we briefly discussed document-oriented databases, otherwise known as NoSQL databases. This concept is imperative to the MEAN stack, as the *M* in the MEAN acronym stands for MongoDB, a widely used NoSQL database implementation. NoSQL databases are conceptually divergent from traditional relational, or SQL, databases.

Non-relational databases have existed for decades, but they did not achieve any widespread use until more recently. This rise in popularity led to the term *NoSQL* first being applied to these types of databases. The reason for the increase in the use of NoSQL databases has primarily been to solve the problem of handling *Big Data*, or massive and complex datasets, and *scaling* that data horizontally in modern web applications.

NoSQL data typing

The term NoSQL means *non-SQL* which implies that it is a non-relational database type. NoSQL databases that are document-oriented, like MongoDB, store their data in documents represented by structured JSON objects. The data *types* in a NoSQL database like this are defined by the data itself, as is the case with standard JSON:

```
{
    "id": 1
}
```

For example, if you have a field in a NoSQL database with the key id and the value is 1, a number, you could easily change the value to myID, a string, without needing to change any other reference to that data type:

```
{
    "id": "myID"
}
```

In this way, the data *type* for that value is entirely dependent upon what it is defined as. In a relational database, making this change would not be so straightforward.

Relational data typing

In contrast to document-oriented databases, traditional SQL databases use tables to structure their data. Each table column is set to a specific data type and the data stored under that column must adhere to the defined type. If you have a large SQL database and wish to change the type for a particular column, it can be potentially problematic and could require the change to be executed on thousands of rows of data. Changing a data type in a JSON document is relatively easy compared to this, as it only involves changing the data itself, and there is no concept of a table column defining the data type across multiple records.

The term *relational* in regard to relational databases refers to the tabular relation of the data stored. Each table of data is considered a relation because the different data stored within it is related to one another in some manner defined by the applications and programs that will be consuming it. A table in a SQL database can be compared to a JSON object in a NoSQL database. The biggest difference between the two, however, is that a table is composed of rows and columns, and the data is further related by column types and rows containing records of related data. In a NoSQL database, there is no concept of rows and columns, and data can be nested with unlimited scope.

In order to retrieve *nested* data within a SQL database, relations must also be identified between tables. Since data cannot actually be nested, references from one or more tables to one or more other tables must be used to create related sets of data for use in application Models and Views. SQL is a programming language used to manage and extract the data from relational database tables and format it in such a way that is required for an application.

ACID transactions

The majority of NoSQL database systems do not support *transactions* which conform to the properties of **ACID**, which stands for **Atomicity**, **Consistency**, **Isolation,** and **Durability**. This set of properties is required for a database to handle transactions in a reliable fashion. A transaction is any change made to a database. That change can be to a single value for a field in one table, or it can be a change that spans multiple tables and affects multiple rows within those tables. Most widely used relational databases support the ACID properties for transactions, no matter the complexity of the operation that is performed.

Atomicity

The Atomicity property of ACID refers to atomic operations within a database, meaning that the changes required for a transaction must all be ensured to occur, otherwise none will occur. This property provides a guarantee that partial changes are not made, which could lead to corrupt data sets. If an atomic transaction fails at any point within a database, the changes made up to that point are rolled back to their previous state.

Consistency

The Consistency property of ACID is the requirement that a transaction only causes *valid* data changes as defined by that database system. This includes ensuring that data is not corrupt, that rollbacks are enforced when necessary, and that all the necessary database triggers related to a transaction are executed.

Isolation

The Isolation property of ACID requires that a simultaneously executed transaction, or concurrency, does not result in database errors in related data. This can involve different levels of strictness, dependent upon the database system being used. The primary goal of Isolation is that the end result of a set of concurrent transactions is the same as if you were to go back and replay them one after another. Isolation is closely tied to Consistency, and it should always ensure that Consistency is maintained.

Durability

The Durability property of ACID requires that a transaction is not *lost* while being executed. You can imagine any number of things going wrong with a computer that could occur during the execution of a transaction, such as a power outage. When something like this occurs, Durability provides that the database system *remembers* the transaction that was in the middle of execution by recording it to disk and ensuring that it isn't lost, even after a reboot.

MongoDB and ACID

It is true that many NoSQL database systems do not conform to the ACID properties; however, MongoDB does to a certain degree. As mentioned, MongoDB is a document-oriented database system, which is a more terse subset of NoSQL databases. In this fashion, MongoDB has the ability to support ACID transactions at the single-document level. It cannot support multi-document transactions, so in this way it falls short of most relational databases, which can support ACID transactions across multiple tables, but MongoDB still stands out among document-oriented databases at the document level.

Write-ahead logging with MongoDB

Another feature that MongoDB touts above others is **Write-Ahead Logging (WAL)**. This is a set of features allowing a database system to conform to the Atomicity and Durability properties of ACID. To do this, MongoDB writes a record of all operations and their results to an internal log before actually executing the operations. This is a simple and effective way to ensure the Durability of document-level transactions because with all operations logged ahead of execution, evidence of what occurred is not lost in the event of a sudden interruption to an operation. Similarly, this feature ensures Atomicity because it gives MongoDB the ability to *undo* and *redo* these operations upon reboot after determining what changes were made and comparing them to the state of the database before the interrupted operation.

When to use SQL versus NoSQL databases

There are clearly major differences between SQL and NoSQL databases, not only in how they are structured, but in how developers and applications interact with them. These differences can have serious implications for the development of an application from both an architectural and a functional perspective. This is why choosing your database type is no small matter and should always be thoroughly evaluated before moving forward with the development of an application.

Scalability

It was mentioned earlier that the needs of modern web applications have led to the rise in popularity of NoSQL databases. *Scalability*, or the ability to continuously handle growing amounts of data and operations on that data, is one of these needs. You can imagine this being the scenario for a social media company such as Facebook or Twitter, and any other social applications that may interact with social data received from resources like this. In the following, scalability is a feature you may need to take under consideration when deciding on the type of database you want to use for your application.

Horizontal scaling

In particular, *horizontal scaling* is a necessity for a growing number of modern-day web applications. This refers to the need for distributed servers and databases geographically with a growing user base. Effective horizontal scaling allows users of an application to receive data from a server that is closest to them, rather than a single server or set of servers that may be in a data warehouse halfway around the world.

Horizontal scaling is certainly not impossible with a relational database, but it is difficult, and it requires the use of a sophisticated **Database Management System** (**DBMS**). NoSQL databases, on the other hand, are simpler in design, and this makes data replication across clusters of machines and networks much simpler as well.

Big Data

Another need for modern web applications is **Big Data**, which can mean exactly what its name implies: a massive amount of data. More often than not, however, Big Data refers to a high degree of complexity among data sets such that it can be difficult to analyze and extract value from them without the aid of sophisticated techniques for doing so.

NoSQL databases lend themselves perfectly to handling Big Data due to their support for *dynamic schema design*, which simply means that you do not have to define a specific schema for a data set before you store it, as is required by traditional relational databases. This goes back to the flexibility of data typing in NoSQL, which doesn't require that the type for a field be governed by a rule, as it is for a column in a tabular data schema. Additionally, the schema for a relational database table cannot be changed without affecting all of the data for that table. In contrast, the schema of a particular data set in a JSON document, for instance, can change at any time without affecting previously stored data sets in that same document.

If Big Data is a foreseeable need for your web application, then the *type* of Big Data is a further consideration you should make before choosing a database type.

Operational Big Data

Operational Big Data refers to data that is consumed and managed in real time to support the operation of currently running processes in distributed applications. Document-oriented databases such as MongoDB are built with operational Big Data support in mind and focus on *speed* of concurrent read and write operations to provide for this.

MongoDB, and other NoSQL systems designed to work with operational Big Data, do so by taking advantage of modern distributed network computing power to increase the efficiency of operations. Traditional relational databases were not built with this ability in mind because computer systems were more isolated when they were developed.

Analytical Big Data

Analytical Big Data contrasts greatly with operational Big Data in that its focus is on **Massively Parallel Processing** (MPP). This means that massive amounts of data are consumed and later analyzed for any number of requirements that give value to the application using it. In contrast to operational Big Data, database systems designed for analytical Big Data focus on massive *throughput* and retrospective processing of that data, rather than speed of concurrent, unrelated operations.

The need to handle analytical Big Data is not always apparent at the outset when developing an application. Anticipation of this requirement is often difficult because when you start out with a small data set, you may not know what massive amounts of data you might want to analyze as your database matures over time. Fortunately, this problem can be handled by the implementation of a solution subsequent to identifying its need. MPP databases are built for this specific purpose, in addition to *MapReduce*, which is an alternative implementation to handle MPP across distributed computers in a cluster.

Overall considerations

When deciding whether to use a SQL or NoSQL database for your application, you should consider the needs of your application both at the initial release and what you foresee further down the line. If you expect a large user base and the potential for viral growth, then you will want to consider a NoSQL database built for handling operational Big Data and scalability.

If you are developing an application that you anticipate having a smaller user base, or perhaps no users other than administrators of the data, then a relational SQL database may be more appropriate. Additionally, if your application may have many users, but has no need for horizontal scalability, a SQL database is likely suitable as well.

Also consider that many modern, distributed web applications started out using only relational databases, and they later implemented NoSQL solutions in congruence with the existing databases to handle growing needs. This is also a use case that can be planned for and adapted to as needed during the life cycle of an application.

Methods of presenting an SPA container

In a Single Page Application, the *container* is the object in which the application is initially loaded and displayed to the user. This concept is different from that of a *software container*, which is an isolated environment that an application lives in, much like a virtual machine.

For a single page web application, the container could be the `<body>` element, or any element within the `<body>` element. For instance, you may have some static welcome text initially loaded on the page in a `<p>` element, and the SPA will then load dynamically below that element in a `<div>` element:

```
<!doctype html>
<html>
    <body>
        <p>This is some welcome text.</p>
        <div class="container">
            The application will be loaded here.
        </div>
    </body>
</html>
```

In a scenario like this, you will always have some fixed content on the page that doesn't need to change based on the user's interaction with the application. This is just a simple example, but the same could be done for a common `<header>`, `<footer>`, and `<nav>` element:

```
<!doctype html>
<html>
    <body>
        <header>Static header content</header>
        <div class="container">
            The application will be loaded here.
        </div>
        <footer>Static footer content</footer>
    </body>
</html>
```

How to define your SPA container

There is no *right* way to define your SPA container; it really just depends on the type of application you are building and what your preference is. It can also depend on the server-side limitations of the system you are using to serve your *layout* – the HTML page used to house your app.

Partial page container

As shown in previous sections, you may want to show some static content in your SPA layout before the application loads. This is useful when you anticipate a long initial load time for an app, or if you require some user interaction to trigger the loading of your app.

Full page container

If your application can be completely controlled through API endpoints accessed by **XMLHttpRequest**, commonly known as **Asynchronous JavaScript and XML (AJAX)**, then there is no need to load any static content in your SPA layout unless you want to. One reason you may load static content in your layout is to have something for the user to view or read while they are waiting for the application to load. This can be particularly useful when you anticipate long initial load times for your app and you want to help deter a user from leaving before the application's initial *state* is ready.

A *state* in a SPA refers to a particular version of the **Document Object Model** (**DOM**), at any point in time. A *loading state* is one you might show within your container element while waiting for it to load the next requested state. A loading indicator of some sort is often enough to let the user know that something is happening and the application will load soon, but when you have any excessive latency in your app, a user may think something has gone wrong and leave the app layout page before the process completes.

How to load your SPA container

The way you initially load your SPA is highly dependent upon the nature of your application. There could be any number of requirements that must be fulfilled before your app can be loaded.

Loading on user interaction

Many web applications require some type of user interaction before the full SPA is loaded. For example:

- User authentication
- User acceptance of an agreement to enter
- Interstitial content that must be shown and either engaged or dismissed by the user, such as an advertisement

Scenarios like these are quite common in web applications, and they can often be challenging to solve in a fluid manner.

Login page transition

In many web applications, the login screen is loaded on a secure page and submitted using HTTP POST to another secure page to authenticate the user and load the actual SPA. This pattern is generally used due to limitations in the server-side framework that is being used to handle authentication.

If you think about a financial application for accessing your bank account that you log in to on your phone, you will likely not see much more than a login screen until you have authenticated with your username and password. This will typically bring you to a second page that loads the full single page application with your sensitive banking information that you would not otherwise want available to someone else who picks up your phone.

A login screen is arguably the most common use case requiring user interaction to load an application, and it is one that is often handled with little elegance. The most fluid way to handle this use case, if your REST framework allows for it, is to load a login screen as part of your SPA and request authentication via a REST endpoint from your login form. When you receive a properly authenticated response from your API request, you can then load the data you need into the existing SPA container and replace the login state with a new *logged in* state.

Loading based on the DOMContentLoaded event

If your SPA does not require user authentication or any other interaction for initial loading, or if you detect a user that is already authenticated at the time the page is loaded and you can skip that step, then you will want a way to automatically load your SPA upon initial page load, and as soon as possible.

The best time to load a single page application is generally as soon as the DOM is completely loaded and can be parsed by the browser. Modern browsers fire an event on the document object when this happens, called DOMContentLoaded, and that can be used for this purpose. To do this, you would simply add an EventListener on the document to detect when the event is fired, and then call a function to load your app:

```
<script>
    document.addEventListener('DOMContentLoaded', function(event) {
        loadMyApp();
    });
</script>
```

Alternatively, if you are using jQuery, you can call the handy jQuery .ready() method to listen for the DOMContentLoaded event and trigger your custom application code within an anonymous function:

```
<script>
    $(document).ready(function() {
        loadMyApp();
    });
</script>
```

Loading based on the document readystatechange event

Modern browsers also provide an event that is fired on the `document` object when you first load a page called `readystatechange`. This event can be used to determine three states of the DOM, which are returned as the following via the `document.readyState` property:

- `loading` – This is when the document is still loading and has not been entirely parsed by the browser.
- `interactive` – This is when all DOM elements have finished loading and can be accessed, but certain external resources may have not fully loaded, such as images and stylesheets. This state change also indicates that the `DOMContentLoaded` event has been fired.
- `complete` – This is when all DOM elements and external resources have fully loaded.

To use the `readystatechange` event to load your application at the same time as the `DOMContentLoaded` event, you would assign a function to be called on the `readystatechange` event and then check whether the `document.readyState` property is set to `interactive`. If it is, then you can call your application code:

```
<script>
    document.onreadystatechange = function() {
        if (document.readyState === 'interactive') {
            loadMyApp();
        }
    };
</script>
```

Using this method to detect the state of the document provides more flexibility in the event that you want to call custom application code for any of the three document states, and not just on the `DOMContentLoaded` event, or `interactive` state.

Loading directly from the document.body

The more traditional way of loading `<script>` tags is by placing them within the document `<head>` element. Adding the `<script>` tags to the `<head>` is fine for loading an SPA if you are using the document `DOMContentLoaded` or `readystatechange` events within your external JavaScript to initialize your application code at the appropriate time:

```
<!doctype html>
<html>
```

```
<head>
    <script src="app.js"></script>
</head>
<body>
    <div class="container">
        The application will be loaded here.
    </div>
</body>
</html>
```

If you want to avoid using these custom DOM events and trigger your application code precisely when you need it, however, a different and more direct approach can be taken.

A common technique for loading JavaScript into a web page today is by placing the <script> tag, which loads your external JavaScript file, directly within the <body> element of the page. The ability to do this lies in the way the DOM is parsed by a browser: from the top to the bottom.

Take this code, for example:

```
<!doctype html>
<html>
    <body>
        <div class="container">
            The application will be loaded here.
        </div>
        <script src="app.js"></script>
    </body>
</html>
```

Loading the external JavaScript app.js file from within the document.body and just above the closing </body> tag will ensure that all DOM elements above the <script> tag are parsed before it is loaded, and the app.js file is loaded precisely after the <div class="container"> element. If that element is where you will load your SPA, then this technique ensures that your application code within app.js will be executed immediately following the container element being parsed.

Another advantage to loading your <script> tags near the bottom of the DOM and below the elements that are required for loading your application is that the loading of those <script> tags will not block the loading of any content above them, due to the browser's top-down parsing of the DOM. Once the <script> tag is reached, there may be some blocking preventing the browser from being usable while it is being loaded, but the user will at least see everything on the page that has been loaded up until that point.

For this reason, loading a `<script>` tag within the `<body>` and near the bottom of the DOM is preferable to loading it with the traditional `<head>` tag insertion so that no blocking occurs before anything is visible on the page.

Using the script tag async attribute

One method for preventing a `<script>` tag from blocking the browser usability while it is loaded is the `async` attribute. This attribute can be added to ensure that your `app.js` file is loaded asynchronously once parsed, and so that the rest of the DOM continues to be parsed and loaded, regardless of when the loading of that script completes:

```
<!doctype html>
<html>
    <body>
        <div class="container">
            The application will be loaded here.
        </div>
        <script src="app.js" async></script>
    </body>
</html>
```

The advantage to this is, again, there is no blocking. The disadvantage to it, however, is that when you are loading multiple scripts asynchronously, there is no guarantee in what order they will finish loading and eventually execute. This is why it also a good practice to load only a single, compressed JavaScript file for your application as much as possible. The fewer `<script>` tags there are, the fewer external resources have to be parsed and downloaded, and in the case of using the `async` attribute, using only one `<script>` tag means waiting for only one asynchronous resource to load and not having to worry about the unpredictable sequence of loading multiples files, which could potentially break your application.

Using the script tag defer attribute

Another method for loading a `<script>` tag directly from the body and not causing the document parser to be blocked is the `defer` attribute. Unlike `async`, this attribute ensures that the `<script>` tag will not be loaded until the document parsing is complete, or upon the `DOMContentLoaded` event.

Using the `defer` attribute, your `<script>` tag can be placed anywhere within the `<body>` and always be guaranteed to load after the `DOMContentLoaded` event:

```
<!doctype html>
<html>
    <body>
        <script src="app.js" defer></script>
        <div class="container">
            The application will be loaded here.
        </div>
    </body>
</html>
```

Managing layouts

As mentioned in `Chapter 2`, *Model-View-Whatever*, a *layout* in relation to an SPA is the server-side HTML page that is used to house, initialize, and display your app. The layout will contain similar HTML markup to the examples in the previous section regarding how to load your SPA container.

The layout is generally the only native server-side component necessary to create an SPA, the other components being the native frontend code and the external API for providing endpoints for data consumption and manipulation.

Static layouts

A layout can be something as simple as a static HTML page that is loaded onto a web server and calls the resources necessary for loading your app within a defined container element on that page. Ideally, once that initial HTML page is loaded, no other server-side HTML pages need to be accessed to run your app, hence the term *Single Page Application*.

If you do not require any server-side framework interaction for setting up environment variables, testing login state, and so on, then a static HTML page is the quickest and easiest way to launch your SPA.

A static HTML layout page could be something as simple as the following example:

```
<!doctype html>
<html>
    <head>
        <title>This is a static HTML page</title>
    </head>
```

```html
    <body>
        <div class="container">
            The application will be loaded here.
        </div>
        <script src="app.js"></script>
    </body>
</html>
```

A drawback to using a static HTML file simply being served on a web server is that you have to go directly to that file in order to load your app. If your app is reached at myapp.com, for instance, and your static HTML layout page is named index.html, most web servers will route the *root* server request to this page automatically, so a user would not need to navigate directly to myapp.com/index.html in order to reach it, but just to myapp.com.

If a user were to go to myapp.com/profile, however, where they might find their user profile information, the app layout would not be loaded and the server would generate a **HTTP 404**, or **Not Found**, response. In order to provide for this use case and allow custom URLs for your app, a *dynamic layout* is necessary.

Dynamic layouts

When you have control over the server-side framework for your single page application, as would be the case when using the MEAN stack, then you may want to develop a more dynamic server layout page that can load variables and some minimal logic from the server side when your app initially loads.

Express is a server-side web framework for Node.js, and it is the *E* in the MEAN stack acronym. When you are developing with the MEAN stack, you will be using Express to define and handle all of your REST API endpoints, but you will also want to handle your main application entry point.

Installing Express

Let's go back to our Node.js environment we have been using to work with NPM, Bower, and Grunt, and install Express:

```
$ npm install express --save
```

In this case, we are using the --save parameter to save Express to our main NPM dependencies, since it is not just being used for development.

Setting up a basic server with Express

Once you have Express installed, create a file called `server.js` in the root directory of your app:

```
$ touch server.js
```

Within this file, add the following code to include the Express module and initialize your application object:

```
var express = require('express');
var app = express();
```

The `app` object within your `server.js` file will allow you to call methods on it for defining routes. In the case of our SPA example, we only need to define one route for the time being.

Basic routing with Express

Routing in Express refers to defining URL paths which are used to respond to server requests. Express can define routes for any type of HTTP request, including GET, POST, PUT, and DELETE requests, which are necessary for creating a REST API. At this point, however, we simply want to define a route for loading a HTML page.

Defining a route for your main application entry point would be a GET request, and this is quite simple to do with Express. In the `server.js` file you just created, add the following code below the `app` object definition:

```
app.get('/', function(request, response) {
    response.sendFile('/index.html', {root: __dirname});
});
```

This command adds a route that will serve the `index.html` file you created earlier as the root response for the app. The second parameter, which defines a `root` property as `__dirname`, simply sets the root server path for the app to the current directory.

Now we want to use Express to serve our app instead of the simple `http-server` module from earlier.

Running a server with Express

Now that you have your `server.js` file set up with a basic route to the root of your application, all that is left is to set up a HTTP port to listen on and to load the app. In your `server.js` file, add the following code to your route definition:

```
app.listen(8080, function() {
    console.log('App now listening on port 8080');
});
```

This tells the server to listen on HTTP `port 8080` for serving the app layout. Now all you have to do is run the server from the command line:

```
$ node server.js
```

This will run the server and display the console message `App now listening on port 8080` in the terminal.

Now go to `localhost:8080` in your browser and you should see the simple SPA page we created in `Chapter 2`, *Model-View-Whatever*. You will notice some errors in your browser console, however, because the local JavaScript files which are linked to in `index.html` are not found. This is occurring because you have not defined a route for loading static asset files.

Loading static assets with Express

First, stop the app by pressing *Ctrl + C* from the command line. Now edit `server.js` again and add the following code *above* the SPA layout page route definition:

```
app.use('/', express.static('./'));
```

This command will set the app to load static assets from the root directory. Now if you run `nodeserver.js` again from the command line and reload the page in your browser, the SPA should load all assets and work just as it did before with `http-server`.

Dynamic routing with Express

As mentioned earlier, our app should allow a user to go to something like
`myapp.com/profile`, or in our case `localhost:8080/profile`, to load a dynamic
request that will trigger a different view than the main root view for the app. If you go to
`localhost:8080/profile` in your app now, you will get the following response in your
browser:

```
Cannot GET /profile
```

To fix this, stop your local server again, edit the `server.js` file and make the following
change to the app layout route definition:

```
app.get('*', function(request, response) {
    response.sendFile('/index.html', {root: __dirname});
});
```

Here, we simply changed the path parameter in the GET route definition from `'/'` to `'*'`.
Express allows for regular expression syntax within route definitions, so what this does is
tell the server to route all dynamic path requests to the `index.html` page, instead of just
the root `'/'` path.

Save this change, and now if you run `node server.js` again on the command line and go
to `localhost:8080/profile` in your browser, you will see the SPA displayed again just
as it did from the root path, and all static asset files should be loaded as expected.

After setting up this basic Node.js Express server, your final `server.js` file should look
like this:

```
var express = require('express');
var app = express();

app.use('/', express.static('./'));

app.get('*', function(request, response) {
    response.sendFile('/index.html', {root: __dirname});
});

app.listen(8080, function() {
    console.log('App now listening on port 8080');
});
```

Our simple SPA has now become a bit more sophisticated, with the ability to serve a
dynamic layout file, and to use dynamic routes for loading the layout via custom URLs.

Summary

You should now have a better understanding of various data interchange formats such as JSON, BSON, XML, and YAML, and how they are used in web applications. You should understand the differences between SQL and NoSQL databases and what the advantages are of using one or the other depending on the needs of your application, and you have also learned about MongoDB and its use of BSON as a binary form of JSON. Additionally, you have learned about using web SPA container elements, and various methods of initializing and loading your app into that container.

These concepts are fundamental to understanding SPA development in general, and to understanding the inner workings of the MEAN stack and how it differs from other application development architectures.

Now that you have gotten a glimpse into the server side of a Node.js application and built a basic server with Express, let's go deeper into working with Express and learn about creating REST API requests for consumption within an SPA.

4
REST is Best – Interacting with the Server Side of Your App

The majority of development work involved in creating a JavaScript single page application is generally going to be on the frontend, but not to be overlooked is the all-important data-transfer layer of your application, which communicates with the server and the database. **Representational State Transfer** (**REST**) is the standard architectural style of data transfer between client and server for the World Wide Web and the **Internet of Things** (**IoT**). Any time you use a web application, chances are that REST is being used to communicate data and transitions of state from the UI.

The beauty of using the REST architectural style for a SPA is that the frontend of your application can be entirely agnostic of what type of software is being used to retrieve requests on your server, as long as your application can be used over **Hypertext Transfer Protocol** (**HTTP**), the standard application protocol for the World Wide Web.

In this chapter, you will learn:

- The fundamental aspects of the REST architectural style
- How to write basic REST API endpoints for performing CRUD operations in a single page web application
- How to work with REST requests on your application frontend using AJAX
- The basics of some alternatives to REST, such as SOAP, WebSockets, MQTT, CoAP, and DDP

Understanding the fundamentals of REST

REST is the architectural style used to serve web pages and make requests on the World Wide Web, or simply the Web. Although the Internet and the Web are often referred to interchangeably, they differ in the fact that the Web is merely a *part* of the Internet.

The Web is a collection of documents, or *web pages*, which are served or hosted on computers all over the world and are connected via *hyperlinks*, or what are commonly referred to as links. These links are served over HTTP, the language of communication for the Web. REST is often confused with HTTP because of its mutual relationship with the Web, but HTTP and REST are far from the same thing.

Understanding an architectural style versus a protocol

REST is an architectural style, while HTTP is an application layer protocol. This means that while HTTP is the language of communication on the Web, REST is simply a set of rules for performing requests and operations on the Web. These operations performed through a REST architectural style are commonly referred to as *Web Services*. In this way, HTTP is simply the method of transport for the Web Services performed by an application using REST.

Architectural style

An architectural style, or architectural pattern, is a set of rules which provides developers with the ability to build abstraction layers as frameworks that are built to achieve a common language of interaction that is to ultimately be consumed by some type of client, or user agent. In the case of the Web, that user agent is a web browser.

A web abstraction layer, or web framework, can be written in any number of languages to provide Web Services via REST, or RESTful services, as long as that language can be hosted on a web server. When that framework follows the REST architectural style, the UI for any application using it can be completely *agnostic*, or unbiased, as to the technology behind the RESTful service.

Protocol

A protocol, as it relates to the Web, is part of an abstraction layer of the **Internet Protocol Suite**, or TCP/IP, providing a common method of communication between connected computers.

Transport layer protocols

The term TCP/IP is a combination of the Internet Protocol Suite's most widely used protocols: **Transmission Control Protocol (TCP)** and **Internet Protocol (IP)**.

TCP

TCP is a transport layer protocol, which lies underneath the application layer. This means that services and information are *transported* up to the top-level application layer of the Internet Protocol Suite.

IP

IP is also a transport layer protocol. You have most likely seen this protocol associated with the term IP address, or Internet Protocol address, which is a unique numerical identifier for a device on a network. On the Web, domain names are commonly used to point to an IP address to make it easier for people to remember how to reach that address.

Application layer protocols

The application layer of TCP/IP is the abstraction layer that defines methods of communication between host computers that are connected through the Web. This layer specifies several protocols, with some of the most common being HTTP, FTP, SSH, and SMTP.

HTTP

HTTP is the primary protocol for data exchange within the application layer of TCP/IP, and it provides the foundation of communication for RESTful web services. HTTP is also responsible for serving a web page for display within a browser, and for sending data from a form on a web page to a server.

FTP

The **File Transfer Protocol (FTP)**, is another standard protocol within the TCP/IP application layer that is used for transferring files between computers. FTP communication requires an FTP server and an FTP client.

SSH

Secure Shell (**SSH**) is another common protocol in the application layer which is used to allow secure remote logins to a non-secure network entry point. For SSH connections to work, a SSH server must be available to receive requests from a SSH client. A SSH client most often comes in the form of a terminal application with a **command line interface** (**CLI**).

SMTP

Simple Mail Transfer Protocol (**SMTP**) is the standard method of sending e-mail, or electronic mail, in the application layer of TCP/IP. SMTP may also be used to receive e-mail and is typically used for this purpose by e-mail servers. SMTP is not typically used by user-level e-mail clients for receiving e-mail, however. Instead, these clients more commonly use POP3 or IMAP.

POP3 is the third version of the **Post Office Protocol**, which is a standard application layer protocol for receiving e-mail over TCP/IP connections. POP3 is generally used to download e-mail to a local computer and then delete it from the host server.

IMAP is the **Internet Message Access Protocol**. It is also a standard application layer protocol for receiving e-mail over TCP/IP connections. IMAP is generally used as way to manage a host server e-mail inbox by multiple clients, and therefore it does not delete the e-mail from the server after downloading it to a local computer like POP3. The latest versions of IMAP also support tracking the state of an e-mail on the host server, such as read, replied to, or deleted.

Using HTTP as a transfer protocol for REST

REST defines a set of rules by which to make HTTP requests for a web application or service. HTTP requests can be made in any number of ways, but they are only RESTful if they follow that set of rules. HTTP provides the transport layer upon which those requests are made.

In the same way that a web application interacting with a REST API is agnostic of the type of software framework being used to serve the API endpoints, HTTP is agnostic of the types of operating systems being used across all of the servers which it communicates with.

The constraints of REST

The REST architectural style is governed by a set of constraints, or rules, that dictate how it should be implemented, interacted with, and handle data. REST was first defined by the American computer scientist Roy Fielding in a doctoral dissertation in 2000, along with these constraints.

REST is considered to be a *hybrid* architectural style in that it borrows from other architectural styles that existed before its conception. These other architectural styles lend greatly to the REST constraints outlined here.

Client-server

The first constraint of REST is the client-server architectural style. This constraint exists to enforce the agnostic nature of REST, or the *separation of concerns* that is so fundamental to it:

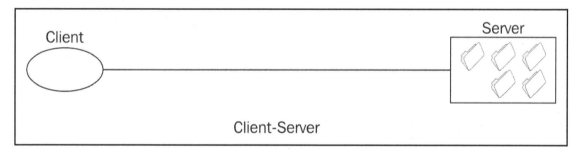

This diagram shows the client-server relationship, and how they are separated. The **client**, or web browser, needs only display the UI for an application. The UI can be as simple or as sophisticated as deemed necessary, without affecting the REST architecture on the server. This REST constraint provides for scalability.

Stateless

The second constraint of REST builds upon the client-server constraint in that the communication between client and server must be stateless. This means that any request from a web browser to the REST server must supply all expected information needed for the context of the request and the current session in order to expect the appropriate response from the server.

The server will have no stored information to help delineate the request, thereby making the REST server *stateless* and putting the burden of session state on the web browser:

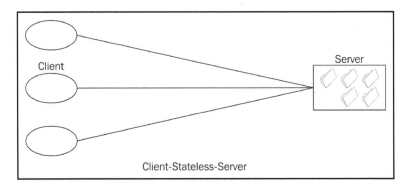

This diagram depicts the client-stateless-server architectural style in which the web browser state can change and the REST server remains consistent. This REST constraint provides for visibility, reliability, and scalability, which are a few of the key benefits of using REST.

Cache

The third constraint of REST builds again upon the client-server and stateless constraints. A cache, or data stored for reuse, can be permitted for use by the browser for any given request based on the cacheability of that request as delegated by the REST server. If the server's cache component indicates that a request is cacheable, then the browser can cache it for future requests. Cacheability is often indicated in the case where a request made multiple times to a particular REST endpoint will likely result in an identical response each time:

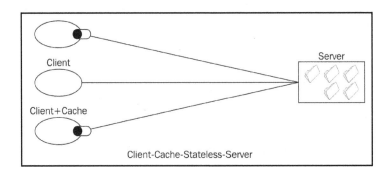

This diagram depicts the client-cache-stateless-server architectural style. This style is just like client-stateless-server, but with the added component of a client cache.

Uniform interface

The fourth constraint of REST is the use of a uniform interface among components of the system. This refers to the simplistic nature of the architecture involved in a REST implementation in which the components are decoupled. This allows each component of the architecture to evolve on its own, without affecting the others:

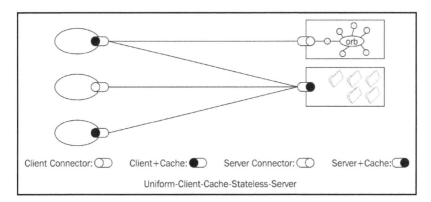

This diagram shows the uniform-client-cache-stateless-server architectural style. This combines the three previous architectural style constraints with the added constraint of uniform interface.

The uniform interface constraint is further subdivided into four of its own constraints.

Identification of resources

A resource in REST is any conceptual mapping of information to a uniquely identifiable object. This object can be a person, place, or thing. An example of this in the case of the Web is a Uniform Resource Identifier (URI). More specifically, a Uniform Resource Locator (URL) is a special type of URI that provides a method to find a web resource and specifies how to obtain a representation of information from that resource. A URL is also commonly referred to as a web address. In relation to REST, a URL may also be referred to as an endpoint.

Manipulation of resources through representations

A representation in REST is a set of data which represents the current state of a resource. In a web architecture using REST, a JSON document can be used as a representation to pass between client and server, and manipulate or change a resource.

Self-descriptive messages

Messages in REST are the communication between components. In keeping with the constraint for a REST server to be stateless, the messages must be self-descriptive, meaning it carries all the information necessary to tell each component how it should be processed.

Hypermedia as the engine of application state

Hypermedia refers to web pages, or hypertext, and the hyperlinks that connect them. In order to remain stateless, a RESTful architecture uses hypermedia to convey the state of the application based on representations received from the server.

Layered system

The fifth constraint of REST is a layered system, which is a hierarchy of architectural components, where each layer provides services to the layer above it and uses the services from the layer below it. In this manner, each layer only has visibility into one layer below it, thus making it agnostic of any layers down.

This concept is applied to distributed servers on the Web that are used to enhance the scalability of an application. For example, a web browser may communicate with any number of *intermediate* servers based on its location, but it is never aware of whether it is connected to the end server or one of those intermediate servers.

A layered system is also used to implement load balancing across servers. This allows additional servers to take on requests when the primary server is inundated with too many requests:

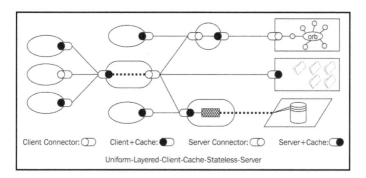

This diagram depicts a uniform-layered-client-cache-stateless-server. This architectural style combines the previous four with the added constraint of a layered system.

Code-on-demand

The sixth and final constraint of REST is the **code-on-demand** architectural style, and it is the only *optional* constraint. In this style, the server provides a set of executable code encapsulated in some form that is consumable by the browser. Some examples of this are Java applets, Flash animations running ActionScript, and client-side widgets running JavaScript.

Using code-on-demand can improve the flexibility of a REST application, but it also reduces *visibility* by encapsulating some functionality. This is why code-on-demand is an optional constraint for REST:

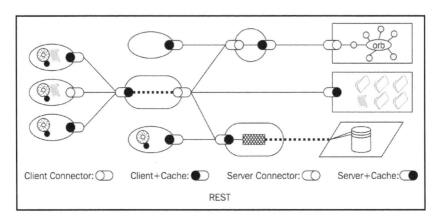

This diagram depicts the final REST architectural style. This combines all previously described constraints, which are required for REST, with the optional constraint of code-on-demand.

Benefits of REST

The REST constraints were designed with separation of concerns and forward-compatibility in mind, and this design allows for the individual components of REST to evolve without compromising the underlying architectural style itself.

By enforcing the constraints of REST, some particular architectural properties are exposed that reveal the beneficial nature of this architectural style. Let's explore some specific benefits of REST more closely.

Performance

Performance is a major benefit of REST, and it is exposed by using cache, simple representations such as JSON, a layered system with multiple servers and load balancing, and the decoupling of components through a uniform interface.

Simplicity

Simplicity is another key benefit of REST, and it is primarily exposed by the uniform resource constraint in which individual components of the system are decoupled. Simplicity is also seen in the server component, which needs only to support HTTP requests, and does not have to support state for any request.

Separation of concerns

Separation of concerns lends to the simplicity of REST, but is also a benefit itself. This is seen in the separate server-client relationship, the burden of caching being put on the frontend, and the use of a layered system. Separation of concerns is a common pattern seen not only in architecture but in software design as well, such as the MVW architectural patterns discussed in Chapter 2, *Model-View-Whatever*.

Scalability

The architectural property of scalability is exposed in REST through the simplicity of the client-server relationship and the separation of concerns properties. By combining these key attributes, the system becomes more scalable because the complexity of relationships between the components is reduced by having specific guidelines around how they should work together.

Portability

Portability is a benefit of REST that is exposed through the client-server separation of concerns. This allows the user interface layer of the application to be *portable* because it is agnostic of the underlying server software being used to host the REST endpoints.

Portability is also exposed through code-on-demand, giving REST the ability to transport application code from server to client.

Visibility

Visibility simply refers to the ability to understand what is happening in a system based on the components' interactions with each other. With REST, high visibility is a benefit because of the decoupled nature of components and the fact that they need little to no knowledge of each other. This allows interactions made within the architecture to be easily understood, such as requests for endpoints. To determine the full nature of a request, one need not look beyond the representation of that request itself.

The code-on-demand constraint of REST is one that actually reduces visibility, but for this reason, it is optional. In following, code-on-demand is not often used by modern-day web applications, aside from simple JavaScript widgets that are found on web pages and used for advertising, social networks, and other third-party interactions.

Reliability

Reliability is a benefit of REST that is exposed primarily through the stateless server constraint. With a stateless server, a failure in the application can be analyzed at the system level because you know that the origin of that failure is from a single, decoupled component of the system.

For example, if you receive an error message in the UI for a web application that indicates to the user that information was entered incorrectly, then this failure can be handled at the UI level. If, on the other hand, you receive a HTTP 400 response code error from the server after entering the correct information, you can further deduce that the REST server endpoint is not configured correctly.

RESTful web services

As mentioned earlier, the REST architectural style is often used to perform , **Read**, **Update** and **Delete** (**Create**, **Read**, **Update**, **and Delete** (**CURD**)) operations in modern web single page applications, and these operations are known as web services. To employ RESTful web services for your own application, you will need not only a HTTP server, but a hosted database or database server in order to perform CRUD operations on the data.

Setting up a simple database with MongoDB

MongoDB is the database used for the MEAN stack. It is an open source, document-oriented database system and can easily be added to your stack via download or package manager, depending upon the operating system you are using.

Installing MongoDB

MongoDB can be installed on systems running Linux, Windows, and OS X. Direct downloads are available for these operating systems and, additionally, MongoDB can be installed using Homebrew on OS X. Homebrew is a popular CLI package manager for OS X. For instructions on installing Homebrew, visit brew.sh.

If you are running OS X and have Homebrew installed, you can use the following instructions to install MongoDB using a CLI. For installation on other systems, you can find instructions on MongoDB's documentation site at docs.mongodb.com/manual/installation/.

Installing MongoDB on Mac using Homebrew

Start by updating Homebrew to the latest version before using it:

```
$ brew update
```

Next, install the mongodb package:

```
$ brew install mongodb
```

Once MongoDB is installed, you will want to add it to your command-line PATH for convenience. To do so, add the following to your user directory .profile, .bash_profile, or .bashrc file if you have one of them already. If you don't have any of these files, then create .profile:

```
export PATH=/usr/local/opt/mongodb/bin:$PATH
```

Once you have added MongoDB to your PATH, you will need to create a directory for storing your data before you can run it. The default data directory for MongoDB is /data/db. You will most likely have to run this command as the superuser.

Creating a MongoDB data directory

First, go to the CLI and create a database directory using `sudo`:

```
$ sudo mkdir -p /data/db
```

Next, you will need to set the permissions on the directory to give you read and write access:

```
$ sudo chown -R $(whoami):admin /data/db
```

Running MongoDB

Now you should be all set and you can go ahead and run MongoDB using the mongod command on the CLI:

```
$ mongod
```

If everything is set up properly, you should see several lines of output with the last line showing something similar to the following line:

```
I NETWORK  [initandlisten] waiting for connections on port 27017
```

Port 27017 is the default port for MongoDB but it can be changed, if necessary, using the `--port` option on the CLI:

```
$ mongod --port 27018
```

To stop MongoDB from running at any time, press *Ctrl + C* at the command prompt where it is running.

Creating a collection with MongoDB

A collection in MongoDB is analogous to a table in a traditional relational database. Let's set up a test database and collection using the `user.json` document we have been working with in our example application. From the root directory of the application, run the following command:

```
$ mongoimport --db test --collection users --file user.json
```

This command will create a database named test and a collection named users, then it will import the data from the user.json file to the users collection. You should see two lines of output after running this command:

```
connected to: localhost
```

```
imported 1 document
```

This output indicates that the user.json document was imported to the MongoDB instance running on localhost.

Installing the Node.js MongoDB driver

MongoDB provides drivers for several programming languages. We will be using the Node.js driver. The Node.js driver for MongoDB can be installed using NPM. Go to the root directory of the application and install it there and save to your local package.json:

```
$ npm install mongodb --save
```

Now you can start using MongoDB within your Node.js application. First, let's add some additional lines to the server.js file we created earlier:

```
var mongo = require('mongodb').MongoClient;
var assert = require('assert');
var url = 'mongodb://localhost:27017/test';

mongo.connect(url, function(err, db) {
    assert.equal(null, err);
    console.log('Connected to MongoDB.');
    db.close();
});
```

This will set up a connection to your local MongoDB test database and output a message to the console if it is successful.

If you added these lines to the additional code we wrote to server.js in *Chapter 3, SPA Essentials – Creating the Ideal Application Environment*, the entire content of the file should look like the following code:

```
var express = require('express');
var app = express();
var mongo = require('mongodb').MongoClient;
var assert = require('assert');
var url = 'mongodb://localhost:27017/test';

mongo.connect(url, function(err, db) {
    assert.equal(null, err);
    console.log('Connected to MongoDB.');
    db.close();
});

app.use('/', express.static('./'));
```

```
app.get('*', function(request, response) {
    response.sendFile('/index.html', {root: __dirname});
});

app.listen(8080, function() {
    console.log('App now listening on port 8080');
});
```

The assert module we added provides a simple set of assertion tests that can be used for testing invariants, or values that cannot change. Now let's save the file and run the server again:

$ node server.js

If everything is working properly and your Node.js server is connected to the database, you should see the following output:

App now listening on port 8080
Connected to MongoDB.

This indicates that your Node.js server is running and connected to MongoDB. If the MongoDB connection is not successful, an error will be thrown in the console.

Now that we've got a Node.js server running with a connection to the test database in MongoDB, we can begin writing some REST API endpoints.

Writing basic REST API endpoints

The most common type of RESTful request on the Web is a HTTP GET or Read operation. An example of this is a simple request to view a web page through a URL. GET requests can be performed to read any kind of data and do not need to be supported by a database, but in order to implement the Create, Update, and Delete operations on data, some type of database or data store must be used, along with a REST **Application Programming Interface (API)**.

CRUD with REST

Performing full CRUD operations with your web application can be done using the simple NPM, Bower, and Grunt application you have been working with thus far; we just need to write some API endpoints now to make this possible. Let's go back to our application CLI to make some changes.

Handling request data with Node.js and Express

Before we can handle any API request data sent to our server, we have to add the ability to parse that data. In most cases, this will be data that is sent from a web page through a form or some other means. This type of data is referred to as the **body** of the request, and in order to parse it we will need to add another Node.js package:

```
$ npm install body-parser --save
```

This will add the Node.js `body-parser` package to our application dependencies. Now let's go back to editing `server.js` and add some additional code:

```
var bodyParser = require('body-parser');

app.use(bodyParser.json());
```

Add the bodyParser variable declaration below the other variable declarations at the top of the file, and then call `app.use(bodyParser.json())` just below it and above all route definitions. This will now allow us to handle and parse any JSON data sent as the body of any request to the server.

Creating with a POST request

Express follows REST vernacular by providing method names for routes that match their respective HTTP request type. In REST, a HTTP POST request is the standard method used for a Create operation. The respective Express method for this is `.post()`. Let's set up a simple POST request with Express that will allow us to add additional records to our users collection in MongoDB.

First, let's remove the MongoDB connection test code in `server.js` and replace it with the following:

```
app.post('/api/users', function(request, response) {
    console.dir(request.body);
    mongo.connect(url, function(err, db) {
        db.collection('users')
        .insertOne(request.body, function(err, result) {
            if (err) {
                throw err;
            }
            console.log('Document inserted successfully.');
            response.json(result);
            db.close();
        });
```

```
        });
    });
```

Make sure this code is *above* the `app.use('/', ...)` and `app.get('*', ...)` definitions we created in *Chapter 3, SPA Essentials – Creating the Ideal Application Environment.*

The entire content of `server.js` should now look like the following code:

```
var express = require('express');
var app = express();
var mongo = require('mongodb').MongoClient;
var assert = require('assert');
var url = 'mongodb://localhost:27017/test';
var bodyParser = require('body-parser');

app.use(bodyParser.json());

app.post('/api/users', function(request, response) {
    console.dir(request.body);
    mongo.connect(url, function(err, db) {
        db.collection('users')
        .insertOne(request.body, function(err, result) {
            if (err) {
                throw err;
            }
            console.log('Document inserted successfully.');
            response.json(result);
            db.close();
        });
    });
});

app.use('/', express.static('./'));

app.get('*', function(request, response) {
    response.sendFile('/index.html', {root: __dirname});
});

app.listen(8080, function() {
    console.log('App now listening on port 8080');
});
```

The .post() request endpoint or handler we added will first log the `request.body` object, which has been parsed and converted from JSON, to the server console on the command line. It will then connect to MongoDB and call the MongoDB `insertOne()` method to insert the `request.body` document into the users collection in our database.

There are many libraries available that can handle this type of interaction and database inserts from a request much more gracefully, but it is important to understand how the Express server is interacting with MongoDB, so for that reason, we are using the native MongoDB API to perform these operations.

Testing the POST request on the frontend

Now that we have a POST handler set up in our server, let's test that it works by sending a request from the frontend. Inserting information is commonly done from user entry in a form, so let's edit the application layout index.html file and add one:

```html
<h2>POST Request</h2>
<form data-url="/api/users" data-method="post">
    <p>
        <label>
            First name:
            <input type="text" name="first_name">
        </label>
    </p>
    <p>
        <label>
            Last name:
            <input type="text" name="last_name">
        </label>
    </p>
    <p>
        <label>
            Title:
            <input type="text" name="title">
        </label>
    </p>
    <p>
        <label>
            Website:
            <input type="text" name="website">
        </label>
    </p>
    <p>
        <button type="submit">Submit</button>
    </p>
</form>
```

Add this HTML code just under the opening `<body>` tag in the page. We will again use the `Payload.js` API for making a request to the server; this time, a simple POST request. Notice that the `data-url` attribute of the `<form>` tag is set to the API endpoint URL, and the `data-method` attribute is set to *post*. When the form is submitted, this will take the form data and convert it to JSON and send it as the request body to the server via a POST request.

Now run the app from the CLI and go to `localhost:8080` in your browser. You should see the form there. Add some sample data to the form inputs:

```
First name: Peebo
Last name: Sanderson
Title: Vagrant
Website: http://salvationarmy.org
```

Now click to submit the form just once. If all goes well, you should see something like the following displayed in your console:

```
App now listening on port 8080
{ first_name: 'Peebo',
  last_name: 'Sanderson',
  title: 'Vagrant',
  website: 'http://salvationarmy.org' }
Document inserted successfully.
```

The JSON document created from the form should now be inserted into the users collection in the MongoDB test database. This means there are now two documents in the collection – the document we inserted originally from the user.json file, and the one we just added from the form POST.

Now that we've got a couple of records in our database, we need a way to retrieve those documents and display them in the browser. We can do this by first creating an endpoint to read data from the database.

Reading with a GET request

A HTTP GET request is the standard method used for a Read operation in REST. The respective Express method for this is `.get()`. We previously set up a GET request in *Chapter 3* to load our layout page, but this time we want to write a REST API request that will return the user records from MongoDB in JSON format.

First, hit *Ctrl + C* on the command line to stop the server, then open up `server.js` again for editing. Just below the `.post()` endpoint we wrote, add the following code:

```
app.get('/api/users', function(req, res) {
    mongo.connect(url, function(err, db) {
        db.collection('users').find()
            .toArray(function(err, result) {
            if (err) {
                throw err;
            }
            console.log(result.length + ' documents retrieved.');
            res.json(result);
            db.close();
        });
    });
});
```

You will notice that this handler is requested through the same URL as the `.post()` handler, but it will be handled differently because of the HTTP request method being a GET instead of a POST.

First, the request will connect to the test database and then call the MongoDB `.find()` method on the users collection, which will return a cursor. A cursor in MongoDB is a pointer to the results of a database query. As we mentioned in *Chapter 3, SPA Essentials – Creating the Ideal Application Environment*, MongoDB uses the BSON data format internally, so in order to format the cursor for use in our application, we have to convert the BSON data to a format that is consumable over HTTP. For this purpose, we chain the `.toArray()` method to the `.find()` operation, which will convert the result set to an array of documents. We can also access the length property of the resulting array and log the number of documents retrieved to the server console.

Next, we pass an anonymous callback function to the `.toArray()` method and return the resulting data as a JSON response.

Testing the GET request on the frontend

Now let's set up some HTML to test our GET request on the frontend. Edit the application layout index.html page and edit the HTML we added to retrieve and display data from the `user.json` file in *Chapter 2, Model-View-Whatever*. This should be right underneath the form we just added for the POST request:

```
<h2>GET Request</h2>
<p>
    <a href="#"
        data-url="/api/users"
```

```
            data-template="users"
            data-selector=".results">Load user data</a>
</p>
<div class="results"></div>
```

We have now changed the URL for the GET request from /user.json to /api/users. Payload.js will handle an API request as a GET by default, so there is no need to add the data-method="get" attribute to this URL, other than to provide more transparency. Additionally, the empty .results <div> is indicated as where we want to display our resulting data.

We also have changed the data-template attribute value here from user (singular) to users (plural). This indicates that we want to load a Handlebars template named users. Create a new file in the root of your app directory called users.handlebars and add the following code to it:

```
{{#each data}}
    <p>{{first_name}} {{last_name}}</p>
{{/each}}
```

Now we need to recompile the Handlebars templates and save them to the templates.js file:

$ handlebars *.handlebars -f templates.js

Run this from the command line and you will be just about ready to load the MongoDB data into the template. First, run the server again, and then go to or refresh localhost:8080 in your browser. Click the Load user data link and you should see only one name show up below it: the first_name and last_name fields from the document you just inserted into the database. If you check the console, you should see output like the following:

App now listening on port 8080
2 documents retrieved.

So two documents were actually retrieved from the database, but only one name is displayed in the browser. Why is this? The reason is quite simple, but easy to overlook. The data from the document we first inserted from user.json looks like the following:

```
{
    "id": 1,
    "name": {
        "first": "Philip",
        "last": "Klauzinski"
    },
    "title": "Sr. UI Engineer",
```

```
    "website": "http://webtopian.com"
}
```

The new document we added from the form POST request, however, looks like this:

```
{
    "first_name": "Peebo",
    "last_name": "Sanderson",
    "title": "Vagrant",
    "website": "http://salvationarmy.org"
}
```

As you can see, the document we created from the form does not have a name object with the first and last properties nested in it like the user.json document, but instead has the explicit first_name and last_name properties, and those are the properties that we are looking to display in the Handlebars template.

This is the reason why the HTML view only displays one name, but how did we overlook this? The reason for this is attributed to the fact that MongoDB is a document-oriented database with no strict data typing, like a relational database. As we discussed in Chapter 3, *SPA Essentials – Creating the Ideal Application Environment*, this is one of the things that makes NoSQL document-oriented databases completely different than traditional SQL databases.

So when we inserted the new data into our collection from the form POST, MongoDB did nothing to check that the format of the new document matched the format of the existing document. Self-defined document structure is a powerful feature of a document-oriented database, but it can also lead to application errors and missing data for the UI when the document collections are not normalized.

Now let's write an Update endpoint to change one of our existing documents and have it match the other.

Updating with a PUT request

In REST, a HTTP PUT request is the standard method used for an Update operation. The respective Express method for this is .put().

Now hit *Ctrl + C* to stop the Node.js server, then open up the server.js file again and add the following code below the .get() handler:

```
app.put('/api/users', function(req, res) {
    mongo.connect(url, function(err, db) {
        db.collection('users').updateOne(
```

```
                    { "id": 1 },
                    req.body,
                    function(err, result) {
                        if (err) {
                            throw err;
                        }
                        console.log(result);
                        res.json(result);
                        db.close();
                    }
                );
            });
    });
```

We are again using the same endpoint URL, but this will only handle a PUT request made from the frontend. This method will first connect to our test database, and then it will call the MongoDB .udpateOne() method to update an existing document. The first argument passed to this method is a filter, or data to look for and find a match. The .updateOne() method will only look for the first document that matches a filter and then end the query.

Notice that the filter passed to the method here is { "id": 1 }. This is the id field that was passed in from the user.json file. Remember that MongoDB actually creates its own internal id for every document if one is not supplied, and this field is called _id. So in the case of our original user object we supplied, it will have an _id field set to a BSON ObjectId and the original *id* field we supplied set to 1. Since we know that the new document we created from the form POST does not have the extraneous *id* field, we can safely filter on that field to find the original document and update it.

The second parameter we are passing to the .updateOne() method is the entire request body, which will be an object produced from a form submission. Typically, with a PUT request, the intention is to update existing fields with new values, but in this case we actually want to change the structure of the document to match the structure of the new record we created using the form POST.

The third parameter passed to the .updateOne() method is an anonymous callback function to which the result of the update request is passed. Here, we log that result to the console and return it as JSON to the frontend.

Testing the PUT request on the frontend

Now let's go back to the application layout index.html file and add some more HTML just below the GET request HTML we added previously. To do this, copy the HTML from the POST request form and change it to look like the following:

```
<h2>PUT Request</h2>
<form data-url="/api/users" data-method="put">
    <p>
        <label>
            First name:
            <input type="text" name="first_name">
        </label>
    </p>
    <p>
        <label>
            Last name:
            <input type="text" name="last_name">
        </label>
    </p>
    <p>
        <label>
            Title:
            <input type="text" name="title">
        </label>
    </p>
    <p>
        <label>
            Website:
            <input type="text" name="website">
        </label>
    </p>
    <p>
        <button type="submit">Submit</button>
    </p>
</form>
```

This code matches the POST request HTML save for a few minor changes. We have edited the `<h2>` title to show that this is the PUT request form, and the `data-method` attribute on the form is now set to `put`. Leave all form inputs as they are because we will want the updated document to match the new document we created.

Now start the server again from the command line and then go to or refresh localhost:8080 in your browser. You should see the new PUT Request form we added below the POST request and GET request areas on the page. Now enter the data from the original `user.json` object into the corresponding form fields:

```
First name: Philip
Last name: Klauzinski
Title: Sr. UI Engineer
Website: http://webtopian.com
```

Now click the submit button once and check your console output. You should see a lot of information printed to the console. At the very top of it, you should see the following:

```
{ result: { ok: 1, nModified: 1, n: 1 }
```

This result indicates that one record was modified. If the update was successful, the original user.json document should now match the format of the second one we added from the form POST. To test this, click on the Load user data link to GET the user documents and list the names using the Handlebars template and the first_name and last_name properties. You should now see each of the two names listed in the browser:

```
Philip Klauzinski
Peebo Sanderson
```

To complete our RESTful API endpoints in server.js, let's add a final Delete handler and use it to remove one of the two user records.

Deleting with a DELETE request

A HTTP DELETE request is the standard method used for the homonymous Delete operation in REST. Naturally, the respective Express method for this is .delete().

Hit *Ctrl* + *C* on the command to stop the server and then open *server.js* again for editing. Add the following code just below the .put() handler:

```
app.delete('/api/users', function(req, res) {
    mongo.connect(url, function(err, db) {
        db.collection('users').deleteOne(
            { "first_name": "Peebo" },
            function(err, result) {
            if (err) {
                throw err;
            }
            console.log(result);
            res.json(result);
            db.close();
        });
    });
});
```

This handler will first connect to the database, then it will call the MongoDB `.deleteOne()` method on the users collection. The first parameter passed to the `.deleteOne()` method is a condition to match against a record to delete. In this case, we want to delete the new record we created earlier from the form POST, so we are using the unique `first_name` value of `Peebo` for this.

The second parameter passed to the `.deleteOne()` method is an anonymous callback function which is passed the result of the delete request. We are again going to log that result to the console and return it to the frontend as JSON.

Testing the DELETE request on the frontend

Open the application layout index.html file again and add the following code below the PUT request form we added previously:

```
<h2>DELETE Request</h2>
<button data-url="/api/users"
        data-method="delete"
        data-template="user"
        data-selector=".delete-response">Delete Peebo</button>
<div class="delete-response"></div>
```

Here we have added a simple button with the Payload.js attributes necessary to send a HTTP DELETE request.

> It should be noted that no request body, such as form data, can be sent with a DELETE request.

Start up the Node.js server again and then go to or reload index.html in your browser. You should see the **Delete Peebo** button at the bottom of the page. Click the button just once and then check the console output. You will see a lot of information from the result. At the very top of the output, you should see the following:

```
{ result: { ok: 1, n: 1 }
```

The n: 1 property shown here indicates that one record was successfully deleted. To verify this, go back to the browser and scroll up to the Load user data link under the **GET Request** title. Click that link, and you should now see only the original `user.json` document `first_name` and `last_name` shown. The console will also indicate that only a single result was found in the users collection:

```
1 documents retrieved.
```

Congratulations, you now have a full RESTful set of endpoints written to perform CRUD operations with Express and MongoDB. Although quite primitive, these example methods should give you a foundation for learning more and building upon them to create a more robust single page application. They should also give you a better understanding of the REST architectural style, and how Node.js interacts with MongoDB.

Alternatives to REST

REST is arguably the most widely used architectural style across the Web and the IoT, but there are many other technologies, protocols, and architectural styles available to use for web services and single page web application data exchange.

TCP versus UDP

As mentioned earlier, TCP is the transport layer protocol upon which HTTP travels to the application layer. Some of the beneficial attributes of TCP connections are that they are reliable, serial, and checked for errors while sending information. These benefits, however, can sometimes lead to undesirable latency:

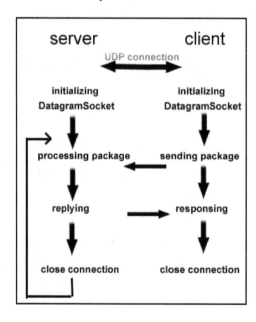

The Internet Protocol Suite includes many other protocols alongside TCP. One of these protocols is **User Datagram Protocol (UDP)**. UDP is also a core member of the *transport layer* of TCP/IP. The primary difference between UDP and TCP is that UDP is *connectionless*. This means that individual units of data are transmitted with self-identifying information and the receiving end of that information has no prior knowledge of when or how it will be received. UDP does nothing to ensure that a recipient endpoint is actually available to receive that information, and thus this risk must be taken into consideration when using UDP.

Since UDP uses no connection, it is inherently not *reliable*, and that is what sets it apart from a connection-based protocol such as TCP. TCP allows for error checking and correction during a transmission because both parties are aware of each other due to their *connection*.

Messages sent over UDP and other connectionless protocols are called *datagrams*. UDP and datagrams should only be used when error checking and correction is not needed or is performed within the application layer itself. Checking errors at the application level is often the model that is used with UDP since error checking and correction is almost always a necessity with any application. Some examples of application types that use UDP are:

- Streaming media
- **Voice over IP (VoIP)**
- Massively multiplayer online games
- **Domain Name System (DNS)**
- Some **Virtual Private Network (VPN)** systems

The most obvious disadvantages with UDP and a connectionless protocol are that there is no guarantee of message delivery, no error checking, and, consequently, no error correction. This can be a major disadvantage in an application where a user is interacting with the system on their own and most events are user generated. In a system where hundreds or thousands of users may be interacting with each other, however, a connectionless protocol allows the application to be free of latency due to error correction. A massively multiplayer online game is a good example of a system in which thousands or even millions of messages may need to be transported across a network consistently, but this cannot be done reliably while also maintaining connections with error checking and correction.

SOAP

REST is often compared to **Simple Object Access Protocol** (**SOAP**), although SOAP is actually a protocol and not an architectural style like REST. The reason for the comparison is because both are used for web services, and in this context, REST is synonymous with HTTP, which is a protocol. Even though SOAP is a protocol, it also interacts with HTTP to transmit messages for implementing web services. It can also be used over SMTP.

The message format for SOAP is XML. An XML message sent with SOAP is referred to as an *envelope*. The structure of a SOAP envelope follows a particular pattern involving elements including a mandatory *body* element and an optional *header* element. The body may also include nested *fault* constructs which carry information regarding exceptions. An example of a SOAP message is shown as follows:

```
<env:Envelope xmlns:env="http://www.w3.org/2003/05/soap-envelope">
<env:Header>
    <n:shipping >
      This is a shipping message
    </n:shipping>
  </env:Header>
  <env:Body>
    <env:Fault>
      <env:Code>
        <env:Value>
          env:VersionMismatch
        </env:Value>
      </env:Code>
      <env:Reason>
        <env:Text xml:lang="en">
          versions do not match
        </env:Text>
      </env:Reason>
    </env:Fault>
  </env:Body>
</env:Envelope>
```

REST can also use XML for data exchange, but more commonly uses JSON in modern-day web applications.

WebSockets

WebSockets is a protocol that allows interactive communication between a web browser and a server. The term *interactive* in this context means that the server can *push* messages to the web browser without the browser needing to periodically *poll* the server for new data, as might typically be done in a web application using HTTP, AJAX, and REST.

You may have heard of *push* technology before. This paradigm is evident in many smartphone applications that push update notifications to a phone as soon as new data is available. This is also referred to as *real-time data*. HTTP is limited in that it does not support open connections that can receive real-time data. Instead, HTTP requires that a request be made and a connection or *socket* is opened, a response is received, information is downloaded, and the connection is then closed. Once new information becomes available, this will not be evident to the application needing that information without making periodic requests to the server, which is referred to as *polling*.

In 2011, WebSockets became officially standardized and supported by modern web browsers. This protocol allows data to be transferred to and from a server by using an *open* socket connection, allowing the client to request data at will but also allowing the server to *push* data to the client in real time:

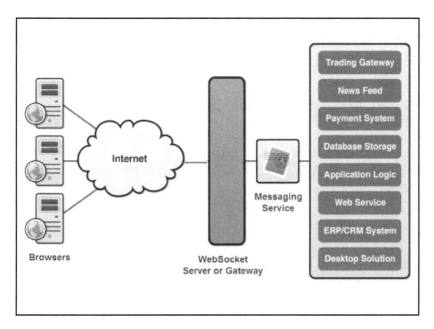

Web applications using REST are limited by the open/close connection constraint with HTTP. This makes sense for many web applications that do not need a server response without a user interaction, or that can implement periodic server polling without too much overhead required. Web applications that want to provide real-time data to the user without an action, however, may be better served by using WebSockets.

MQTT

MQTT originally stood for **MQ Telemetry Transport**. It is a messaging protocol designed to be used on top of TCP/IP, or the Internet Protocol Suite. MQTT employs a *publish-subscribe,* or PubSub, messaging pattern in which events or messages are published by publishers and available to any number of subscribers. In following, subscribers receive messages from any number of publishers. In this paradigm, publishers are entirely agnostic of subscribers.

In contrast to SOAP and WebSockets, MQTT is not designed to be used for web services over HTTP, but instead is primarily use for **machine-to-machine** (**M2M**) communication. MQTT is often used for satellite communications, home or **smart home** automation, and for mobile applications. MQTT is considered to be lightweight and have a small code footprint, making it ideal for mobile applications which may be using slower, wireless mobile network connections.

The "MQ" in MQTT was originally derived from IBM's **Message Queuing** (**MQ**) protocol. Message queuing is not actually a requirement for MQTT, however, which is why it is no longer a true acronym and is simply referred to as MQTT.

MQTT is an **Organization for the Advancement of Structured Information Standards** (**OASIS**) standard. OASIS is an organization that defines standards for the IoT and other areas of technology.

Any software that implements MQTT is referred to as an MQTT broker, which is a type of message broker architectural pattern that translates messages sent from an application to the proprietary format of the receiver, or the message broker itself:

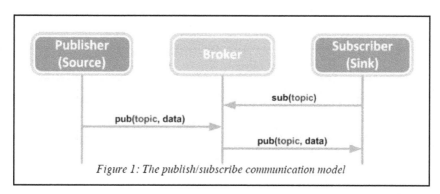

Figure 1: The publish/subscribe communication model

The purpose of the message broker is to take the messages received by an application and perform some type of action on them. For example, some actions might be:

- Initiating web service requests
- Forwarding messages to other destinations
- Transforming messages to a different type of representation for consumption by anther application or endpoint
- Storing messages to be used for publish-subscribe events and responses
- Logging and/or responding to application errors

There are many popular message broker applications and services that can be used for message exchange in single page applications. Some of these are Mosquitto, CloudMQTT, IBM MessageSight, and ActiveMQ.

AMQP

Advanced Message Queuing Protocol (AMQP) is similar to MQTT. It is an open standard application layer protocol for use with message brokers.

One of the most popular open source message brokers for modern-day web applications is RabbitMQ, which employs AMQP. In an AMQP architecture using something like RabbitMQ, messages are *produced* by an application and then *queued* or stored in the RabbitMQ server. A queue is also, in a sense, a *buffer* because it can store any amount of information for any amount of time until it is needed:

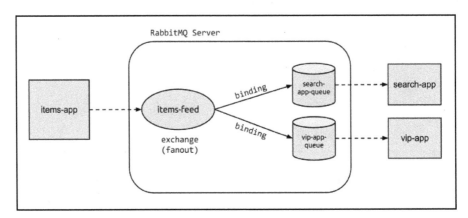

Although it uses AMQP, RabbitMQ also includes an adapter for MQTT. It additionally supports HTTP and **Streaming Text Oriented Messaging Protocol (STOMP)**. The fact that RabbitMQ is open source and that it also includes adapters for other protocols, most notably HTTP, contributes greatly to its popularity today.

CoAP

Constrained Application Protocol (CoAP) is a web transfer protocol designed for M2M communication. The machines primarily targeted for CoAP services are IoT devices.

CoAP is actually quite similar to HTTP and employs the REST architectural style as part of its specification. The difference with CoAP is that it strictly adheres to REST principles, while HTTP merely supports REST but does not require it.

Since CoAP uses the REST architectural style, it can actually be connected to over HTTP because, like with any RESTful architecture, the client is agnostic of the RESTful server it is accessing. In this scenario, a cross-protocol proxy is used to make the CoAP services available to a HTTP client:

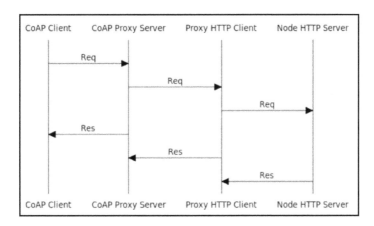

DDP

Distributed Data Protocol (DDP) is not commonly used but gaining ground through the popular Meteor JavaScript framework. DDP is a simple protocol used for explicitly retrieving representations from a server, and also receiving updates regarding modifications on those representations in real time.

DDP allows Meteor applications to use WebSockets for services, providing a framework around those services to be connectionless. JSON data is used, but instead of being explicitly requested like it is with a RESTful architecture, the JSON data messages can be *pushed* in real time to an application.

DDP was originally developed for Meteor by its founders; however, it is not specific to Meteor and can be used in other frameworks. Meteor's implementation of DDP is written entirely in JavaScript and is open source.

Summary

You have now learned the fundamental aspects of the REST architectural style, the differences between an architectural style and a protocol, the relationship between REST and the HTTP protocol, and the constraints of REST. You have also learned to write some basic REST API endpoints using Express and MongoDB. A good understanding of REST and the server side of a single page application is paramount to becoming a skilled web SPA developer. In the next chapter, we will transition our focus to the frontend of SPA development, learn a few things about SPA UI frameworks and best practices, and take everything we have learned so far and apply it to the View layer.

5
Its All About the View

The UI layer, or **View**, is the most visible component of any application. No matter what is going on underneath the hood, be it REST, Websockets, MQTT, or SOAP, the view is where everything culminates for a full, interactive application experience. Just as with the server side, the view has its own set of complexities and myriad of architectural choices to make from a development perspective. We will now explore some of these choices along with some different design patterns that can be used in the all-encompassing view layer.

In this chapter, we will cover the following images:

- The differences among various JavaScript templating engines
- The advantages of precompiling JavaScript templates
- How to optimize your application layout

JavaScript templating engines

Maintaining the view on the frontend of your application goes a long way toward keeping it server-side agnostic. Even if you are using a MVC framework underneath to serve REST endpoints for your application, keeping the view templates and logic on the frontend will ensure that you can more easily swap out the MVC backend in the future without significantly altering the logical and architectural structure of your application. JavaScript templating engines provide an effective way to manage view templates entirely on the frontend.

There are many open source JavaScript templating engines available. Next, we will cover the basics of some of the more popular ones:

- Underscore.js
- Mustache.js
- Handlebars.js
- Pure.js
- Pug
- EJS

Underscore.js

The **Underscore.js** library is well known for its useful JavaScript functional programming helpers and utility methods. One of those utility methods is `_.template()`. This method is used to compile strings with expressions into functions that replace those expressions with dynamic values.

Underscore.js template syntax delimiters resemble those of the **ERB**, or **Embedded Ruby** template syntax, with an **equals** sign following the opening tag:

```
<p>Hello, <%= name %>.</p>
```

An Underscore.js template expression used within HTML looks like the preceding example. The variable name would be dynamically passed in to the compiled function for this template.

The `_.template()` method can also be used to parse and execute arbitrary JavaScript code within a template. JavaScript code within Underscore.js templates is delimited by using the ERB style tags *without* an equals sign following the opening tag:

```
<ul>
    <% _.each(items, function(item) { %>
        <li><%= item.property %></li>
    <% } %>
</ul>
```

As you can see in this example, the ERB tags within the template give the script access to the global _ object and allow it to iterate over a given object or array contained in that context or even up the scope chain from that context using the library's `_.each()` method. The fact that the script has access to the _ object shows that any global variable attached to the `window` namespace is available to the script.

Giving templates the ability to execute arbitrary JavaScript code is a subject that has met with much debate in the community, and the general consensus is that the practice is frowned upon. This is due to the lessons learned from other web scripting languages, such as PHP.

Mixing code for dynamic business logic with HTML directly in your templates can lead to a codebase that is difficult to maintain and debug by other developers and future generations. This type of code also violates the principles of MVC and MVW architectural patterns. It should go without saying that it is up to the developer writing the code how much or how little business logic they choose to include in their templates, but for the creators of many JavaScript templating engines, leaving that door open was not an option. For these reasons, the concept of *logic-less* templates was born.

You can learn more about Underscore.js at `underscorejs.org`.

Mustache.js

Mustache.js is an implementation of the popular **Mustache template system** for JavaScript templating. Mustache touts itself as a *logic-less* template syntax. The idea behind this concept is not necessarily to have templates completely void of logic, but more to discourage the practice of including a large amount of business logic within your templates.

Mustache gets its name from the use of double curly braces, which resemble the shape of a mustache, as the default delimiter tags for templates. The major difference between Mustache templates and Underscore.js templates is that Mustache does not allow for the placement of arbitrary JavaScript within an alternate form of its tags; it only allows for expressions.

In its simplest form, a Mustache template maps values from a JavaScript object directly to their respective template expressions, represented by the keys for those object values. Take an object such as the one shown here, for example:

```
{
    "name": {
        "first": "Udis",
        "last": "Petroyka"
    },
    "age": "82"
}
```

The values from this object can be represented in a Mustache template like this:

```
<p>{{name.first}} {{name.last}}</p>
<p>Age: {{age}}</p>
```

In this example, you can see that even nested object values can be accessed by using JavaScript dot notation, as shown with `{{name.first}}` and `{{name.last}}`:

```
<p>Udis Petroyka</p>
<p>Age: 82</p>
```

Sections

Mustache templates also include the ability to render *sections*, or *blocks of text*. This involves using an alternate expression syntax that includes an opening and closing tag syntax. How a section is rendered depends on the value of the key being called for it.

Boolean values

Given a Boolean value, a section will render or not render depending on if that Boolean is `true` or `false`:

```
{
    "name": {
        "first": "Jarmond",
        "last": "Dittlemore"
    },
    "email_subscriber": false
}
```

The delimiter syntax for sections consists of opening curly braces followed by the pound # symbol and the name of the property to start the section, and closing curly braces followed by the / symbol and the property name to end the section. This syntax is similar to HTML opening and closing tags:

```
<p>{{name.first}} {{name.last}}</p>
{{#email_subscriber}}
    <p>Content here will not be shown for this user.</p>
{{/email_subscriber}}
```

In this example, the `email_subscriber` property is set to false, so the template would render the following HTML:

```
<p>Jarmond Dittlemore</p>
```

Essentially, the use of a section with a Boolean value is equivalent to an `if` conditional statement. Such a use case does indeed include logic, though in its most basic form. In this way, the term *logic-less* is proven to not be as stringent as it may initially be perceived.

Lists

Additionally, sections can be used to iterate over a list of items set as the value for a given object key. Within a section, the context, or variable scope, is shifted to that of the key that is being iterated over. Take the following parent key and corresponding list of values, for example:

```
{
    "people": [
        { "firstName": "Peebo", "lastName": "Sanderson" },
        { "firstName": "Udis", "lastName": "Petroyka" },
        { "firstName": "Jarmond", "lastName": "Dittlemore" },
        { "firstName": "Chappy", "lastName": "Scrumdinger" }
    ]
}
```

Given a list of people and their names, a section can be used to render each person's name in an HTML unordered list:

```
<ul>
{{#people}}
    <li>{{firstName}} {{lastName}}</li>
{{/people}}
</ul>
```

This template code would render the following HTML, given the preceding example object:

```
<ul>
    <li>Peebo Sanderson</li>
    <li>Udis Petroyka</li>
    <li>Jarmond Dittlemore</li>
    <li>Chappy Scrumdinger</li>
</ul>
```

Lambdas

Object property values can also be returned from *lambdas,* or functions that are passed to return values as data, to the current section's context:

```
{
    "people": [
        { "firstName": "Peebo", "lastName": "Sanderson" },
        { "firstName": "Udis", "lastName": "Petroyka" },
        { "firstName": "Jarmond", "lastName": "Dittlemore" },
        { "firstName": "Chappy", "lastName": "Scrumdinger" }
    ],
    "name": function() {
        return this.firstName + ' ' + this.lastName;
    }
}
```

In the case of a list, a lambda will return a value based on the context of the current list item for an iteration:

```
<ul>
{{#people}}
    <li>{{name}}</li>
{{/people}}
</ul>
```

In this manner, the preceding template will produce the same output as the previous example:

```
<ul>
    <li>Peebo Sanderson</li>
    <li>Udis Petroyka</li>
    <li>Jarmond Dittlemore</li>
    <li>Chappy Scrumdinger</li>
</ul>
```

Inverted sections

An inverted section in a Mustache template is one that is rendered only when the value for that section's key is `false` or *falsy,* such as `null`, `undefined`, 0, or an empty list `[]`. Take the following object, for example:

```
{
    "name": {
        "first": "Peebo",
        "last": "Sanderson"
```

```
        },
        "email_subscriber": false
    }
```

An inverted section begins with a caret ^ symbol following the opening curly braces, rather than the pound # symbol used for a standard section. Given the preceding example object, the following template syntax can be used to render HTML for the `false` property value:

```
<p>{{name.first}} {{name.last}}</p>
{{^email_subscriber}}
    <p>I am not an email subscriber.</p>
{{/email_subscriber}}
```

This template would render the following HTML, based on the `false` property value in the object:

```
<p>Peebo Sanderson</p>
<p>I am not an email subscriber.</p>
```

Comments

Mustache templates also give you the ability to include comments within your templates. The advantage to using the Mustache syntax for your comments over HTML comments is that they will not be rendered in the HTML output, as would be the case with standard HTML comments:

```
<p>Udis likes to comment{{! hi, this comment won't be rendered }}</p>
<!- This is a standard HTML comment ->
```

Mustache comments are denoted by a *bang*, or exclamation point, following the opening curly braces. The preceding template code would render the following:

```
<p>Udis likes to comment</p>
<!- This is a standard HTML comment ->
```

As shown, the Mustache template comment is not part of the rendered HTML, but the standard HTML comment is. The advantage to using Mustache template comments is in the payload size of the rendered HTML, which you want to keep as small as possible, and there are probably not many cases in which you would actually want to render comments in dynamic HTML. This allows you to have helpful comments for other developers in your template code without it putting a burden on the frontend of the application.

Partials

One of the most useful features of Mustache templates is the ability to include *partials*, or separate templates rendered at runtime within a compiled template. Conceptually, this feature is similar to *includes* for server-side template languages.

The syntax for partials uses a greater than > sign after the opening curly braces followed by the name of the partial. A common file naming convention is to prepend the uncompiled partial filenames with an underscore _. Consider the following two files:

user.hbs

```
<h3>{{name.first}} {{name.last}}</h3>
{{> user-details}}
```

_user-details.hbs

```
<ul>
    {{^email_subscriber}}
    <li>I am not an email subscriber</li>
    {{/email_subscriber}}
    <li>Age: {{age}}</li>
    <li>Profession: {{profession}}</li>
</ul>
```

The call to include the partial file is indicated on the second line of user.hbs. This will parse _user-details.hbs in the same context as user.hbs. In a standard compiler setup, the underscore on the partial filename would be excluded from the key name, and the template would be stored within the partials namespace:

```
{
    "name": {
        "first": "Jarmond",
        "last": "Dittlemore"
    },
    "email_subscriber": false,
    "age": 24,
    "profession": "Student"
}
```

Given the preceding example object, the fully rendered HTML from the template would look like the following:

```
<h3>Jarmond Dittlemore</h3>
<ul>
    <li>I am not an email subscriber</li>
    <li>Age: 24</li>
```

```
    <li>Profession: Student</li>
</ul>
```

As you can see in the example, the key names from the object were used directly in the partial from the same context as the parent template.

Set alternative delimiters

One of the more unusual features of Mustache templates is the ability to set *alternative* delimiters from inside standard Mustache delimiter tags in a template. This is done by using an equals sign = following the opening standard delimiter tags, inserting the new opening delimiter followed by the new closing delimiter, and an equals sign followed by the standard closing delimiter tags:

```
{{=<% %>=}}
```

If this code is placed anywhere inside of a Mustache template, the delimiter tags from below that point will then use the new syntax:

```
{
    "name": {
        "first": "Chappy",
        "last": "Scrumdinger"
    },
    "email_subscriber": false,
    "age": 96,
    "profession": "Oilman"
}
```

Given the preceding object, a template could be constructed using that data combined with alternative delimiter tags for parsing it:

```
<p>Standard tags: {{name.first}} {{name.last}}</p>
{{=<% %>=}}
<p>New tags - Age: <%age%></p>
<%={{ }}=%>
<p>Standard tags again - Profession: {{profession}}</p>
```

In this example, the standard tags are used once, then the set delimiters feature is used to change the tags to use the ERB style delimiters, then the tags are again changed back to the original standard delimiters:

```
<p>Standard tags: Chappy Scrumdinger</p>
<p>New tags - Age: 96</p>
<p>Standard tags again - Profession: Oilman</p>
```

The resulting HTML would look like the preceding code, rendered with two entirely different sets of delimiters inside of one template.

You can learn more about Mustache.js at `github.com/janl/mustache.js`, or learn about the original Mustache templates at `mustache.github.io`.

Handlebars.js

Handlebars.js templates are also considered *logic-less* and are largely based on Mustache templates, but provide some additional features. They also exclude some of the features of Mustache templates that the creators did not consider useful.

Handlebars is one of the more prominent templating engines in the JavaScript community. It is used by several major open source JavaScript frameworks including Backbone.js, Ember.js, and the popular Meteor.js framework. It uses their own reactive flavor of Handlebars templating engine called Spacebars. Due to its popularity, we will cover Handlebars in a bit more depth here.

Explicit path lookup versus recursive path lookup

One of the features that differentiates Handlebars templates from Mustache templates is that Handlebars does not support recursive path lookup as Mustache templates do. This concerns sections, or blocks, as they are referred to in Handlebars. When you are in the context of a child property of an object, Handlebars will not automatically look up the scope chain for an expression reference. Instead, you must explicitly define the path to the scope for the variable that you are looking for. This makes the scope in Handlebars templates more meaningful and understandable:

```
{
    "name": {
        "first": "Peebo",
        "last": "Sanderson"
    },
    "email_subscriber": false,
    "age": 54,
    "profession": "Singer"
}
```

Given this object, the following template syntax would work with Mustache templates:

```
<!-- Mustache template -->
<p>{{name.first}} {{name.last}}</p>
{{#profession}}
<p>Profession: {{profession}}</p>
{{/profession}}
```

This template would render the value for the `profession` key inside of the block scope for `#profession` because Mustache supports recursive path lookup. In other words, a nested context always has access to variables on the parent context above it. This is not the case by default, however, with Handlebars:

```
<!-- Handlebars template -->
<p>{{name.first}} {{name.last}}</p>
{{#profession}}
<p>Profession: {{this}}</p>
{{/profession}}
```

As shown in this example, the `this` keyword is used to reference the variable for which the current block context is set. If the `profession` variable itself were referenced, this would throw an error in Handlebars.

```
<!-- Handlebars template -->
<p>{{name.first}} {{name.last}}</p>
{{#profession}}
<p>Profession: {{../profession}}</p>
{{/profession}}
```

Additionally, Handlebars can look up the scope chain for a variable with an **explicit path** reference using the `../` syntax shown in the preceding code. This syntax mimics that of recursive file path lookups in command-line interfaces. In this example, the `../profession` reference simply looks up the variable for which the current block context is set:

```
<p>Peebo Sanderson</p>
<p>Profession: Singer</p>
```

The reason Handlebars does not support recursive path lookup by default is for speed. By limiting the path lookup to the current block context, Handlebars templates can render more quickly. A compile time `compat` flag is provided to override this functionality and allow recursive path lookups, but the creators of Handlebars advise against this and note that there is a performance cost in doing this.

Helpers

Handlebars templates do not support the use of lambdas defined in objects such as Mustache templates, but instead use helpers for added functionality. Helpers in Handlebars are a way to abstract away view logic that might otherwise be done directly in the templates when using a less restrictive templating engine such as Underscore.js. Instead, you can write a helper in the form of a regular JavaScript function, register it on the Handlebars namespace, and in your template, use it as a single expression or a block expression:

```
{
    "name": {
        "first": "Udis",
        "last": "Petroyka"
    },
    "age": "82"
}
```

Given this example object, a helper can be written to return the user's full name based on the object properties:

```
Handlebars.registerHelper('fullName', function(name) {
    return name.first + ' ' + name.last;
});
```

As shown here, the `Handlebars` object provides a `registerHelper` method that gives you the ability to define a helper by defining the name as the first argument and a lambda as the second argument. Arguments to the lambda can be provided directly from the template context at the point the helper is invoked; in this case, as an expression:

```
<p>Hi, my name is {{fullName name}}.</p>
```

The syntax for the helper, as shown in the preceding example, uses the name of the helper immediately following the opening Handlebars tags followed by any arguments to be passed to the helper; in this case, the `name` argument:

```
<p>Hi, my name is Udis Petroyka.</p>
```

The template would then be rendered as HTML with the full name returned from the helper by passing the required object property from the template context.

Helpers as block expressions

Handlebars templates use block expression syntax to invoke helpers as well. The context for the block expression, however, is entirely dependent upon the way the helper is written. Several built-in block helpers are provided with Handlebars.

#if block helper

A simple `#if` block helper is provided with Handlebars for rendering content or not based on Boolean values or truthy versus falsy value resolution. This means that values such as 0, `null`, `undefined`, and empty lists `[]` will resolve as false.

Consider the following object:

```
{
    "name": {
        "first": "Jarmond",
        "last": "Dittlemore"
    },
    "email_subscriber": false
}
```

Rather than using the standard Mustache style section implementation, the `#if` helper can be invoked on a Boolean value here:

```
<p>{{name.first}} {{name.last}}</p>
{{#if email_subscriber}}
    <p>I am an email subscriber.</p>
{{/if}}
```

This template would not render the portion inside of the `#if` block because `email_subscriber` is `false`. The built-in `#if` helper also provides the ability to include an `{{else}}` section within the `#if` block that will render if the passed variable evaluates to `false`:

```
<p>{{name.first}} {{name.last}}</p>
{{#if email_subscriber}}
    <p>I am an email subscriber.</p>
{{else}}
    <p>I am not an email subscriber.</p>
{{/if}}
```

Given the example object, this template would render the following:

```
<p>Jarmond Dittlemore</p>
<p>I am not an email subscriber.</p>
```

Another difference between the `#if` helper in Handlebars and a section in Mustache templates is that the context inside of the `#if` helper does not change, whereas the context inside of a section is changed to the object property for which it is called.

#unless block helper

The `#unless` block helper in Handlebars is similar to the inverted section feature in Mustache templates, and it can also be considered the inverse of the Handlebars `#if` helper. If the value passed to the `#unless` helper is falsy, the block will be rendered:

```
{
    "name": {
        "first": "Chappy",
        "last": "Scrumdinger"
    },
    "email_subscriber": false

}
```

Consider a template similar to the previous `#if` example and based on the preceding object:

```
<p>{{name.first}} {{name.last}}</p>
{{#unless email_subscriber}}
    <p>I am not an email subscriber.</p>
{{/if}}
```

This template would render the content inside of the `#unless` block because the value of `email_subscriber` is `false`:

```
<p>Chappy Scrumdinger</p>
<p>I am not an email subscriber.</p>
```

#each block helper

The `#each` block helper is used to iterate over both lists and objects. In its most basic form, it works just like a Mustache section in the context of a list, but it has additional features that make it much more powerful:

```
{
    "people": [
        { "firstName": "Peebo", "lastName": "Sanderson" },
        { "firstName": "Udis", "lastName": "Petroyka" },
        { "firstName": "Jarmond", "lastName": "Dittlemore" },
        { "firstName": "Chappy", "lastName": "Scrumdinger" }
    ]
}
```

In the `#each` context for a list, the `this` keyword can be used to refer to the current value in the list:

```
<ul>
{{#each people}}
    <li>{{this.firstName}} {{this.lastName}}</li>
{{/each}}
</ul>
```

This is similar to the lambda example of iteration for Mustache templates, except that no lambda property value is needed to access the iterated object properties in this case.

Since the scope for each iteration is constrained to the object that is currently being iterated over in this example, the preceding template could also be more simply written as follows:

```
<ul>
{{#each people}}
    <li>{{firstName}} {{lastName}}</li>
{{/each}}
</ul>
```

As you can see, the `this` keyword is not necessary to access the properties for each object since the context for each iteration is set to that object.

#with block helper

The `#with` block helper works much like a standard section in Mustache templates by constraining the context of the current block to the parent key that is passed in:

```
{
    "name": {
        "first": "Peebo",
        "last": "Sanderson"
    },
    "email_subscriber": false,
    "age": 54,
    "profession": "Singer"
}
```

Given this example object, a template can be constructed using the `#with` helper to constrain a block to the context of the `name` key:

```
<h1>User Information</h1>
<dl>
    <dt>Name</dt>
    {{#with name}}
    <dd>{{first}} {{last}}</dd>
```

```
    {{/with}}
    <dt>Age</dt>
    <dd>{{age}}</dd>
    <dt>Profession</dt>
   <dd>{{profession}}</dd>
 </dl>
```

This template would render the following HTML:

```
<h1>User Information</h1>
<dl>
    <dt>Name</dt>
    <dd>Peebo Sanderson</dd>
    <dt>Age</dt>
    <dd>54</dd>
    <dt>Profession</dt>
    <dd>Singer</dd>
</dl>
```

Other differences in Handlebars from Mustache templates

Many of the features in Handlebars.js that differentiate it from Mustache.js are designed to make the templates render more quickly in a browser. One of the main features in Handlebars that allows this is the ability to precompile templates, as we covered in Chapter 2, *Model-View-Whatever*.

Precompiling templates

Precompiling the templates converts them to the JavaScript functions that are normally compiled in an application before rendering with other templating engines. Using this feature increases the speed of an application by skipping that step, and it additionally reduces the load on the browser for the application because the JavaScript compiler does not need to be included in the frontend asset payload.

No alternative delimiters

The creators of Handlebars also decided that the ability to set alternative delimiters within a template is not necessary. This further reduces the asset payload for an application if you are not precompiling your templates.

Usually, the only reason you would want to change the delimiter style for templates, other than personal preference, is to avoid conflicts with another templating language, for example, a server-side templating language that uses the same delimiters. If you were to include your Handlebars templates inside of JavaScript blocks within a server-side template, this issue would materialize. If you precompile your templates or abstract them from your server-side templates by keeping them in their own external JavaScript files, however, that issue can be avoided entirely and there is no need to set alternative delimiters.

You can learn more about Handlebars.js at `handlbarsjs.com`.

Pure.js

Pure.js is a JavaScript templating engine that takes the concept of logic-less templates to an even greater extreme than Mustache and Handlebars do. Pure.js uses no special template expression syntax that has to be interpolated before rendering. Instead, it uses only pure HTML tags and CSS selectors, combined with JSON data, to render values in the DOM. In this way, Pure.js uses entirely logic-less views because there is no template markup in which to include any logic.

Markup

Using plain HTML, a simple Pure.js template can be constructed like this:

```
<p class="my-template">
    Hello, my name is <span></span>.
</p>
```

The empty `<span>` element is where you might add data for a particular template, but you can use any HTML tag.

```
var data = {
    name: 'Udis Petroyka'
};

var directive = {
    'span': 'name'
};
```

In this example, we provide the data for the template in the `data` variable, and then provide what is called a `directive` that tells the templating engine how to map that data:

```
$p('.my-template').render(data, directive);
```

Pure.js provides a global `$p` object upon which methods for interacting with templates are available. In this case, we are calling the `render()` method and passing the `data` and the `directive` as the arguments:

```
<p class="my-template">
    Hello, my name is <span>Udis Petroyka</span>.
</p>
```

This would be the rendered result of this simple example. You can learn more about Pure.js at `beebole.com/pure/`.

Pug

Pug, formally named Jade, is a JavaScript templating engine that is prominent in the Node.js community. It is largely influenced by **HTML abstraction markup language (Haml)**, which was originally designed to make authoring ERB templates easier by using a cleaner and less verbose syntax than raw HTML. In this way, Pug requires the compilation of not only its expressions, but of the markup language itself.

Pug is similar to YAML in that hierarchy is denoted by whitespace with indentation for delimiters. This means that no closing element tags are necessary:

```
doctype html
html(lang="en")
  head
    title= pageTitle
body
  h1 This is a heading
  if thisVariableIsTrue
    p This paragraph will show.
  else
    p This paragraph will show instead.
```

As shown in this example, Pug can be used as a simple shorthand syntax for HTML. It can also include simple conditionals with variables, all following the same fluid syntax. HTML element attributes are added by including parenthesis after the tag name with the attributes defined inside them, such as `html(lang="en")` in the example. Elements populated with variables are indicated by placing an equals sign after the tag name and following it with a JavaScript key name, as shown by `title= pageTitle` in the example:

```
{
    pageTitle: 'This is a dynamic page title',
    thisVariableIsTrue: true
}
```

Using this example JavaScript object, the preceding template would render the following HTML:

```
<!DOCTYPE html>
<html lang="en">
  <head>
    <title>This is a dynamic page title</title>
  </head>
  <body>
    <h1>This is a heading</h1>
    <p>This paragraph will show.</p>
  </body>
</html>
```

Inline variables can also be used with another syntax that allows for accessing top level properties and nested properties. Consider the following object:

```
{
    "name": {
        "first": "Jarmond",
        "last": "Dittlemore"
    },
    "email_subscriber": false,
    "age": 24,
    "profession": "Student"
}
```

A Pug template can be written to access all variables in this object as follows:

```
h1#title Hello, my name is #{name.first} #{name.last}.
if email_subscriber
  p I am an email subscriber.
else
  p i am not an email subscriber.
h2.age Age
```

```
p= 24
h2.profession Profession
p I am a #{profession}.
```

In this template, you can see that the inline variable syntax #{ } is used along with a conditional and an element populated with a variable using the = syntax.

You will also notice that the h1 tag has a # symbol immediately following it with the word title, and the h2 tags have .className following them. This demonstrates another feature of Pug which allows the use of standard CSS selector syntax to include IDs and classes. The rendered HTML from this template would look as follows:

```
<h1 id="title">Hello, my name is Jarmond Dittlemore.</h1>
<p>I am not an email subscriber.</p>
<h2 class="age">Age</h2>
<p>24</p>
<h2 class="profession">Profession</h2>
<p>I am a Student.</p>
```

This example shows how much less verbose writing with Pug can be compared to standard HTML combined with another type of template syntax, and that is probably the reason it has become so popular. You can learn more about Pug at pug-lang.com.

Embedded JavaScript (EJS)

EJS is a JavaScript templating engine that works much like Underscore.js and also uses ERB <% %> style delimiters. Alternatively, it also allows the use of [% %] style tags for delimiters.

Just like Underscore.js, EJS allows arbitrary JavaScript to be parsed when used with the standard <% %> ERB style syntax, and allows the evaluation of expressions using an equals sign = following the opening delimiter tag <%= %>:

```
<ul>
<% for (var i = 0; i < people.length; i++) { %>
    <li><%= firstName %> <%= lastName %></li>
<% } %>
</ul>
```

This template can be used to iterate over a list of objects from which key names are evaluated as variables with different values:

```
{
    "people": [
        { "firstName": "Peebo", "lastName": "Sanderson" },
        { "firstName": "Udis", "lastName": "Petroyka" },
        { "firstName": "Jarmond", "lastName": "Dittlemore" },
        { "firstName": "Chappy", "lastName": "Scrumdinger" }
    ]
}
```

Iterating over this object with the example template would render the following HTML:

```
<ul>
    <li>Peebo Sanderson</li>
    <li>Udis Petroyka</li>
    <li>Jarmond Dittlemore</li>
    <li>Chappy Scrumdinger</li>
</ul>
```

Synchronous template loading

In a typical EJS use case, each template is stored in a file with the proprietary `.ejs` extension. A template is compiled from JavaScript code by creating a new `EJS` object, supplying the path to the template file, and calling the render method with the data you want to be interpolated.

Let's assume the EJS template is saved in a file located in your project at `templates/people.ejs`. The following JavaScript could then be written to render it as the HTML shown for this example:

```
var data = {
    "people": [
        { "firstName": "Peebo", "lastName": "Sanderson" },
        { "firstName": "Udis", "lastName": "Petroyka" },
        { "firstName": "Jarmond", "lastName": "Dittlemore" },
        { "firstName": "Chappy", "lastName": "Scrumdinger" }
    ]
};
var html = new EJS({url: 'templates/people.ejs'}).render(data);
```

The global `EJS` object is a constructor for which you create a new instance to parse a template and call methods on it for rendering. Note that since the path to the file is referenced in the JavaScript, a *synchronous* call must be made to initially load the template for parsing. This keeps the initial page load for your application low, but can lead to longer response times when interacting with your app, depending upon both the complexity of the template being loaded and the speed of the server upon which your app is running.

Once you have the rendered HTML created in your JavaScript code, you simply insert it into the DOM in your application:

```
var html = new EJS({url: 'templates/people.ejs'}).render(data);
document.body.innerHTML = html;
```

Asynchronous data loading

One unique feature of EJS is the ability to render a template using asynchronous data loaded from an external source. Using the previous example, imagine the JSON data is in an external file named `people.json`:

```
new EJS({url: 'templates/people.ejs'}).update('element_id', 'people.json');
```

In this example, the `.update()` method is called instead of `.render()`. The object instance is also not assigned to a variable because the DOM insertion is handled by the `.update()` method as well by passing a DOM node ID. For this method to work, no other CSS selectors can be used for injecting the HTML into the DOM; only an ID will work.

Caching

EJS caches templates by default after the first time they are loaded synchronously. This provides an advantage in that templates used multiple times will always load more quickly after the first request, and unused templates will not take up any memory. This approach is in stark contrast to precompiling in which all templates are loaded into memory at the initial page load of the application. Both of these approaches have advantages and disadvantages, so care must be taken to choose the best approach for your particular app.

Caching can be also be turned off for any template by including a `cache` key in the object of options passed into any template instantiation:

```
var html = new EJS({url: 'templates/people.ejs', cache:
false}).render(data);
```

View helpers

EJS includes some view helpers that are similar to the concept of helpers in Handlebars templates. They allow the use of shorter syntax for some common HTML elements. We will illustrate a few examples here.

The link_to view helper

The link_to view helper provides a simple template syntax for insuring HTML hyperlinks:

```
<p>Here is a <%= link_to('link', '/link/path') %> to a path.</p>
```

The first parameter to the link_to view helper is the displayed text for the link, and the second parameter is the path to be passed to the href attribute for the link. Also notice that the delimiters for view helpers use the opening expression delimiter syntax. This example would render the following HTML:

```
<p>Here is a <a href="/link/path">link</a> to a path.</p>
```

The img_tag view helper

This img_tag view helper provides an easy syntax for including images in your rendered HTML:

```
<p><%= img_tag('/path/to/image.png', 'Description text') %></p>
```

The first parameter to the link_to view helper is the path to the image, and the second parameter is the text for the image's alt attribute. This example would render the following HTML:

```
<p><img src="/path/to/image.png" alt="Description text"></p>
```

The form_tag view helper

The form_tag view helper provides a syntax for building HTML forms and can be used in conjunction with other view helpers for creating input elements:

```
<%= form_tag('/path/to/action', {method: 'post', multipart: true}) %>
    <%= input_field_tag('user_input', 'value text here') %>
    <%= submit_tag('Submit') %>
<%= form_tag_end() %>
```

In this example, four view helpers are used to construct the form. The `form_tag` view helper creates the opening form body providing the form action to the first parameter, and other form attributes in the second parameter using a JavaScript object syntax with curly braces. The `input_field_tag` view helper is used to create a standard input text field, taking the input name as the first parameter, and optionally, the input value as the second parameter. The `submit_tag` view helper creates a form submit input with the button text passed as the first parameter. Finally, the `form_tag_end` view helper is used to close the body of the form. This example would render the following HTML:

```
<form action="/path/to/action" method="post" enctype="multipart/form-data">
    <input type="text" id="user_input" name="user_input" value="value text
here">
    <input type="submit" value="Submit">
</form>
```

EJS also includes many other view helpers for common HTML elements using the _tag suffix.

Partials

EJS has its own implementation of partials that works using its synchronous template loading technique inside of template delimiter tags. To use this feature, a call to the partial template file is made directly inside of the parent template. Consider the following two template files:

templates/parent.ejs

```
<p>This is the parent template.</p>
<%= this.partial({url: 'templates/partial.ejs %>
```

templates/partial.ejs

```
<p>This is the partial template.</p>
```

Notice that the call to the partial template references the URL inside of the parent template using the expression syntax delimiters and a call to the `this.partial` method. To load the partial template inside of another, only the parent template has to be initialized from your JavaScript code:

```
var html = new EJS({url: 'templates/parent.ejs'}).render();
document.body.innerHTML = html;
```

The final rendered HTML would look like the following:

```
<p>This is the parent template.</p>
<p>This is the partial template.</p>
```

These examples provide a brief overview of EJS, but we will use this templating engine in more depth later. For additional information on EJS templates, visit embeddedjs.com.

Optimizing your application layout

Building a JavaScript SPA can often involve many layers of abstraction including custom application code, third party libraries, frontend frameworks, task runners, transpilers, and more. All of this can end up amounting to a whole lot of JavaScript to be downloaded for the application on the frontend, so steps should always be taken to minimize this impact as much as possible.

Let's go back to the Node.js example application we have been working with so far. In Chapter 2, *Model-View-Whatever* we wrote the index.html layout page for the app with the following script tags included for third party libraries and the compiled templates:

```
<script src="/bower_components/jquery/dist/jquery.min.js"></script>
<script
src="/bower_components/handlebars/handlebars.runtime.min.js"></script>
<script src="/bower_components/payloadjs/payload.js"></script>
<script src="/templates.js"></script>
```

This is actually a minimal example compared to how many JavaScript files a full-scale application might include.

UglifyJS and grunt-contrib-uglify

A common tool for minifying and concatenating JavaScript files is **UglifyJS**. We can leverage this tool on the command line and automate it using the Grunt task runner and the **grunt-contrib-uglify** task:

```
$ npm install grunt-contrib-uglify --save-dev
```

Once installed, open up Gruntfile.js and add the following task to existing tasks immediately above the watch task:

```
uglify: {
    options: {
        preserveComments: false
    },
    main: {
        files: {
            'js/all.min.js': [
                'bower_components/jquery/dist/jquery.js',
                'bower_components/handlebars/handlebars.runtime.js',
                'bower_components/payloadjs/payload.js',
                'js/src/templates.js'
            ]
        }
    }
}
```

This sets up the uglify task to remove all comments with the `preserveComments` option set to false, to mangle or shorten variable and function names, and to concatenate the indicated list of JavaScript files into the single target filename of `all.min.js`. With this setup, UglifyJS will create the smallest possible download size for your JavaScript based on the input files.

Next, make sure to load the new uglify task at the bottom of Gruntfile.js with the other tasks:

```
grunt.loadNpmTasks('grunt-contrib-uglify');
```

Now, all you have to do is run the task on the command line:

```
$ grunt uglify
```

After running the task, you should see output similar to the following:

```
Running "uglify:main" (uglify) task
File all.min.js created: 322.28 kB → 108.6 kB
>> 1 file created.
Done, without errors.
```

You will notice that the CLI output indicates the original size of the JavaScript files, and what it is reduced to in the final output on the second line; in this example, showing 322.28 kB → 108.6 kB. In this case, it is compressed to less than half of its original size.

Now, you can change your index.html layout file to make a call to only one JavaScript file:

```
<!doctype html>
<html>
    <head>
        <title>My Application</title>
    </head>
    <body>
        <div id="app"></div>
        <script src="/js/all.min.js"></script>
    </body>
</html>
```

Placing the `<script>` tag at the bottom of the page also ensures that anything above it will be loaded and visible to the user before the JavaScript is entirely downloaded. This is another common practice in optimizing SPAs by preventing a delay before the user sees anything.

grunt-contrib-handlebars

If you are using Handlebars templates in an application, the **grunt-contrib-handlebars** task is available for precompiling them easily from the command line and via the watch task. In Chapter 2, *Model-View-Whatever* we created the example user.handlebars file in the root directory of the project, and in Chapter 4, *REST is Best – Interacting with the Server Side of Your App* we created users.handlebars. Let's now create a new directory in js/templates and move the files there. Next, rename the files user.hbs and users.hbs for brevity. The .hbs extension is also widely accepted for Handlebars files:

```
/
js/
    templates/
                    user.hbs
                    users.hbs
```

Next, install the grunt-contrib-handlebars plugin:

```
$ npm install grunt-contrib-handlebars --save-dev
```

Once installed, add the following task configuration to Gruntfile.js, just above the uglify task configuration:

```
handlebars: {
    options: {
        namespace: 'Handlebars.templates',
        processName: function(file) {
```

```
                    return file.replace(/js\/templates\/|\.hbs/g, '');
            },
            partialRegex: /.*/,
            partialsPathRegex: /\/partials\//
        },
        files: {
            src: 'js/templates/**/*.hbs',
            dest: 'js/src/templates.js'        }
    }
```

The Grunt plugin for Handlebars makes fewer assumptions for you than the Handlebars command-line tool does out of the box, so this configuration does several things for you.

Options configuration

First, the `options` object is passed four parameters. The `namespace` option simply tells the compiler what global namespace to use to store the compiled Handlebars template functions. `Handlebars.templates` is the default namespace for this with the command line utility, so we will go with that.

The `processName` parameter is passed a function that takes a Handlebars file as the argument and uses it to create the key name for that template in the `Handlebars.templates` namespace. In this case, we are using a regex to take the path and filename and remove everything except for the prefix of the filename, so the compiled template function for `user.hbs`, for example, would be available at `Handlebars.templates.user`.

The `partialRegex` option accepts a regex that is used to identify a pattern for partial filenames. The default for this is a file prefixed with an underscore _, but in this case, we will be using a directory for partials, so the `partialRegex` option is set to `.*`, meaning it will identify any file on the given path as a partial.

The `partialsPathRegex` options accepts a regex that is used to identify the path to a directory of partials. We have set it to `/\/partials\//`, which will be evaluated as the `/partials` directory beneath the main template path that is passed in. Combined with the `partialRegex` option, this tells the compiler to parse every file in the `/partials` directory as a partial and add its compiled template function to the `Handlebars.partials` namespace.

Files configuration

The files configuration object passed to the Handlebars Grunt task is used to tell the compiler what file pattern to use for finding templates for compiling, and for defining the output filename of the compiled templates:

```
files: {
    src: 'js/templates/**/*.hbs',
    dest: 'js/src/templates.js'
}
```

In this case, we have defined the templates `src` directory to be located in the `js/templates/` under the root path, and to parse all files with the extension `.hbs` in that directory and every directory underneath it. The recursive directory lookup is indicated by the `/**/*.hbs` syntax.

The `dest` key tells the compiler to create the `js/src/templates.js` file with the final compiled output of all the templates.

Running the Grunt Handlebars task

In order to run the handlebars task, we first need to load the plugin at the bottom of Gruntfile.js:

```
grunt.loadNpmTasks('grunt-contrib-handlebars');
```

Next, run the grunt handlebars command from the CLI:

```
$ grunt handlebars
```

After running the task, you should see output similar to the following:

```
Running "handlebars:files" (handlebars) task
>> 1 file created.
Done, without errors.
```

Now, if you look in the `js/src/` directory, you should see that a `templates.js` file has been created there next to the `app.js` file we created in Chapter 1, *Getting Organized with NPM, Bower, and Grunt*. Now that we are storing the `templates.js` file here, go ahead and delete the original `templates.js` file in the root directory and edit the `files` object in the Grunt uglify task to look as follows:

```
files: {
    'js/all.min.js': [
        'bower_components/jquery/dist/jquery.js',
```

```
        'bower_components/handlebars/handlebars.runtime.js',
        'bower_components/payloadjs/payload.js',
        'js/src/templates.js'
    ]
}
```

Now we have added the new `templates.js` file to the uglify task so it is included in the full minified application JavaScript.

Watching for changes

Now that you are loading the minified JavaScript file, you will probably want to add a watch task to create the file while you are developing so that you do not have to constantly run the command from the CLI.

For this example, let's assume that we want to detect changes to any files in the `js/src` directory where we are actively working. Edit the `watch` task configuration in `Gruntfile.js` and add the following directly underneath the `jshint` target for that task:

```
uglify: {
    files: ['js/src/*.js'],
    tasks: ['uglify:main']
}
```

This tells Grunt to run the `uglify` task `main` target when it detects changes to files matching the pattern. Additionally, change the `jshint` watch task above the `uglify` watch task to the following:

```
jshint: {
    files: ['js/src/*.js', '!js/src/templates.js'],
    tasks: ['jshint']
}
```

This tells the watch task to ignore changes to `templates.js` for running the jshint task. We want to ignore this file because it is compiled and will not pass JSHint tests.

Add the same file ignore path to the *main* `jshint` task `files` configuration near the top of the file:

```
files: {
    src: [
        'Gruntfile.js',
        'js/src/*.js',
        '!js/src/templates.js'
    ]
```

```
}
```

This will prevent JSHint from checking `templates.js` against its defined rules when the `jshint` task is run.

We also need a `watch` task for changes to Handlebars template files. Add the following configuration underneath the `uglify` target in the `watch` task:

```
handlebars: {
    files: ['js/templates/**/*.hbs'],
    tasks: ['handlebars']
}
```

This will watch for any changes to the Handlebars templates and partials and run the `handlebars` task accordingly. Doing so will generate the `templates.js` file, which will then trigger the uglify watch task to run and compile the full application JavaScript to `all.min.js`.

Next, run the Grunt `watch` command from the CLI:

```
$ grunt watch
Running "watch" task
Waiting...
```

Now open `user.hbs` and change the markup to look like the following example. Note that the `{{name.first}}` and `{{name.last}}` expressions are updated to the properties we created in MongoDB in `Chapter 4`, *REST is Best – Interacting with the Server Side of Your App* :

```
<h3>{{first_name}} {{last_name}}</h3>
<p>{{title}}</>
```

Save the file, then check your console where you are running the `watch` task. You should see output similar to the following:

```
>> File "js/templates/user.hbs" changed.
Running "handlebars:files" (handlebars) task
>> 1 file created.
Done, without errors.
Completed in 0.979s - Waiting...
>> File "js/src/templates.js" changed.
Running "uglify:main" (uglify) task
File all.min.js created: 322.28 kB → 108.6 kB
>> 1 file created.
Done, without errors.
```

The change to user.hbs set off a chain reaction of two tasks to run and your application JavaScript is compiled to the latest version. If you open the compiled templates.js file, you will see that both a user and a user's property have been created with associated template functions:

```
this["Handlebars"]["templates"]["user"] = Handlebars.template({...}});
this["Handlebars"]["templates"]["users"] = Handlebars.template({...}});
```

Next, while the handlebars task is still running, move the user.hbs file to the js/templates/partials directory. This will again trigger the watch task. When it has completed, open templates.js again and you will notice that the Handlebars.templates.user property is no longer defined. Instead, a function call to .registerPartial() is made instead:

```
Handlebars.registerPartial("user", Handlebars.template({...});
```

This will invoke the user.hbs partial when it is included in a parent template using the Handlebars partials syntax. Now open up users.hbs and change it to use the user.hbs partial:

```
{{#each data}}
    {{> user}}
{{/each}}
```

This will iterate over the user's data provided. In Chapter 4, *REST is Best – Interacting with the Server Side of Your App* we left the test database with only one entry, so let's add another one now to make this example more illustrative.

In a separate console session, run your local Node.js server with Express:

```
$ node server.js
App now listening on port 8080
```

Now go to localhost:8080 in your browser and add another entry to the database using the POST Request form:

```
First name: Peebo
Last name: Sanderson
Title: Singer
```

Once you've added an additional record, click on the Load user data link under the GET Request form. You should see output similar to the following:

```
Philip Klauzinski
Sr. UI Engineer

Peebo Sanderson
Singer
```

This content was rendered by looping over the user data from MongoDB in `users.hbs` and populating the expressions in the `user.hbs` partial.

Putting it all together

Using a single, minified JavaScript file for your application code, precompiling your JavaScript templates, and loading your JavaScript at the bottom of your application layout page are all good practices to follow in optimizing the download time of your SPA. Including all of the JavaScript in one file versus multiple files is just as important as minifying the JavaScript because it reduces the number of HTTP requests a client has to make in order to load your SPA. This same practice should be used with CSS and can be done with Grunt using plugins such as `grunt-contrib-cssmin` and `grunt-postcss`.

Summary

You should now have a good understanding of the differences among some of the more popular JavaScript templating engines, how to use them for basic views, and some of their advantages and disadvantages. You should also understand the difference between using precompiled templates and templates that are compiled in the browser. Additionally, you have learned about optimizations to use in your layout file to minimize the download size of your app including minification, concatenation into one file, and including JavaScript at the bottom of the document. In the next chapter, we will dive further into the View layer by deconstructing the technique of data binding.

6
Data Binding, and Why You Should Embrace It

The View layer of a single page application goes far beyond statically displaying HTML and data through JavaScript templating engines or other means. A modern JavaScript application must handle real-time updates and be imbued with reactivity. Some of the protocols described in Chapter 4, *REST is Best – Interacting with the Server Side of Your App* such as WebSockets, MQPP, and DDP can be used to actively retrieve updates to data for an application, but the ability to bind those changes to the DOM and display them in the View must be handled on the frontend of the application. This is where data binding comes into play.

In this chapter, you will learn:

- What data binding is?
- The differences between one-way and two-way data binding
- The AngularJS implementation of data binding
- Other popular implementations of data binding
- How to implement data binding with native JavaScript?
- What some use cases of data binding are?

What is data binding?

At a high level, data binding is a software design pattern specifying the ability to directly tie changes to your underlying application data, or Model, to the View by visually reflecting those changes automatically. This can be done by any number of means using JavaScript, and it is really dependent upon what version of JavaScript you are using and its abilities and limitations. In the case of a web application, those abilities and limitations are governed by the user's browser, of course, and this is why there are so many implementations of data binding in the JavaScript community.

If you have worked with any popular JavaScript frameworks, or at least have read about any of them, you have probably heard of data binding. You also have probably never attempted to implement it on your own, considering the number of libraries and frameworks out there that provide this capability. The advantage that some of these implementations give you is cross-browser compatibility by using multiple methods and feature detection in the browser for the delegation of those methods. Other frameworks, such as Ember.js and Knockout.js, use their own proprietary implementation of data binding that works across most browsers, but requires loading a potentially large library when all you want is the data binding feature.

Using a library or framework for complex data observation is often more desirable than writing custom JavaScript to do it yourself, which speaks to the popularity of frameworks such as AngularJS – often touted for its data binding features. Leveraging these features is one thing, but understanding how they work and what is going on under the hood of a framework is quite another. First, let's break down the concept of data binding a bit more.

One-way data binding

One-way, or unidirectional, data binding is when a change to an application's data model is updated and subsequently reflected in the View. The initial change to the data model can come from anywhere, be it the submission of a form from the current user, the edit of a post of a different user on another computer, or a change in current data pushed directly from the application's host server. When the change in that data is automatically merged with a dynamic template and updated in the View without intervention from the user, it is known as one-way data binding:

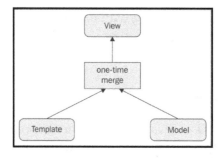

One-way data binding is visualized in a View from the merging of a ViewModel with a Template.

Here, you can see a simple representation of the one-way data binding design pattern. The manner in which the update to the View ultimately takes place relies entirely on how the application's frontend JavaScript is written, and can be done in any number of ways, but the conceptual pattern itself remains unvarying.

Using a JavaScript templating engine, like the ones discussed in `Chapter 5`, *Its All About the View* provides one-way data binding at the template level when expressions in the compiled templates are bound to dynamic data. Updating the view to reflect real-time changes to that data, however, must be handled with additional code that observes for model changes and triggers updates to the view accordingly.

Two-way data binding

Two-way, or bidirectional, data binding includes the one-way data binding pattern but additionally allows changes to the representation of data in the View by the user to be reflected in the underlying Model itself. With this pattern in place, the data displayed in the View is always a representation of the current state of the Model, even when the user makes changes to that data in the View without explicitly submitting it via forms or other means:

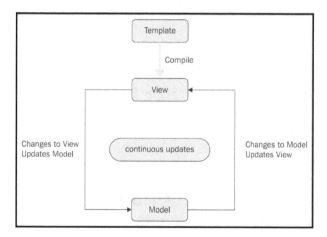

Two-way data binding is visualized in a View from changes to the ViewModel merged with a template, and changes by the user to the representations of the data in the View are merged back into the ViewModel.

This diagram shows the two-way data binding design pattern. In order for this pattern to work, there must be some type of observer in place that is continuously watching for changes to the data and syncing it in both directions. This naturally requires a more complex frontend architecture, and popular frameworks such as AngularJS can be leveraged to take the reins.

Data binding with modern JavaScript frameworks

Due to the complexity that comes with data binding design patterns, there are some standalone JavaScript libraries, such as Rivets.js and Knockout.js, that can provide it for you. Many full-fledged JavaScript frameworks also include their own implementations of data binding as a core feature.

Data binding with AngularJS

AngularJS, which is maintained by Google, is one of the most popular modern JavaScript frameworks. As discussed in *Chapter 2*, *Model-View-Whatever* it is a self-avowed MVW framework. In addition to its MVW architectural pattern implementation, it includes a powerful data binding design pattern, which is often its most touted feature.

One-way data binding with AngularJS

One-way data binding with AngularJS is achieved when an expression in the View is populated by a value from the Model associated with the Controller for that View. Consider the following Controller and Model data:

```
var myApp = angular.module('myApp', []);
myApp.controller('UserController', function UserController($scope) {
    $scope.user = {
        firstName: 'Peebo',
        lastName: 'Sanderson'
    };
});
```

The user Model that is defined on the scope for this Controller can be represented in the View with the following template markup:

```
<body ng-app="myApp">
    <div ng-controller="UserController">
        <p>
            <strong>First Name:</strong> {{user.firstName}}<br>
            <strong>Last Name:</strong> {{user.lastName}}
        </p>
    </div>
</body>
```

Just like with many other JavaScript templating engines, the double curly brace syntax is used to represent expressions to be evaluated in an AngularJS template. Additionally, AngularJS allows for the use of the ng-bind attribute on empty HTML elements to be used in place of the double curly brace syntax for expressions:

```
<body ng-app="myApp">
    <div ng-controller="UserController">
        <p>
            <strong>First Name:</strong>
            <span ng-bind="user.firstName"></span><br>
            <strong>Last Name:</strong>
            <span ng-bind="user.lastName"></span>
        </p>
    </div>
</body>
```

This syntax is more verbose, but may be preferable to some. In either case, changes to the Model properties will be automatically updated in the View where those properties are bound by their respective template expressions. In this way, AngularJS provides the underlying DOM manipulation layer that wires Model changes to be updated in the View without any further code being necessary.

Two-way data binding with AngularJS

Two-way data binding with AngularJS is achieved when an editable value in the View, such as a text input, is assigned to a property on the Model for the current Controller scope. When the value for that property is changed by the user, the Model will be updated automatically, and that change will be propagated back to the View for any expression that is bound to that Model property.

Using the Controller and Model from the previous example, consider the following template markup:

```
<body ng-app="myApp">
    <div ng-controller="UserController">
        <p>
            <strong>First Name:</strong> {{user.firstName}}<br>
            <strong>Last Name:</strong> {{user.lastName}}
        </p>
        <p>
            <label>
                <input type="text" ng-model="user.firstName">
            </label><br>
            <label>
                <input type="text" ng-model="user.lastName">
            </label>
        </p>
    </div>
</body>
```

The text inputs are given the ng-model attribute to assign a Model property as the value when the View is initially loaded. When the user changes the value for either of these inputs, the $scope.user Model will be updated, and the change will then be reflected in the paragraph block above the inputs where the same properties are bound to the DOM by their respective expressions. This round-trip from a change in the View to the Model and back to the View again is a simple example of two-way data binding.

Dirty checking with AngularJS

AngularJS uses a method of polling for changes to find differences between the Model and the View, and this method is referred to as dirty checking. This checking is done on a defined interval, which is referred to as the digest cycle. For each digest cycle, special methods called watches are registered with listeners by the scope to watch for changes to bound expressions that are passed to them:

```
$scope.$watch(watchExpression, listener);
```

As explained in `Chapter 2`, *Model-View-Whatever* the *scope* is a JavaScript object that defines the Model context for variable expressions in the View. The watches compare bound Model expressions with their previous values and if any of them are found to be *dirty*, or different, the listener callbacks are executed and the changes are then synced to the View.

AngularJS allows dirty checking to be performed at multiple levels of depth for an object, depending on your needs. There are three types of watch provided for this, with three respective depths. These levels provide for flexible data binding features, but with more depth comes more performance concerns.

Dirty checking by reference

The standard method of dirty checking in AngularJS watches for the entire value of a bound expression to change to a new value. This is referred to as dirty checking by reference. If the expression represents an object or an array, and only changes to its properties or members are made, the change will not be detected. This is the lowest depth of dirty checking, and thereby the most performant.

As an example, consider a user object with multiple properties is applied to the scope:

```
$scope.user = {
    firstName: 'Peebo',
    lastName: 'Sanderson',
    age: 54
};
```

Now a watch expression can be bound by reference to one of the object's properties:

```
$scope.$watch('user.firstName', listener);
$scope.user.firstName = 'Udis';
```

Since user.firstName has changed, this will be picked up in the subsequent digest cycle and the listener function will be triggered. Now consider instead that we watch the user object itself:

```
$scope.$watch('user', listener);
$scope.user.lastName = 'Petroyka';
// The entire value of $scope.user has not changed
```

In this case, nothing is picked up by the watch after user.lastName is changed. This is because the watch is looking for the user object itself to change – not one of its individual properties:

```
$scope.user = {
    firstName: 'Udis',
    lastName: 'Petroyka,
    age: 82
};
// The entire value of $scope.user has changed
```

If you were to instead replace the entire user object itself, the watch would find the value to be *dirty* and would then invoke the listener during the next digest cycle.

Dirty checking by collection contents

If you need to watch for shallow changes to an object or an array, AngularJS provides another method for watching called `$watchCollection`. In this context, *shallow* means that the watch will only respond to changes at the first level of the object or array – **deep** property changes, or those of nested objects or arrays, will not be detected. AngularJS calls this dirty checking by collection contents:

```
$scope.$watchCollection(obj, listener);
```

In this case, changing a property of the user object from the previous example would be picked up by the watch and trigger the `listener`:

```
$scope.$watchCollection('user', listener);
$scope.user.firstName = 'Jarmond';
// A property of the object has changed
```

Dirty checking by collection contents is not as performant as checking by reference because a copy of the watched object or array must be kept in memory.

Dirty checking by value

AngularJS also allows you to watch for changes on any nested data within an object or array. This is referred to as dirty checking by value:

```
$scope.$watch(watchExpression, listener, true);
```

You can implement this method of watching using the `$watch` method, just as you would with checking by reference, but with an added third parameter set to true. This parameter tells the watch whether you want to check for object equality or not, and it defaults to false. When the watch checks for equality by reference, it performs a simple `!==` conditional. When the third parameter of $watch is set to true, however, it uses the internal angular.equals method for a deep comparison.

The `angular.equals` method can be used to compare any two values, and it supports value types, regular expressions, objects, and arrays. If a property being compared is a function or its name begins with $, it will be ignored. The reason for ignoring functions is obvious, and as for the $ prefix, it is likely done to avoid AngularJS internal functionality from being overwritten.

Dirty checking by value is the most comprehensive form of data binding in AngularJS, but it is also the least performant. This is because a full copy of any complex object or array being compared must be held in memory, as is the case with dirty checking by collection contents, but additionally, a deep traversal of the entire object or array must be performed on each digest cycle. To maintain memory efficiency in your application, care should be taken when using this type of data binding with AngularJS.

When to use dirty checking for data binding

The dirty checking approach to data binding has its pros and cons. AngularJS assures us that memory is not a concern as long as you are not doing several thousand bindings in a single view. A downside is, however, that changes to the Model will not always show up in real time due to the latency of the digest cycle. If you are designing an application in which you would like to display true real-time, two-way data binding, then AngularJS may not be the solution for you.

Data binding with Ember.js

Ember.js is a popular open source JavaScript framework for building web applications. It is similar to AngularJS in its provided features, but it takes quite a different approach to data binding.

Ember.js runs an internal loop, similar to the digest cycle in AngularJS, called the **run loop**. It does not use dirty checking on bound Model data, but it maintains the run loop for other internal functionality, such as scheduling work queues to be performed in a particular order. The main reason behind scheduling operations within the run loop is to provide memory management and optimize the efficiency of the framework.

Ember.js uses property accessors to provide data binding, which means it uses direct object properties to get and set bound Model values. With this mechanism in place, it can forgo dirty checking to employ data binding.

Computed properties

Ember.js uses computed properties via object property accessors internally for setting and getting values. This means that properties are defined as functions that perform some type of manipulation to produce the final values that are returned. To do this, the native JavaScript object type is extended with the internal `Ember.Object.extend` method, and computed properties are returned using the `Ember.computed` method:

```
var User = Ember.Object.extend({
    firstName: null,
    lastName: null,
    fullName: Ember.computed('firstName', 'lastName', function() {
        return `${this.get('firstName')} ${this.get('lastName')}`;
    })
});
```

For this extended `User` object, the `firstName` and `lastName` properties are static, but the `fullName` property is computed with the `'firstName'` and `'lastName'` strings passed to it as parameters. This tells the computed method that those properties of the extended object are to be used in computing the returned value for `fullName`.

Now, to access the value that is returned by `fullName`, a new User object must first be created with the static `firstName` and `lastName` properties defined:

```
var currentUser = User.create({
    firstName: 'Chappy',
    lastName: 'Scrumdinger'
});
```

Once a `currentUser` object is created with a given `firstName` and `lastName` value, the `fullName` property can be computed and returned:

```
currentUser.get('fullName'); // returns "Chappy Scrumdinger"
```

This convention of extending objects is a bit verbose, but it allows Ember.js to handle the computed properties internally and track bound objects while also normalizing JavaScript inconsistencies across various user agents, or browsers.

One-way data binding with Ember.js

Ember.js uses computed properties in its data binding implementation, which means that direct property accessors can be used and no dirty checking is necessary. For one-way bindings, you can get the property for an object, but you cannot set it:

```
var User = Ember.Object.create({
    firstName: null,
    lastName: null,
    nickName: Ember.computed.oneWay('firstName')
});
```

In this example, the `Ember.computed.oneWay` method is used to apply a one-way binding for the `nickName` property as an *alias* of the `firstName` property:

```
var currentUser = User.create({
    firstName: 'Peebo',
    lastName: 'Sanderson'
});
```

When a new User object is created, the `nickName` property for it can then be accessed:

```
currentUser.get('nickName'); // returns "Peebo"
```

Since this is only a one-way binding, however, the `nickName` property cannot be used to set the aliased `firstName` property:

```
currentUser.set('nickName', 'Chappy');
currentUser.get('firstName'); // returns "Peebo"
```

Often, you may only need to return bound values in an application and not implicitly set them from the View. Wither Ember.js, the `Ember.computed.oneWay` method can be used for this purpose and will save you additional performance concerns.

Two-way data binding with Ember.js

Two-way data binding is also available with Ember.js via computed properties. This uses an alias paradigm as well; however, a computed two-way alias allows for both getting and setting an aliased property:

```
var User = Ember.Object.extend({
    firstName: null,
    lastName: null,
    nickName: Ember.computed.alias('firstName')
});
```

In this instance, we are using the Ember.computed.alias method to employ two-way data binding for the aliased `firstName` property via the computed `nickName` property:

```
var currentUser = User.create({
    firstName: 'Udis',
    lastName: 'Petroyka'
});
```

When a new User object is created now, the `nickName` property can be accessed to both set and get the aliased `firstName` property:

```
currentUser.get('nickName'); // returns "Udis"
currentUser.set('nickName', 'Peebo');
currentUser.get('firstName'); // returns "Peebo"
```

Now, with two-way data binding, View synchronization comes into play. One thing to note about Ember.js in this scenario is that, although it does not use dirty checking, it will not immediately update values bound to the Model after they are changed. Property accessors are indeed used to aggregate changes to bound data, but they are not synchronized until the next run loop, just as with AngularJS and its digest cycle. In this respect, you could surmise that data binding with AngularJS versus Ember.js is really no different, and neither framework provides any benefit over the other in this regard.

Keep in mind that the internal looping mechanisms implemented in these frameworks are designed around performance optimization. The difference in this case is that AngularJS uses its digest cycle to check for changes to bound values, in addition to its other internal operations, while Ember.js is always aware of changes to its bound values and only uses its run loop to synchronize them.

It is likely that each of these frameworks provides certain advantages over the other, depending upon what type of application you are building. When choosing a framework to build an application, it is always important to understand these internal mechanisms so that you can consider how they may affect performance in your particular use case.

Data binding with Rivets.js

Sometimes it is desirable to build an SPA with smaller, more modular libraries that provide you with specific functionality, rather than using a full-fledged frontend framework such as AngularJS or Ember.js. This could be because you are building a simple application that does not necessitate the complexity of an MVW architectural pattern, or you may just not want to be constrained by the conventions of a framework.

Rivets.js is a lightweight library that is primarily designed around data binding, and although it does provide some additional features, it makes very few assumptions about your application architecture. In this respect, it is a good choice if you are only looking to add a data binding layer to a modularized application.

One-way data binding with Rivets.js

Rivets.js uses an internal construct called a *binder* to define how the DOM should be updated in response to a change in a bound property's value. The library comes with a variety of built-in binders, but also allows you to define your own custom binders.

One-way binders in Rivets.js update the DOM when a property on a bound Model changes. As you would expect in a one-way scenario, updating the View will not update the Model.

Consider the following object:

```
var dog = {
    name: 'Belladonna',
    favoriteThing: 'Snacks!'
};
```

Using the binder syntax of Rivets.js, these properties can be bound to the View as follows:

```
<h1 rv-text="dog.name"></h1>
<p>
    My favorite thing is:
    <span rv-text="dog.favoriteThing"></span>
</p>
```

Rivets.js uses the `rv-` custom attribute prefix on HTML elements to define behaviors for different types of binders. The `rv-text` attribute is a built-in binder that inserts a bound value directly into the DOM, just as any JavaScript templating engine might do. To that point, there is also an expression interpolation syntax that uses single curly braces:

```
<h1>{ dog.name }</h1>
<p>My favorite thing is: { dog.favoriteThing }</p>
```

With either of these examples, the View would render the following HTML:

```
<h1>Belladonna</h1>
<p>My favorite thing is: Snacks!</p
```

Changing any properties on the bound Model would also update the View:

```
dog.name = 'Zoe'; // binder in View is updated
dog.favoriteThing = 'Barking!'; // binder in View is updated
```

The rendered HTML in the View would then reflect these changes:

```
<h1>Zoe</h1>
<p>My favorite thing is: Barking!</p>
```

Defining your own one-way binder

If none of the many predefined binders in Rivets.js fits your needs, you can always define your own:

```
rivets.binders.size = function(el, val) {
    el.style.fontSize = val;
};
```

In this example, we have created a binder called size, which can be used to dynamically change the CSS font-size property for an element based on a Model value:

```
var dog = {
    name: 'Belladonna',
    favoriteThing: 'Snacks!',
    size: '2rem'
};
```

The custom binder can then be used in the View as follows:

```
<h1>{ dog.name }</h1>
<p>
    My favorite thing is:
    <span rv-size="dog.size">{ dog.favoriteThing }</span>
</p>
```

This would render the View with the dog.favoriteThing value displayed at twice the font-size of the body text, as defined in the bound dog Model.

Two-way data binding with Rivets.js

Two-way binders in Rivets.js behave just as one-way binders do when a Model is updated by synchronizing the bound values in the View, but they will also update the Model when bound values in the View are changed by the user. This behavior could be triggered by form input or some other type of event, such as clicking a button.

There are some predefined two-way binders included with Rivets.js. As you might expect, it provides for the most common use case – a text input:

```
<input type="text" rv-value="dog.name">
```

Using the `rv-value` attribute to bind a Model property to an input element will prepopulate the value for that input with the bound Model value, and it will also update the Model value when the user changes the value of the input.

Defining your own two-way binder

To define a custom two-way binder in Rivets.js, a much more explicit approach must be taken, in contrast to one-way binders. This is because you must define how to bind and unbind to an element, as well as the data binding routine to run when the bound value changes:

```
rivets.binders.validate = {
    bind: function(el) {
        adapter = this.config.adapters[this.key.interface];
        model = this.model;
        keypath = this.keypath;

        this.callback = function() {
            value = adapter.read(model, keypath);
            adapter.publish(model, keypath, !value);
        }

        $(el).on('focus', this.callback);
    },

    unbind: function(el) {
        $(el).off('blur', this.callback);
    },

    routine: function(el, value) {
        $(el)[value ? 'removeClass' : 'addClass']('invalid');
    }
};
```

Using the special property definitions shown in this example, we are telling Rivets.js to bind to an input `onfocus` and to unbind from the input `onblur`. Additionally, we define a routine to run when the value changes in which a `className` of invalid is added to the input when the value is empty, and removed when it is populated.

Implementing data binding with native JavaScript

Writing your own implementation of data binding can be done fairly easily using native JavaScript. If you don't feel the need to use a comprehensive framework or library for your application and simply want the benefit of the data binding design pattern baked in, using native JavaScript to implement it is a logical course to take. This will provide you with several benefits, including the following:

- You will understand how the data binding actually works under the hood
- You will have a less bloated frontend that doesn't include extraneous library code that you may not even use
- You won't be pigeonholed into an architecture defined by a particular framework when all you want is the added benefit of data binding

Object getters and setters

The `Object` type in JavaScript has native `get` and `set` properties that can be used as `getters` and `setters` for any property name on a particular object. A `getter` is a method that returns a dynamically computed value from an object, and a `setter` is a method that is used to pass a value to a given property on an object as if you were assigning it that value. When a setter is defined and passed a value, the property name for that setter cannot actually hold a value itself; however, it can be used to *set* the value on a completely different variable.

The `get` and `set` properties default to `undefined`, just like any unassigned property on an object, so they can easily be defined as functions for any user-defined object without affecting JavaScript's native `Object` prototype. This can be a powerful tool when used in an appropriate manner within an intuitive design pattern such as data binding.

The object initializer

`Getters` and `setters` can be defined for an object using an object initializer, which is most commonly performed by defining an object in literal notation. For example, suppose we want to create a `getter` and a `setter` for the `firstName` property on an object named user:

```
var firstName = 'Udis';
var user = {
    get firstName() {
        return firstName;
    },
    set firstName(val) {
        firstName = val;
    }
};
```

In this instance, we can use the `user.firstName` property to `get` and `set` the value for the `firstName` variable by simply using standard object literal syntax:

```
console.log(user.firstName); // Returns "Udis"
user.firstName = 'Jarmond';
console.log(user.firstName); // Returns "Jarmond"
console.log(firstName); // Returns "Jarmond"
```

In this example, setting `user.firstName = 'Jarmond'` does not actually change the value of the `user.firstName` property; rather, it calls the property's defined setter method and instead sets the value for the standalone `firstName` variable.

The Object.defineProperty() method

It may often be the case that you would like to modify an existing object to provide data binding for that object in your application. To do this, the `Object.defineProperty()` method can be used to add the getter and setter for a particular property on a predefined object:

```
var user = {};
Object.defineProperty(user, 'firstName', {
    get: function() {
        return firstName;
    }
    set: function(val) {
        firstName = val;
    },
    configurable: true,
```

```
    enumerable: true
});
```

This method takes the object you want to define a property for as the first argument, the property name you are defining as the second argument, and a `descriptor` object as the third argument. The descriptor object allows you to define the `getter` and `setter` for the property using the `get` and `set` key names, and it additionally allows some other keys to further describe the property.

The `configurable` key, if `true`, allows the property's configuration to be changed and the property itself to be deleted. It defaults to `false`. The `enumerable` key, if `true`, allows the property to be visible when iterating over the parent object. It also defaults to `false`.

Using `Object.defineProperty()` is a more concise way to declare the `getter` and `setter` for an object's property because you can explicitly configure the behavior for that property, in addition to being able to add the property to a predefined object.

Designing a getter and setter data binding pattern

Now we can take this example further by creating a two-way binding between a DOM element and the `user` object for which we have defined a `getter` and `setter`. Let's consider a text input element that is prepopulated with the `firstName` value initially when the page loads:

```
<input type="text" name="firstName" value="Jarmond">
```

Now we can define our `getter` and `setter` based on the value of this input so that there is a reactive binding between the Model and the View:

```
var firstName = document.querySelector('input[name="firstName"]');
var user = {};
Object.defineProperty(user, 'firstName', {
    get: function() {
        return firstName.value;
    },
    set: function(val) {
        firstName.value = val;
    },
    configurable: true,
    enumerable: true
});
```

If you create a page with the input element and run the code above, you can then use the developer console in your browser to set the value of `user.firstName` and see it automatically update in the DOM for the value of the input element:

```
user.firstName = 'Chappy';
```

Additionally, if you change the value in the text input and then check the value of the `user.firstName` property in the developer console, you will see that it reflects the changed value of the input. With this simple use of a `getter` and `setter`, you have architecturally implemented two-way data binding with native JavaScript.

Synchronizing data in the View

To further extend this example so that representations of the Model in the View always remain synchronized and work much like the Rivets.js data binding pattern, we can simply add an oninput event callback to our input to update the DOM in the desired fashion:

```
firstName.oninput = function() {
    user.firstName = user.firstName;
};
```

Now, if we want other places in the DOM where this data is represented to be updated upon changing the value of this input, all we need to do is add the desired behavior to the setter for the property. Let's use a custom HTML attribute called `data-bind` to convey the property's representation in the DOM outside of the text input itself.

First, create a static file with the following HTML:

```
<p>
    <label>
        First name:
        <input type="text" name="firstName" value="Udis">
    </label>
</p>
```

Then, below the HTML and just before the closing `</body>` tag of your document, add the following JavaScript within `<script>` tags:

```
var firstName = document.querySelector('input[name="firstName"]');
var user = {};
Object.defineProperty(user, 'firstName', {
    get: function() {
        return firstName.value;
    },
    set: function(val) {
        var list = document.querySelectorAll(
```

```
                '[data-bind="firstName"]'
            ), i;
            for (i = 0; i < list.length; i++) {
                list[i].innerHTML = val;
            }
            firstName.value = val;
        },
        configurable: true,
        enumerable: true
    });
    user.firstName = user.firstName;
    firstName.oninput = function() {
        user.firstName = user.firstName;
    };
```

Now load the page in your browser and observe that the `<strong data-bind="firstName">` element will be populated with the name `Udis` from the value of the input. This is achieved by calling the setter for the `user.firstName` property and assigning it to its corresponding `getter` as `user.firstName = user.firstName`. This may seem redundant, but what is actually occurring here is the code defined in the setter method is being executed with the given value from the text input, which is obtained from the `getter`. The setter looks for any element on the page with the `data-bind` property set to `firstName` and updates that element's content with the `firstName` value from the input, which is represented in the model as `user.firstName`.

Next, place your cursor in the text input and change the value. Notice that the name represented within the `<strong>` element changes as you type, and each representation is in sync with the model. Finally, use your developer console to update the value of the model:

```
    user.firstName = 'Peebo';
```

Notice that the representations both in the text input and the `<strong>` element are automatically updated and in sync. You have successfully created a two-way data binding and View synchronization design pattern using a small amount of native JavaScript.

Abstracting the design pattern to a reusable method

You can further abstract your data binding design pattern by creating a method that can be used to apply this behavior to a property for any predefined object:

```
    function dataBind(obj, prop) {
        var input = document.querySelector('[name="' + prop + '"]');
        input.value = obj[prop] || input.value;
        Object.defineProperty(obj, prop, {
```

```
        get: function() {
            return input.value;
        },
        set: function(val) {
            var list = document.querySelectorAll(
                '[data-bind="' + prop + '"]'
            ), i;
            for (i = 0; i < list.length; i++) {
                list[i].innerHTML = val;
            }
            input.value = val;
        },
        configurable: true,
        enumerable: true
    });
    obj[prop] = obj[prop];
    input.oninput = function() {
        obj[prop] = obj[prop];
    };
}
```

Here, we have created a method called `dataBind`, which takes an object and a property as its arguments. The property name is used as an identifier for elements in the DOM that are to be bound to the Model:

```
// For the input
var input = document.querySelector('[name="' + prop + '"]');
// For other elements
var list = document.querySelectorAll('[data-bind="' + prop + '"]');
```

Next, simply define an object and call the `dataBind` method on it, additionally passing in the property name you want to bind to the DOM. This method also allows you to set the initial value for the property in the Model, and it will be reflected in the View upon binding if it is set. Otherwise, it will display the value set on the input itself, if any:

```
var user = {};
user.firstName = 'Peebo';
dataBind(user, 'firstName');
```

If you modify the code in the page you just created to use the abstracted `dataBind` method, you will see that it works exactly as before, but it can now be reused to bind multiple object properties with multiple corresponding elements in the DOM. This pattern can certainly be further abstracted and combined with a modeling pattern in which it could be used as a powerful data binding layer within a JavaScript SPA. The open source library inbound.js is a good example of this pattern taken to the next level. You can learn more about it at inboundjs.com.

Accounting for DOM mutations

One downfall of the previous example, when it comes to View synchronization, is that only user input will trigger the setting of the Model from the View. If you want comprehensive, two-way data binding in which any changes to bound values in the View sync to their respective Model properties, then you must be able to observe DOM mutations, or changes, by any means.

Let's take a look at the previous example again:

```
var user = {};
user.firstName = 'Peebo';
dataBind(user, 'firstName');
```

Now if you edit the value of the text input, the `firstName` property on the Model will update, and the `<strong data-bind="firstName">` element's contents will be updated as well:

```
<input type="text" name="firstName" value="Jarmond">

console.log(user.firstName); // returns "Jarmond"
```

Now let's instead use the developer console and change the `<strong data-bind="firstName">` element's `innerHTML`:

```
document.querySelector('strong[data-bind="firstName"]')
    .innerHTML = 'Udis';
```

After doing this, you will notice that the value of the input has not updated, and neither has the Model data:

```
console.log(user.firstName); // returns "Jarmond"
```

The DOM mutation you created by using the console has now broken your two-way data binding and View synchronization. Fortunately, there is a native JavaScript constructor that can be used to avoid this pitfall.

MutationObserver

The `MutationObserver` constructor provides the ability to observe changes to the DOM no matter where they are triggered from. In most cases, user input is likely sufficient for triggering Model updates, but if you are building an application that may have DOM mutations triggered from other sources, such as data being pushed via Websockets, you may want to sync those changes back to your Model.

MutationObserver works much like the native addEventListener by providing a special type of listener that triggers a callback upon DOM mutation. This event type is unique in that it is not often triggered by direct user interaction, unless the developer console is being used to manipulate the DOM. Instead, application code is typically what will be updating the DOM, and this event is triggered directly by those mutations.

A simple `MutationObserver` can be instantiated as follows:

```
var observer = new MutationObserver(function(mutations) {
  mutations.forEach(function(mutation) {
    console.log(mutation);
  });
});
```

Next, a configuration must be defined to pass to the observe method of the new observer object:

```
var config = {          ·
    attributes: true,
    childList: true,
    characterData: true
};
```

This object is called `MutationObserverInit`. It defines special properties that are used by the `MutationObserver` implementation to specify how closely an element is to be observed. At least one of `attributes`, `childList`, or `characterData` must be set to true, or an error will be thrown:

- `attributes`: Tells the observer whether mutations to the element's attributes should be observed or not
- `childList`: Tells the observer whether the addition and removal of the element's child nodes should be observed or not
- `characterData`: Tells the observer whether mutations to the element's data should be observed or not

There are also four additional, but optional, `MutationObserverInit` properties that can be defined:

- `subtree`: If true, tells the observer to watch for mutations to the element's descendants, in addition to the element itself
- `attributeOldValue`: If true in conjunction with attributes set to true, tells the observer to save the element attributes' old values before mutation.

- `characterDataOldValue`: If true in conjunction with `characterData` set to true, tells the observer to save the element's old data values before mutation.
- `attributeFilter`: An array specifying attribute names that should not be observed in conjunction with attributes set to true.

With the configuration defined, an observer can now be called on a DOM element:

```
var elem = document.querySelector('[data-bind="firstName"]');
observer.observe(elem, config);
```

With this code in place, any mutations to the element with the attribute `data-bind="firstName"` will trigger the callback defined in the observer object's instantiation of the `MutationObserver` constructor, and it will log the mutation object passed to the iterator.

Extending dataBind with MutationObserver

Now let's further extend our `dataBind` method with the `MutationObserver` constructor by using it to trigger callbacks when elements with the data-bind attribute are mutated:

```
function dataBind(obj, prop) {
    var input = document.querySelector('[name="' + prop + '"]');
    var observer = new MutationObserver(function(mutations) {
        mutations.forEach(function(mutation) {
            var val = mutation.target.innerHTML;
            if (obj[prop] !== val) {
                console.log(
                    'Inequality detected: "' +
                    obj[prop] + '" !== "' + val + '"'
                );
                obj[prop] = mutation.target.innerHTML;
            }
        });
    });
    var config = {
        attributes: true,
        childList: true,
        characterData: true
    };
    var list = document.querySelectorAll(
        '[data-bind="' + prop + '"]'
    ), i;
    for (i = 0; i < list.length; i++) {
        observer.observe(list[i], config);
    }
    input.value = obj[prop] || input.value;
```

```
Object.defineProperty(obj, prop, {
    get: function() {
        return input.value;
    },
    set: function(val) {
        var list = document.querySelectorAll(
            '[data-bind="' + prop + '"]'
        ), i;
        for (i = 0; i < list.length; i++) {
            list[i].innerHTML = val;
        }
        input.value = val;
    },
    configurable: true,
    enumerable: true
});
obj[prop] = obj[prop];
input.oninput = function() {
    obj[prop] = obj[prop];
};
}
```

The `MutationObserver` constructor takes a callback function as its only parameter. This callback is passed a mutations object, which can be iterated over to define callbacks for each mutation:

```
var observer = new MutationObserver(function(mutations) {
    mutations.forEach(function(mutation) {
        var val = mutation.target.innerHTML;
        if (obj[prop] !== val) {
            console.log(
                'Inequality detected: "' +
                obj[prop] + '" !== "' + val + '"'
            );
            obj[prop] = mutation.target.innerHTML;
        }
    });
});
```

Note that in the `MutationObserver` instantiation callback, we perform an inequality comparison of the bound Model property to the `mutation.target.innerHTML`, which is the content of the DOM element being observed, before we set the Model property. This is important because it provides that we only set the bound Model property when there is a DOM mutation triggered directly on this particular DOM node, and not as a result of a setter. If we did not perform this check, all setters would trigger the callback, which calls the setter again, and infinite recursion would ensue. This is, of course, not desirable.

Using the new version of the `dataBind` method, test the HTML page in a browser again and update the input value:

```
<input type="text" name="firstName" value="Chappy">
```

```
console.log(user.firstName); // returns "Chappy"
```

Next, use the developer console to change the bound Model property and you will see it update in the DOM for both the input and the `<strong data-bind="firstName">` element, as originally expected:

```
user.firstName = 'Peebo';
```

Finally, use the developer console to change the innerHTML of the `<strong data-bind="firstName">` element and trigger a mutation event:

```
document.querySelector('strong[data-bind="firstName"]')
    .innerHTML = 'Udis';
```

This time, you will see the value of the input element update as well. This is because the mutation event was triggered and detected by the observer object, which then fired the callback function. Within that callback function, the `obj[prop] !== val` comparison was made and found to be true, so the setter was called on the new value, subsequently updating the input value and the value returned from the `user.firstName` property:

```
console.log(user.firstName); // returns "Udis"
```

You have now implemented two-way data binding and comprehensive view synchronization using native `getters` and setters and the `MutationObserver` constructor. Keep in mind that the examples given here are experimental and have not been used in a real-world application. Care should be taken when employing these techniques in your own application, and testing should be paramount.

Why use data binding?

Data binding provides a layer of abstraction that can eliminate the need for a lot of additional application wiring, custom event publishing and subscribing, and Model evaluation against the View. These things are usually handled with custom application code that is specific to the application itself, when a framework or some type of data binding is not being used. Without careful planning and the use of defined architectural patterns, this can lead to a lot of adjunct code, and subsequently a code base that is not extensible, does not scale well, and is difficult for new developers to take on and learn.

If you feel that data binding is a component you'd like to include in your application, then consider your options, some of which we have laid out here, and choose accordingly. You may see the need to build your application with a full-fledged JavaScript framework such as AngularJS, or you may only want the added abstraction layer of data binding in combination with your own custom architecture. Also, consider the performance implications of your choices, and whether you need two-way data binding, which is more memory-intensive, or only one-way data binding, which will help to keep your application more performant.

Use cases for one-way data binding

The most common form of data binding in modern single page applications is one-way data binding. At its most basic, one-way data binding need only consist of binding dynamic Model values to their respective expressions in a template at render time. If the model changes after a template has already been rendered, the synchronization of that data to the View is an added benefit of some frameworks such as AngularJS, Ember.js, and Rivets.js.

If you are building an application in which you want to display real-time, frequently changing data to a user, and that data does not need to be manipulated by the user, this is a good use case for one-way data binding with View synchronization. A more specific example of this is an application for tracking stock quotes and displaying the prices as they change in real time. The Model data in this case is meant entirely for viewing by the user, but no changes to the Model from the View are necessary since the stock quotes cannot be changed by the user. In a scenario like this, two-way data binding listeners would not be useful and would only generate additional and unnecessary overhead.

Use cases for two-way data binding

Two-way data binding is not as commonly used as one-way data binding in single page applications, but it does have its place. It is important to fully understand the needs of your application before you decide to attach two-way data binding behaviors to the DOM and use additional memory.

A live chat, or live messaging, application is one of the most common examples of two-way data binding. Whether the application provides one-to-one messaging or multiuser messaging, two-way data binding can be used to synchronize the View in both directions for each user. As a user is viewing the application, new messages from other users are added to the Model and displayed in the View. Likewise, the user viewing the application enters new messages in the View and they are added to the Model, downloaded to the server, and then displayed to the other users in their own Views.

Summary

You have now learned what data binding is, the differences between one-way and two-way data binding, how data binding is implemented in some modern JavaScript frameworks and libraries, and what some use cases for data binding are in the real world. You have also learned about the architectural differences between one-way and two-way data binding implementations, and how to write your own data binding implementation using modern native JavaScript with getters and setters. Additionally, you have learned about the `MutationObserver` constructor and how it can be used to trigger behaviors in the DOM based on mutation events.

Next, we will take everything that we have learned so far about different architectural components, including MongoDB, Express, AngularJS, and Node.js, and learn how to begin putting them all together to leverage the full MEAN stack.

7
Leveraging the MEAN Stack

The MEAN stack is an acronym for MongoDB, Express, AngularJS, and Node.js. It represents full stack development using practically nothing but JavaScript alone. Naturally, you will need some HTML and CSS to render things to the browser and make them look pretty.

MongoDB is a document-based NoSQL database that stores data in ways that can be treated like plain JavaScript objects. As the data and database methods are essentially JavaScript, MongoDB plays well with JavaScript-based applications.At this point, if you typed the code correctly, there will be no output in the console other than a new line. Open your favourite browser

Express is a web application framework, written in JavaScript that runs beautifully on Node.js. It's similar to other frameworks, such as Sinatra, but less obtrusive and opinionated. Express is essentially routing and middleware that handles web requests and responses.

AngularJS is a frontend JavaScript framework that is primarily used to build Single Page Web applications. It's a powerful and prescriptive framework curated by Google, which has become one of the more popular JavaScript MV* toolkits.

In this chapter, you'll explore each of the following components of the MEAN stack while starting to build the framework of your very own Single Page Application:

- Running Node.js code from the command line using the REPL
- Writing and running Node.js scripts
- Installing MongoDB and basic CRUD operations from the Mongo shell
- Installing Express via the standard method and the Express generator
- Express routing, middleware, and view rendering
- Building the basic components of a frontend application with Angular

The Node.js environment

Node.js is a runtime environment built to execute JavaScript. With it, you can build powerful software, such as full-fledged backend web servers. In Chapter 1, *Getting Organized with NPM, Bower, and Grunt,* you began to use some Node.js-based tools, such as Grunt, NPM, and the Node Package Manager.

Node.js is powerful, and extremely fast. It is based on the V8 JavaScript engine that's used in the Chrome browser and is tuned for speed. It uses a non-blocking I/O that allows it to handle many requests simultaneously.

This chapter assumes that you have already installed the Node runtime. If not, go to https://nodejs.org, and follow the installation instructions for your operating system Node version 4.3.2 has been used in this book.

Running the REPL

Node.js provides a way to enter a run JavaScript code from the command line called the Read-Eval-Print Loop or REPL. You can start the REPL simply by typing node at the command line in a console. It's a great way to begin exploring some of the possibilities with Node.js, as shown in the following command:

```
$ node
> var sum = 1 + 2;
undefined
> sum
3
console.log(sum);
3
undefined
```

 The variable assignment in JavaScript returns undefined.

Here, it might appear that there are two return values, the first being 3 and the second being undefined. In this case, console.log() is a function that is used to write things out to the screen, but the function actually returns undefined. This will be useful in writing Node.js code where you want to log things to the screen, similar to print statements in other programming languages.

To quit out of the REPL, hit *Ctrl + C* twice.

Writing a hello Node.js script

Using the REPL on its own will not be incredibly useful. Node.js allows developers to create programs by writing them out and saving them as text files with a .js file extension.

One of the advantages of this is that you can use any text editor and practically any IDE to write Node.js programs.

To show you how powerful Node.js can be, let's start by building a simple web server. It will not do much, other than handling HTTP requests, but it's a great start.

Let's create a new file, call it hello.js, and open it in your favorite text editor or text-based IDE. Then, type the following lines of code:

```
var http = require('http');
var serverResponse = function(req, res){
    res.end("Hello Node");
}

var server = http.createServer(serverResponse);
server.listen(3000);
```

Save the file and navigate it to the directory where it is stored with a console program. Then, type the following command:

```
$ node hello
```

At this point, if you typed the code correctly, there will be no output in the console other than a new line. Open your favorite browser and type localhost:3000 in your address bar.

You should see **Hello Node** in your browser's main window. And just like that, you have written a web server.

You can stop the server by typing Ctrl + C in the console.

There's a lot going on in a small piece of code, so let's walk through what the program is doing:

- In the first line of the varhttp=require('http'); code, similar to import statements in some programming languages, Node.js uses require to import code modules. Node.js ships with a number of built-in code modules. The HTTP module is a built-in module that provides, as you might assume, HTTP services. Built-in modules can be required using a string containing the name of the module. Generally, they will be used by assigning them to a variable. Non-built-in modules are required using a string containing the full path to the module.

- In the next two lines, `var serverResponse = function(req, res)` and `res.end("Hello Node")`, the `serverResponse` function here is a callback function that we will pass to the web server we are creating. We will cover the request and response objects in more detail when we get into `Express.js`, but it's important to realize that we are setting up `req` to deal with the HTTP request object, and `res` to deal with the response. The end function on the response object sends whatever text is passed to it and tells the server that the response is done.

- In the next code line, `varserver=http.createServer(serverResponse);`, we are actually creating a web server by invoking the `createServer` function on the HTTP object we required earlier. We pass the `serverResponse` function to the `createServer` function, which becomes a callback function for the server. We will store a reference to the server we just created in the variable called *server*.

- In the last line of the code, `server.listen(3000);`, we will invoke the `listen` function on the server object we just created. We will pass to it an integer representing the port number we want it to use to listen to requests. This bit of code actually starts up the server, and has it listen to requests on port `3000`.

Setting up a Node.js project with NPM

As Node.js projects become larger, having a tool to mange it properly is important. Concerns such as consistent dependency management, version management, and environment management are made easier using **Node Package Manager** and the `package.json` file.

Fortunately, the smart people who created Node.js created a method of doing that using NPM. Running `npm init` from the command line will set up a Node.js project and build out a `package.json` file, which is used to manage your node projects. Let's try it with your `hello` Node project. Note that some of the prompts are optional and can be left blank, as shown in the following commands:

```
$ npm init
This utility will walk you through creating a package.json file.
It only covers the most common items, and tries to guess sensible
defaults.
See `npm help json` for definitive documentation on these fields
and exactly what they do.
Use `npm install <pkg> --save` afterwards to install a package and
save it as a dependency in the package.json file.
Press ^C at any time to quit.
name: (SPA-js) hello-node
```

```
version: (1.0.0)
description: my new program
entry point: (hello.js)
test command:
git repository:
keywords:
author: Your Name
license: (ISC)
About to write to /Users/your-home/helloNode/package.json:
{
  "name": "hello-node",
  "version": "1.0.0",
  "description": "my new program",
  "main": "hello.js",
  "scripts": {
    "test": "echo "Error: no test specified" && exit 1"
  },
  "author": "John Moore",
  "license": "ISC"
}
Is this ok? (yes)
```

Pressing Enter at this point will create the `package.json` file in the directory you're in. Open it in your IDE or text editor and take a look. While you're in there, let's make the following small change to the scripts section:

```
"scripts": {
  "test": "echo "Error: no test specified" && exit 1",
  "start": "node hello"
}
```

The scripts section of `package.json` allows you to run code using NPM. In this case, typing npm `start` will run the `node hello` command and start your web server. It's not a super efficient shortcut at this point, but you can create efficient and useful aliases for lots of commands this way.

One of the very important things that NPM does is manage dependencies. In the next section, on Express, you'll see how to store references to NPM modules and their versions in the `package.json` file. This is important when working as part of a group or team. By taking a copy of a project's `package.json` file, a developer can recreate the environment for the project just by running NPM installation.

Getting started with Express

Express describes itself as a fast, unopinionated, minimalist web framework for Node.js. Express is a very powerful and flexible framework that operates on top of Node.js, but still allows you access to all of the features of Node. At its core, Express operates as a set of routing and middleware functionality.

We'll get into routing and middleware in detail in later chapters. Basically, routing handles web requests. Middleware consists of functions that have access to the request and response objects and call the next piece of middleware in the stack.

If it's so easy to just throw up a web server using Node,js, why do we need something like Express?

The answer is, you don't. You could, all on your own, build a fully featured web application by just writing your own Node.js. Express has done a lot of the grunt work and heavy lifting for you. Because of the middleware that's easy to plus into Express, adding things such as security, authentication, and routing is fairly simple. And, who wants to build that stuff from scratch when you have an exciting new web application to build?

Installing Express

Of course, you will use NPM to install Express. There are two ways to do this.

The standard method is just to use NPM to pull the Express project down and add a reference to it in `package.json`. This is just adding the module into a Node.js project. You will build an application script, require it in Express, and utilize it in that WAR file.

The second method is to install the Express generator and use it to generate a starter web application. This method is simple to employ but it does structure your whole application, including folder structure, for you. Some people would prefer to do all of this on their own to get their setup precisely a certain way.

We will try both methods, and use the Express generator to build the framework for the Single Page Application that you will build throughout the rest of this book.

Standard method

Again, the standard method will just be to pull the module down and add it to your project. In your console, in the directory with the `package.json` file we just created, type the following command:

```
$ npm install express --save
```

On a Mac, you may have to type `sudo` before `npm install`. If you're on a Mac, I would just go ahead and use `sudo` each type you are installing something with NPM.

The `-save` part tells npm to add Express as a dependency to your `package.json` file. Go ahead and open your `package.json` file and look at the dependencies section.

If you are using `git` or another source control system to share a code base with other developers, you, typically, will not store the dependencies in the remote repository. Instead, the `package.json` file will hold a reference to the required modules and their version.

Another developer can pull down your code, run `npm install`, and install all of the dependencies.

If you look in the folder where your `package.json` file resides, you will see a new folder called `node_modules`. This is where all of your dependencies installed with `npm` are stored. It's important not to move this or change it as the require function will look in here for modules. Typically, this folder will be added to a `.gitignore` file to ensure that its files aren't stored on a remote `git` repository.

Express generator

There is another method of setting up an Express application. Express has created a generator that is a tool for rapidly setting up the framework for an Express application. It assumes some common conventions used in Express applications and configures things such as the main application, the `package, json`, and even the directory structure.

The generator is installed globally rather than in a specific project using the following command:

```
$ npm install express-generator -g
```

The -g tells NPM to install the module and its dependencies globally. They won't be installed in the npm_modules folder in your project, but in a global modules folder on your system.

Setting up your Express application

Now that we have the express generator installed globally, let's use it to start building the application we'll be building out in the rest of the book. Pick a folder where you want this project to live. The Express generator will create a new folder inside this folder, so it's fine if it is a home or projects folder containing other things.

Navigate to this folder in your console using the following command:

```
$ express -e giftapp
   create : giftapp
   create : giftapp/package.json
   create : giftapp/app.js
   create : giftapp/public
   create : giftapp/public/javascripts
   create : giftapp/public/images
   create : giftapp/routes
   create : giftapp/routes/index.js
   create : giftapp/routes/users.js
   create : giftapp/public/stylesheets
   create : giftapp/public/stylesheets/style.css
   create : giftapp/views
   create : giftapp/views/index.ejs
   create : giftapp/views/error.ejs
   create : giftapp/bin
   create : giftapp/bin/www
   install dependencies:
     $ cd giftapp && npm install
   run the app:
     $ DEBUG=giftapp:* npm start
```

As you can see, the express generator has created a number of files including app, js, your main app file.

The -e modifier we typed after the express command told the generator that we want to use ejs (embedded JavaScript) frontend templates. Express supports a number of templating languages, including Handlebars and Jade. If you add no modifier, the Express generator will assume you want to use Jade. For this project, we will use ejs, which is essentially real HTML with embedded JavaScript code.

The final output of the generator tells you the next steps you need to actually stand up your application. Navigate to your new `giftapp` directory and run `npm install` (remember `sudo` if you're on a Mac or Linux box). The `npm install` command at this point might take a few minutes as it's installing a number of dependencies.

The next command starts your new Express application in `DEBUG` mode—you will see all requests logged to the console. Navigating to `localhost:3000` in your browser will display a **Welcome to Express** page.

Congratulations, this page is being served from your very own robust Express web application. It's not doing much yet, but a lot of pieces are already in place for you.

Exploring the main script

Open giftapp's new `package.json` file. Note the following scripts object:

```
"scripts": {
  "start": "node ./bin/www"
}
```

This is saying that when the `npm` start is run, the script that's actually invoked is at `./bin/www`. So, let's open the `www` file in your bin directory and take a look.

You'll see that this file is requiring a number of things, including `app.js`; this is your main application file:

```
var app = require('../app');
```

The next bit of code set's the port number of the app. It looks to see if there's an environment variable set containing the desired port number. If not, it sets it to `3000`. When deploying an application to production, typically, you will use `port 80` for HTTP or `port 443` for HTTPS:

```
var port = normalizePort(process.env.PORT || '3000');
app.set('port', port);
```

The next bit creates the server and starts listening on the correct port:

```
var server = http.createServer(app);
...
server.listen(port);
```

For now, we'll skip over the rest of this file and take a look at what's in the `app.js` file. Go ahead and open it up.

Looking at the main application

`App.js` is the main application file that loads the routes and middleware and configures the application. There are a number of important sections of this file. In general, in Express applications, the order of loading and utilization, and the order middleware is invoked in this file, is important. Let's take a look.

Loading dependencies

When you open `app.js`, you will first encounter a number of calls to the require function, as follows:

```
var express = require('express');
var path = require('path');
var favicon = require('serve-favicon');
var logger = require('morgan');
var cookieParser = require('cookie-parser');
var bodyParser = require('body-parser');
var routes = require('./routes/index');
var users = require('./routes/users');
```

This system is known as `CommonJS`. The first set of modules includes the dependencies, such as Express, and a parser for cookies. The routes and users modules were created by the Express generator for routing. The routes you create will be required in the main file as well.

Configuring the application

Next, an `app` variable is declared by invoking the express function, and a couple of configuration variables are set, as follows:

```
var app = express();
...
app.set('views', path.join(__dirname, 'views'));
app.set('view engine', 'ejs');
```

The first configuration, views, tells Express where to look for the view templates. These are the templates that are normally rendered into HTML as the result of requests to the web application.

The second configuration sets the view engine. As we discussed earlier, we will use `ejs` or embedded JavaScript templates.

Application-level middleware

The next thing we will see in this file is a bunch of calls to the app object's use function, which is as follows:

```
app.use(logger('dev'));
app.use(bodyParser.json());
app.use(bodyParser.urlencoded({ extended: false }));
app.use(cookieParser());
app.use(express.static(path.join(__dirname, 'public')));
app.use('/', routes);
app.use('/users', users);
// catch 404 and forward to error handler
app.use(function(req, res, next) {
  var err = new Error('Not Found');
  err.status = 404;
  next(err);
});
```

In Express, calls to the application object's use function are application-level middleware. Requests sent to the application will execute every function matching the path set in app.use. If no path is set, the middleware function defaults to the root path /and will be invoked for every request.

For example, app.use(cookieParser()); means that the cookieParser function will be invoked for every request sent to the application because it defaults to the root path. However, app.use('/users',users); will only apply when the request begins with /users.

Middleware is invoked in the order it's declared. This will become very clear later, when we add authentication to our application, or want to handle POST data. If you don't parse cookies before you try to manage a request requiring authentication, it won't work.

Our first Express route

Express uses a mechanism called routing, using its Router object, to handle HTTP requests, such as those from web browsers. In a later chapter, we will take a more in-depth look at Express routing. It bears examining the first route that the Express generator created for us. Open your routes/index.js file, as shown in the following code block:

```
var express = require('express');
var router = express.Router();

/* GET home page. */
```

```
router.get('/', function(req, res, next) {
  res.render('index', { title: 'Express' });
});
module.exports = router;
```

To create a new set of routes, we must create a new router object by invoking the `Expresses Router` function. You will see that we require Express first, then do exactly that.

The next expression is a call to the router object's get function. This, in Express, is router-level middleware. This function sets up middleware, in the form of the enclosed anonymous function, which responds to HTTP GET requests, such as typing a URL in a browser's address bar or clicking on a link.

The first argument to the function is a path to match. When the path matches, in this case the root path, the function is invoked. The anonymous function here receives the request object, the response object, and the next object.

The function invokes the response object's render function. This function looks in the views directory for a template called index and renders it, passing it the object in the second argument. The template has access to all the properties of that object, in this case, just the title, and can render them to in the response.

Finally, we will see the `module.exports=router;` expression. This allows the Node.js module system to load this code using the required function and assign the router object to a variable. Near the top of our `app.js` file, you'll see `varroutes=require('./routes/index');`.

Rendering the first view

When you started the Express server, navigated to `localhost:3000`, and saw the default Express page, what happened?

The request came into the web application and was routed to index based on the request type, GET, and the path, /. The middleware then called the response object's render function and told it to get the index template, passing it an object with a property called title.

Open your `views/ index.ejs` file to see the following template code:

```
<!DOCTYPE html>
<html>
  <head>
    <title><%= title %></title>
```

```
      <link rel='stylesheet' href='/stylesheets/style.css' />
    </head>
    <body>
      <h1><%= title %></h1>
      <p>Welcome to <%= title %></p>
    </body>
</html>
```

If you've used other dynamic templating languages before, you probably already understand that this is normal HTML that contains some dynamic elements. Those dynamic elements that are contained by `<%...%>` are processed by the server. These *tags* are not sent to the browser, just clean HTML.

In this case, the three tags are identical, all rendering the title property of the object passed in the call to the response object's render method. As a quick experiment, change the value of the title passed in.

Exploring MongoDB

Remember that the *M* in the MEAN stack, is an open source document-based database. It's considered a NoSQL database because it doesn't use SQL and is not relational. It integrates well with JavaScript-based tools because, instead of tables, it stores data in documents that can be treated by our Node.js application as JSON.

 Technically, MongoDB stores data in a format called BSON, short for Binary JSON.

Setting up MongoDB

The first step in getting MongoDB running on your system is installation. Head over to `htt ps://www.mongodb.org/downloads#production`, and you will find the most updated installation download for Windows, Mac, Linux, or Solaris. There are also links to instructions there to install MongoDB with tools such as Homebrew for Mac and yum for Linux.

Up-to-date installation instructions for each operating system can be found at `https://doc` `s.mongodb.org/manual/`. There are differences between the operating systems, and installation instructions may change with newer versions. I suggest following the official installation instructions.

Once installed, you can start the MongoDB service by typing `mongod` in a console.

You will not be able to type any other commands in that console while the MongoDB daemon is running. By default, this process will run on `port 27017` and bind to the IP address, `127.0.0.1`. Both of these can be changed with command flags at start up, or with a `.conf` file. For our purposes, the defaults will do.

Working with the MongoDB shell

We'll begin to work with MongoDB with the command-line shell included with the Mongo installation. As you must have the MongoDB daemon running to work with the database, you'll need to open a new console.

In the application we are building, we will rely on Node.js plugins to handle our database operations. It is beneficial, however, to gain an understanding of how MongoDB works and how it differs from SQL databases.

The best way to do that is to get our hands dirty and run some basic operations from the command line of MongoDB's shell.

Selecting a database

Let's select the database that we want to work with. Open your command line and enter the following command:

```
$mongo
> use test
switched to db test
>
```

Running `mongo`, as opposed to `mongod`, from the command line starts the MongoDB shell, which allows typing commands directly to the running MongoDB daemon.

The `use` command selects which database we are currently using. But, wait a minute; we never created a test database. That's correct, and we still haven't. We can use the `showdbs` command to list all of the databases on our computer that MongoDB knows about:

```
> show dbs
local   0.078GB
```

If you've done all the previous examples, you would already have created a local database name `test`. Local stores a `startup` log and replica information in replicated environments. We can use local and add our own data to it, but that's not really a great idea. Let's create a database of our own.

Inserting documents

Remember that records in MongoDB are referred to as documents. They loosely relate to rows in a traditional relation database but are much more flexible.

If we insert a document now, the new database will be created use the following commands:

```
> db.cat.insert({name:"Tom",color:"grey"})
WriteResult({ "nInserted" : 1 })
> show dbs
local   0.078GB
test    0.078GB
```

The `db.cat.insert()` command adds the document in the argument to insert to a collection called cat.

In MongoDB, a collection is a set of documents. This is similar to a table in a relational database, which is a set of records. Unlike relational databases, the documents in a collection do not have to all be the same type or have the same set of data.

You may get notices that the document we inserted looks like a plain old JavaScript object. Essentially, it is. This is one of the nice things about working with MongoDB as part of the MEAN stack—it's JavaScript from the frontend all the way to the database.

When we type `showdbs`, we will see that the test database is now created. We also created a cat collection in the test database by inserting a document into it. This is something to be cautious of when working with the shell. It's easy to accidentally create unwanted databases and collections with a typo.

Finding documents

Now that we have a database, a collection in that database, and have inserted a document into that collection, we need to be able to retrieve the document. The most basic way to do that is using the find method of MongoDB.

Let's take a look at our document:

```
> db.cat.find()
  { "_id" : ObjectId("565c010dd9d61e2dc614181f"), "name" : "Tom", "color"
: "grey" }
```

The `db.collection.find()` method is MongoDB's basic method to read data. It is the *R* in MongoDB's CRUD—Create, Read, Update, Delete—operations.

As you can see, MongoDB has added an _id field to our object, which is as follows:

```
> db.cat.insert({name:"Bob",color:"orange"})
WriteResult({ "nInserted" : 1 })
> db.cat.find({},{_id:0,name:1})
{ "name" : "Tom" }
{ "name" : "Bob" }
```

We've inserted a new orange cat named Bob here and, this time, the find method we're using is a little different. It's taking two arguments.

The first argument is the query criteria. This tells MongoDB which documents to select. In this case, we've used an empty object so all documents are selected.

The second argument is a projection that limits the amount of data MongoDB returns. We told MongoDB that we want the name field, but to suppress the _id field, which will be returned by default.

In a later chapter, we will explore how to limit the number of documents returned and sort them.

Take a look at following command:

```
> db.cat.find({color:"orange"},{_id:0,name:1})
{ "name" : "Bob" }
```

We've adjusted our query to contain query criteria that selects only cats that have a color of orange. Bob is the only orange cat, so this is the only document returned. Again, we will suppress _id and tell MongoDB that we only want to see the name field.

Updating documents

What if we want to change a record in our database? There are several methods to do this, but we'll start with the simplest one. MongoDB provides the appropriately named update method to modify documents in a database, as follows:

```
> db.cat.update({name:"Bob"},{$set:{color:"purple"}})
WriteResult({ "nMatched" : 1, "nUpserted" : 0, "nModified" : 1 })
> db.cat.find({color:"orange"},{_id:0,name:1})
> db.cat.find({color:"purple"},{_id:0,name:1})
{ "name" : "Bob" }
```

Similar to the find method, the first argument to the update method tells MongoDB which documents to select. By default, however, MongoDB will only update one document at a time. To update multiple documents, we will add a third argument, a modifier object, {multi:true}.

We have selected documents where the name field equals Bob (there is only one). Then, we will use the $set operator to change color of Bob to purple.

We can verify that this has worked by querying for orange cats using the following command:

```
> db.cat.find({color:"orange"},{_id:0,name:1})
> db.cat.find({color:"purple"},{_id:0,name:1})
{ "name" : "Bob" }
```

No documents are returned. A query for purple cat now returns our document for a cat named Bob.

Removing documents

No set of CRUD operations is complete without the *D* or Delete operation. MongoDB provides the remove method for this, which is as follows:

```
> db.cat.remove({color:"purple"})
WriteResult({ "nRemoved" : 1 })
> db.cat.find({},{_id:0,name:1})
{ "name" : "Tom" }
```

The remove method has a fairly similar signature to the other MongoDB CRUD methods. The first argument, as you may have surmised, is a selector to choose which documents MongoDB should be removed.

In the preceding example, we removed all documents containing the `purple` value for the color property. There was only one, so goodbye poor `Bob`. We verified with our call to the find method which now only returns `Tom`.

The default for the remove method is to delete all found documents, so use caution. Passing an empty selector will delete all documents in a collection, as follows:

```
> db.cat.remove({})
WriteResult({ "nRemoved" : 1 })
> db.cat.find()
>
```

And with that, we have no cats.

MongoDB has no built-in rollback functionality, so there's no real way to undo such a deletion. In production, this is one reason why replication and regular database backups are important.

Create your SPA database

So, now that we have mucked about with MongoDB a little bit, let's create the development database we will use for the SPA we are building.

In a later chapter, we will use a Node.js plugin called *mongoose to model* to validate, query, and manipulate our data.

For now, let's just get the database set up. In your mongo shell, type the following command:

```
> use giftapp
switched to db giftapp
```

Remember, we haven't actually created the database yet. For that, we will need to stick a document into a collection. As we'll let Mongoose do all of the heavy lifting for us later, we'll just put something in a test collection to get started. Let's consider the following code as an example:

```
> db.test.insert({test:"here is the first document in the new
database"})
WriteResult({ "nInserted" : 1 })
```

```
> db.test.find()
{ "_id" : ObjectId("565ce0a2d9d61e2dc6141821"), "test" : "here is the
first document in the new database" }
> show dbs
giftapp    0.078GB
local      0.078GB
test       0.078GB
```

Here, we will insert a document into the test collection. We can verify it's there with a call to the find method. Finally, we will run showdbs and see that our giftapp database is successfully created.

Starting with AngularJS

We've got most of the pieces of our application stack in place now. We have a runtime environment, Node.js. We've installed and set up a web application framework, Express. We just set up our database, MongoDB.

The one piece that's missing is pretty crucial in any SPA—no matter what the backend stack looks like, there's a frontend framework to make the SPA magic happen.

There are numerous frontend libraries and frameworks used for SPAs, but one of the most popular, and the *A* in MEAN, is AngularJS, otherwise known as Angular.

Angular is an open source frontend framework, particularly well-suited to building SPA. It's extremely popular and currently maintained by Google.

 In this book, we will use AngularJS version 1.4.8, which was released in November, 2015. AngularJS 2.0 was announced in 2014 and is, at the time of publication, just made available in a production version. The 2.0 version introduced breaking non-backward-compatible changes. Most development today is done using some version on the 1.x branch, and the plan is to continue support for the foreseeable future.

Installing AngularJS into the application

Ultimately, Angular is a single JavaScript file with some optional plugin files. There are a few ways to add Angular to your frontend application. You can download the package you're interested in or load it with a tool such as Bower.

The simplest way for us to get started is to simply point to the Angular file on a publicly available CDN. We can include Angular 1.4.8 from `https://cdnjs.cloudflare.com/ajax /libs/angular.js/1.4.8/angular.js`.

Let's open our `index.ejs` file and include a script tag linking to the following file:

```
<!DOCTYPE html>
<html>
  <head>
    <title><%= title %></title>
    <link rel='stylesheet' href='/stylesheets/style.css' />
  </head>
  <body>
    <h1><%= title %></h1>
    <p>Welcome to <%= title %></p>
    <script
src="https://cdnjs.cloudflare.com/ajax/libs/angular.js/1.4.8/angular.js"></
script>
  </body>
</html>
```

It's good practice, when possible, to include script tags linking to external JavaScript files right before the closing body tag in HTML. This is done for performance reasons. You can find out more and see some examples showcasing the reasoning for this at `http://stevesouders.com/hpws/ru le-js-bottom.php`.

If you restart the server and load the default page at `localhost:3000`, you won't see very much. You are loading AngularJS, but there's no visible effect yet. We will build up some example frontend code in layers.

The first thing we want to do after adding the AngularJS script is to change the `html` tag to read as shown in the following code:

```
<html ng-app>
```

The `ng-app` attribute on the head element is what is called an Angular directive. When Angular loads in a page, it goes through a bootstrapping phase looking for directives such as `ng-app`. This directive tells Angular where the root element of the application is.

You can think of this attribute as a way of marking out an area of interest that Angular will manage. In our case, we'd like to use Angular components on the whole page, so we'll declare the HTML element as the root element.

In the next section, we will build a module that will become our root application.

Building the first AngularJS module

AngularJS was designed to be modular and includes a function to register modules. Modules act as containers for other objects, such as Angular services, directives, and controllers.

Angular modules are also injectable. This means that modules can be injected into and consumed by other modules. Angular has a unique dependency injection system, which we will see shortly and use a lot.

Create a new JavaScript file in the `public/javavscripts` directory of `giftapp` called `app.js` and type the following code into it:

```
var giftAppModule = angular.module('giftAppModule', []);

giftAppModule.value('appName', 'GiftApp');
```

The first line creates and registers an Angular module using the `angular.module()` function. The first argument to this function is a string that Angular will use as the name of the module, `giftAppModule`. The second argument is an array of dependencies we wish to inject into this module. For now, we don't have any, so the array is empty.

We then assign the module to the `giftAppModule` variable. This variable name, even though it happens to be identical to the module name, is unrelated; we could have called it anything else. You don't have to assign a module to a variable name, but it's useful as it allows us to more cleanly add assets to the module.

The next line, `giftAppModule.value('appName', 'GiftApp');`, creates a new service on the module by calling the `value` function. A service in Angular is a singleton, which is injectable. Angular includes a number of types of services. A value service is the simplest type and creates a name value pair that can be injected and used. We will use this in our controller.

Finally, we want to load our new module and `Bootstrap` it as the root Angular application in our `index.ejs` template.

Take a look at the following code:

```
<!DOCTYPE html>
<html ng-app="giftAppModule">
  <head>
    <title><%= title %></title>
    <link rel='stylesheet' href='/stylesheets/style.css' />
  </head>
  <body>
```

```
    <h1><%= title %></h1>
    <p>Welcome to <%= title %></p>
    <script
src="https://cdnjs.cloudflare.com/ajax/libs/angular.js/1.4.8/angular.js"></
script>
    <script src="/javascripts/app.js"></script>
  </body>
</html>
```

There are two important changes to note here. First, in the HTML element we added a reference to the `giftAppModule` we just created by setting it as the value of the `ng-app` directive. The next change is that we've added a new `script` tag before the closing body tag that loads the `app.js` file that we just created.

Load order is important here, and Angular must be loaded before `app.js` or it will fail. Note the path that we're using to load `app.js`: `/javascripts/app.js`. This works because of piece of code in the Express `app.js` that points requests for static files at the public directory, `app.use(express.static(path.join(__dirname, 'public')));`.

Starting the server up, if it's stopped, and reloading the page does nothing visible at this point. To start making changes to the page, we need to add a controller and an Angular expression.

Adding a controller

In Angular, a controller is a JavaScript object that exposes data and functionality to the view. It does this through Angular's `$scope` object.

Open your `app.js` file and add the following code:

```
var giftAppModule = angular.module('giftAppModule', []);

giftAppModule.value('appName', 'GiftApp');

giftAppModule.controller("GreetingController", ['$scope','appName',
function($scope)
{
        $scope.name = appName;
        $scope.greeting = "Hello Angular"
    }
]
);
```

The additional code has created a controller constructor on `giftAppModule` called `GreetingController`. This isn't an actual controller until it is invoked in the page using the `ng-controller` directive.

The first argument to the function is the name of the controller. The second argument is an array consisting of the dependencies we wish to inject. The final item in the array is the function itself. Angular documentation refers to this as array annotation and it is the preferred method of creating constructors.

The module name strings of the first part of the array map to the arguments of the function. The order of each must be the same.

Next, we will need to add the controller to our `index.ejs html`, as follows:

```
<!DOCTYPE html>
<html ng-app="giftAppModule">
  <head>
    <title><%= title %></title>
    <link rel='stylesheet' href='/stylesheets/style.css' />
  </head>
  <body>
    <h1><%= title %></h1>
    <p>Welcome to <%= title %></p>
    <div ng-controller="GreetingController">

    </div>
    <script
src="https://cdnjs.cloudflare.com/ajax/libs/angular.js/1.4.8/angular.js"></
script>
    <script src="/javascripts/app.js"></script>
  </body>
</html>
```

Here, we will add a `div` tag and give it an `ng-controller` attribute with a value of `GreetingController`. When we load this page, Angular will create a new `GreetingController` object and attach a child scope to this part of the page.

Again, if you hit reload on your browser, you will not see anything different. Generally, to display data to the user, you will use Angular expressions.

Displaying data with Angular expressions

Angular expressions are code snippets that are placed between double curly braces ({{ }}). Angular evaluates these (the JavaScript eval() function is not used as it's not a safe mechanism).

The Angular documentation refers to expressions as JavaScript as there are some pretty major differences. For example, Angular expressions don't have control loops.

Angular expressions are evaluated within the context of the current scope.

Let's make the following changes to index.ejs:

```
<!DOCTYPE html>
<html ng-app="giftAppModule">
  <head>
    <title><%= title %></title>
    <link rel='stylesheet' href='/stylesheets/style.css' />
  </head>
  <body>
    <h1><%= title %></h1>
    <p>Welcome to <%= title %></p>
    <div ng-controller="GreetingController">
        {{ greeting }} from {{ name }} {{ 2+3 }}
    </div>
    <script
src="https://cdnjs.cloudflare.com/ajax/libs/angular.js/1.4.8/angular.js"></
script>
    <script src="/javascripts/app.js"></script>
  </body>
</html>
```

We've added some Angular expressions inside div, where we invoked GreetingController. Angular makes the GreetingController scope object available inside this div.

Now, if you reload this page, under **Welcome to Express**, you should see the following line of code:

```
Hello Angular from GiftApp 5
```

Angular has evaluated the expressions and displayed them as strings. The expressions containing greeting and name are pulling those values from the scope. The final expression is just doing a little bit of arithmetic.

Two-way data binding

One of the main features that Angular provides is called two-way data binding. This means that changing data in the view updates the data on the model. Likewise, data changed in the model is reflected in the view.

Open `app.js` and add the following property to the scope:

```
var giftAppModule = angular.module('giftAppModule', []);

giftAppModule.value('appName', 'GiftApp');

giftAppModule.controller("GreetingController", ['$scope','appName',
function($scope, appName){
        $scope.name = appName;
        $scope.greeting = "Hello Angular";
        $scope.newName = "Bob";
    }]
);
```

We've added a `newName` property and assigned to it the string, `Bob`.

Now, we will need to make the following changes to `index.ejs`:

```
<!DOCTYPE html>
<html ng-app="giftAppModule">
  <head>
    <title><%= title %></title>
    <link rel='stylesheet' href='/stylesheets/style.css' />
  </head>
  <body>
    <h1><%= title %></h1>
    <p>Welcome to <%= title %></p>
    <div ng-controller="GreetingController">
        {{ greeting }} from {{ name }} {{ 2+3 }} {{ newName }}
        <p><input type=""text" ng-model="newName"></p>
    </div>
    <script
src="https://cdnjs.cloudflare.com/ajax/libs/angular.js/1.4.8/angular.js"></
script>
    <script src="/javascripts/app.js"></script>
  </body>
</html>
```

We've made two changes to this file. The first is that we've added the `{{newName}}` expression after the arithmetic expression. This renders the `Bob` string to the screen. The second change is that we've added a text input control and added the `ng-model="newName"` directive. This directive binds the value in the text box to the `newName` property on the scope.

When the page loads, the value in the text box is `Bob`. But what happens if we type something besides `Bob` in the text box? The value rendered by the expression changes nearly instantly.

This is a clear example of what is meant by two-way data binding. Changes to the data in the view affect the model seamlessly.

Summary

In this chapter, you learned how to build a full stack application from database to frontend using nothing but JavaScript-based tools. In the previous chapters we looked at the MEAN stack components. Now we've started to put them together.

You started by looking at Node.js, our JavaScript-based runtime environment. You used the Node.js REPL to execute JavaScript code on the command line. You then wrote a script, a small web server, which could be run by Node.js

You learned the two methods to set up an Express application. Additionally, you also used the express generator to build out a functioning framework to build an application. You learned about routing and middleware—the two key components of Express.

MongoDB is a NoSQL database that stores data as flexible documents in collections as opposed to the records/table model of relational databases. You ran each of the basic CRUD (Create, Read, Update, Delete) methods in Mongo with insert, find, update, and remove.

In the next chapter, we will dive deeply into MongoDB, gaining experience with the command-line interface.

8
Managing Data Using MongoDB

MongoDB is the database for the MEAN stack, and we have already explored some of its more basic features. It is an extremely powerful, scalable, NoSQL database that has gained wide popularity for big data and web applications. It happens to be open source and supported on a wide variety of operating systems and platforms.

MongoDB can be accessed using the MongoDB shell, a command-line interface that uses JavaScript-like syntax.

In this chapter, we will explore MongoDB in greater depth and begin to incorporate it into our SPA. You will explore the various CRUD operations in the MongoDB shell, as well as using a Node.js plugin to access a database inside your single page application.

We will cover the following topics:

- NoSQL databases
- Commanding MongoDB using the shell
- Incorporating MongoDB into the SPA
- MongoDB performance

Exploring the NoSQL database model

MongoDB is one of a number of NoSQL databases. Currently, it happens to be the most popular NoSQL database in use, according to statistics gathered by those who watch databases. SQL-based, relational databases have served us well for decades, so what's the big deal with NoSQL?

Defining NoSQL

MongoDB is often referred to as a NoSQL database. NoSQL is a popular buzzword that applies to MongoDB and several other database engines. But what does it mean?

First, there is no standard definition by some governing body defining what NoSQL means. The term was first used in 1998 by Carlo Strozzi to describe an open source relational database that did not have an SQL interface. However, today the term is used differently. NoSQL databases tend to have two defining features.

NoSQL

As the name might imply, most NoSQL databases do not use SQL to access the database. There are some NoSQL databases, however, that allow languages that are SQL-like or derived from SQL. Therefore, some take NoSQL to mean *not only SQL*.

MongoDB databases are normally accessed through JavaScript-like syntax.

Non-relational

NoSQL databases do not use the relational model, where data is stored in structured tables of columns or rows. In the case of MongoDB, data is stored as documents in collections.

In relational databases, data is stored in tables, much like a table in a spreadsheet.

Distributed

MongoDB, and other NoSQL databases, are designed to be distributed to work well in clusters. This makes hosting NoSQL databases in the cloud among numerous servers easier and provides for security, backup, performance, and scaling.

MongoDB supports sharding. Sharding is a process where portions of the database are hosted on different servers. This can make MongoDB extremely fast and highly scalable.

While it's beyond the scope of this book, the distributed nature of MongoDB makes it appealing for big data projects. Certainly, it makes MongoDB a compelling solution for web applications, which is its most popular use currently.

Features of MongoDB

Mongo has a number of features you should be aware of that make it different from other databases. They are explained as follows.

Document model

There are a number of models used by NoSQL databases. Some of these include the graph model, key-value model, object model, and others. These other models are beyond the scope of this book.

MongoDB uses the document model. Data is stored in collections of documents in a MongoDB database.

Here's an example of a MongoDB document:

```
{
"_id" : ObjectId("566d9d4c1c09d090fd36ba82"),
"name" : "John",
"address" : {
"street" : "77 Main street",
"city" : "Springfield" }
}
```

As you can see, documents in MongoDB are a form of JSON. In this case, the document even contains a subdocument, the address.

The database itself binary encodes the documents and stores them in a form referred to as BSON. Not to worry, though, you will not have to be concerned about encoding or decoding any of the data yourself, that is all handled behind the scenes.

One of the main differences between JSON and BSON is that BSON supports a number of data types not supported by JSON. This includes binary data, regular expressions, symbols, dates, and so on. For example, a date may be represented in JSON output as a simple string. However, storing a date as date type in BSON allows efficient date comparisons and operations as part of queries or insertions.

For the most part, this is not something you'll need to worry about. MongoDB will seamlessly convert the data into usable JSON. However, when we get to Mongoose, data validation will be an important feature that will be handled by middleware.

Schemaless

One of the features of MongoDB, and some other NoSQL databases, is that it doesn't have a fixed schema.

In MongoDB, documents are stored in groups called *collections*. Documents stored in a collection should be related conceptually, but there is no restriction in the database software itself that enforces this. This is in stark contrast to databases where schemas strictly define the data which can be entered into a table.

There is a danger here that random documents can be placed into any collection making the organization of the collections meaningless. You could insert a document reflecting data for a car into a collection called pets, but this wouldn't make much sense and could render the data in that collection difficult to query meaningfully.

It bears some thought.

Open source

MongoDB is an open source database. A number of various licenses apply to the server itself, the drivers, tools, and the documentation.

Complete licensing information for MongoDB is available at `https://www.mongodb.org/licensing`.

Why use MongoDB?

There are many choices of databases you could use to build a single page web application. For example, MySQL is a popular database for web applications overall. Why would you want to choose MongoDB over something like MySQL?

Ultimately, almost any database will do the job, but there are certain features in MongoDB that make it particularly attractive for use in SPAs.

Well supported

MongoDB enjoys wide support on a number of operating systems and platforms. MongoDB has downloads and installers for Windows, multiple flavors of Linux, Mac, and Solaris.

One of the popular ways to run MongoDB in the cloud is on a **Platform as a Service** (**PaaS**). PaaS is a service, normally provided by a vendor such as Amazon, that allows developers to build web applications in the cloud without the hassle of managing infrastructure. MongoDB maintains a list of supported platforms at https://docs.mongodb.org/ecosystem/platforms/.

MongoDB is supported in many popular languages. A quick visit to MongoDB's drivers page at `https://docs.mongodb.org/ecosystem/drivers/` shows that, as of the time of writing this book, MongoDB has supported drivers for C, C++, C#, Java, Node.js, Perl, PHP, Python, Motor, Ruby, and Scala. Additionally, community-supported drivers for Go and Erlang, undoubtedly, may will be on the way.

Data model

Because MongoDB's data model is based on JSON, it is ideal for use in web applications. JSON output can be consumed directly through frontend JavaScript and JavaScript frameworks such as AngularJs and others.

Because JSON is an object-oriented data format, the data works well with languages that are object-oriented themselves. The data structures can be modeled in the software you're writing very easily.

Popularity

As a developer, the popularity of the tools you are using is relatively important. For one thing, unpopular frameworks don't get the attention from development communities that popular ones get. Using a popular open source tool ensures that there is active development going on.

This extends to things such as books and learning resources, platform availability, and language support.

Popularity can also be an indication of quality or, at least, the quality of fit for popular types of applications. MongoDB has become very popular in **Big Data** circles, where unstructured data is the bread and butter or day-to-day operation. However, MongoDB really shines when it comes to some of the most popular types of web applications – such as CMS and geo-spatial data.

MongoDB is extremely popular. According to the 2015 press release from MongoDB (`https ://www.mongodb.com/press/mongodb-overtakes-postgresql-4-most-popular-dbms-db -engines-ranking`), MongoDB has surpassed PostgreSQL as the fourth most popular database. As of the press release, it was the only non-relational database in the top five. According to the same release, MongoDB has grown over 160% in popularity over the previous 2 years.

MongoDB is being used more and more in much wider places than many other databases. All indications are that it is going to be around, and be supported on all of the most popular platforms, for a long time.

Commanding MongoDB

MongoDB comes with an interactive shell, which we have already used briefly in the previous chapter. To refresh your memory, after starting the MongoDB daemon by typing `mongod`, you access the shell in a separate terminal window by typing `mongo`.

Primarily, you will be accessing MongoDB using native code in your application. However, understanding the MongoDB shell is invaluable to using it. There will be times when you want to access the shell directly, particularly for debugging. You may also need to manage a MongoDB instance in the cloud.

You should have a good grasp of the MongoDB shell.

Getting information

One of the most important things you can do in the MongoDB shell is to manage your databases. Getting *meta* information out of MongoDB is most easily accomplished using shell commands. The following are some of the basic commands you can use in the MongoDB shell to get information.

`help` – This will output a list of basic commands available in the MongoDB shell. For help with methods that operate on a database, you will use the `db.help()` method. Typing help into the MongoDB shell outputs the following:

- `db.help()`: Help on db methods
- `db.mycoll.help()`: Help on collection methods
- `sh.help()`: Sharding helpers
- `rs.help()`: Replica set helpers

- `help admin`: Administrative help
- `help connect`: Connecting to a db help
- `help keys`: Key shortcuts
- `help misc`: Misc things to know
- `help mr`: Mapreduce
- `show dbs`: Show database names
- `show collections`: Show collections in current database
- `show users`: Show users in current database
- `show profile`: Show most recent system.profile entries with time *s*>= *1 m*
- `show logs`: Show accessible logger names
- `show log [name]`: Prints out last segment of log in memory; `global` is default
- `use <db_name>`: Set current database
- `db.foo.find()`: List objects in the `foo` collection
- `db.foo.find( { a : 1 } )`: List objects in foo where a == 1
- `it`: Result of the last line evaluated; use to further iterate
- `DBQuery.shellBatchSize = x`: Set default number of items to display on shell
- `exit`: Quit Mongo shell

Some of the most important commands for gathering info from a database are the commands that begin with `show`. For example, `showdbs` will give you a list of the currently accessible database names on the system. `showcollections` will list the collections in the current database.

One thing that isn't listed here is a method for retrieving the database on which you are currently operating. To do that, simply type `db` and the shell will output the name of the current database.

Inserting and updating data

In the last chapter, we inserted some records using the insert method. You're going to do that a little differently here so that you can set up and load some data into your `giftapp` database, one that we created in the last chapter for the SPA you're building.

We're going to use two methods to insert data that you haven't used yet. One will be to execute a JavaScript file in the MongoDB shell which will set up and execute commands. We'll use this to insert some documents. The other method we'll use is a bulk operation that will allow us to set up some data and then execute and bulk insert it.

Running scripts in the MongoDB shell

The MongoDB shell allows you to load and execute JavaScript files. In your `giftapp` directory, create a new folder called `scripts` and create a JavaScript file called `db-init.js`:

```
db = db.getSiblingDB('giftapp');

var user1 = {firstName:"Mark", lastName:"Smith",
email:"msmith@xyzzymail.org"};

var user2 = {firstName:"Sally", lastName:"Jones",
email:"sjones@xyzzymail.org"};

var users = [user1, user2];

db.users.insert(users);
```

The first line, `db=db.getSiblingDB('giftapp')`, tells the MongoDB shell which database to work with in case you haven't already selected the `giftapp` database in some way. We need to use this method because the `use` command isn't valid JavaScript.

Next, you create two objects, `user1` and `user2`, using JavaScript object literal notations. These objects represent user data for the users' `Mark Smith` and `Sally Jones`. You then create an array called users that contains the two user objects.

Next, we invoke the `insert` method on the users collection and pass it the users array. If there is no users collection in the `giftapp` database, one will be created when we execute this script.

Note that when an array is passed to the insert method, MongoDB will insert each document separately. This is a powerful feature allowing for easy and efficient multiple document inserts.

There are two ways we can load and execute this script.

From the command-line in a terminal not running the MongoDB shell, navigate to the directory where the script is stored and type the following:

```
$ mongo localhost:27017/test db-init.js
MongoDB shell version: 3.0.4
connecting to: localhost:27017/test
```

Unfortunately, there won't be any really useful output to tell you that the inserts were completed. If you start the MongoDB shell, or use a terminal where it's already running, you can verify by doing the following:

```
> db.users.count()
2
> db.users.find()
{ "_id" : ObjectId("566dcc5b65d385d7fa9652e3"), "firstName" : "Mark",
"lastName" : "Smith", "email" : "msmith@xyzzymail.org" }
{ "_id" : ObjectId("566dcc5b65d385d7fa9652e4"), "firstName" : "Sally",
"lastName" : "Jones", "email" : "sjones@xyzzymail.org" }
```

The count method returns the number of documents in a collection. Here, there are two. We've already explored the find method. Here we invoke find with no arguments, which returns all the documents in the collection. You can see that Mark and Sally are now documents stored separately in the users collection.

If you run this script multiple times, it will create numerous Mark and Sally documents. If you want to clean out the collection and start over, you can use the drop method and verify using the following command:

```
> db.users.drop()
true
> db.users.count()
0
> db.users.find()
>
```

I promised you a second method of running scripts, and we'll get to that. Let's make a small modification to the script first:

```
db = db.getSiblingDB('giftapp');
var now = new Date();

var user1 = {firstName:"Mark", lastName:"Smith",
email:"msmith@xyzzymail.org", created: now};
var user2 = {firstName:"Sally", lastName:"Jones",
email:"sjones@xyzzymail.org", created: now};

var users = [user1, user2];

db.users.insert(users);
```

We added a variable called `now` that contains a new `Date` object. Creating a `Date` object in this way sets the date and time in the object to the current date and time. Next, we add a field called `created` to `Mark` and `Sally`, and give it the value of now, our date object.

In a terminal running the MongoDB shell, do the following:

```
> db.users.drop()
true
> db.users.count()
0
> load('/[path to your directory]/giftapp/scripts/db-init.js')
true
> db.users.count()
2
> db.users.find()
{ "_id" : ObjectId("566dd0cb1c09d090fd36ba83"), "firstName" : "Mark",
"lastName" : "Smith", "email" : "msmith@xyzzymail.org", "created" :
ISODate("2015-12-13T20:10:51.336Z") }
    { "_id" : ObjectId("566dd0cb1c09d090fd36ba84"), "firstName" : "Sally",
"lastName" : "Jones", "email" : "sjones@xyzzymail.org", "created" :
ISODate("2015-12-13T20:10:51.336Z") }
```

Here, we use the load method to run the script, passing it the path to the script. We see that the two users have been added to the collection, and the find method retrieves their documents.

If you look at the created field on `Mark` and `Sally` documents you'll see something new. The `Date` may look a little different. Internally, MongoDB stores dates as a 64-bit integer representing the number of milliseconds since January 1st, 1970. Negative numbers are used to represent dates before that.

Storing dates and times as integers likes this, instead of strings, allows things such as date calculations and comparisons.

Fortunately, MongoDB outputs dates in a somewhat usable and readable format. We will explore displaying dates in a more human friendly way in a later chapter.

Running bulk operations

Another way to insert multiple documents into a MongoDB collection in a single pass is to use MongoDB's `Bulk` API. This allows us to set up a list of ordered or unordered operations and then run them all when we choose to execute We can experiment with this using the MongoDB shell commands.

Take a look at the following commands:

```
> var bulk = db.users.initializeUnorderedBulkOp()
> bulk.insert(
... { firstname: "John",
... lastname: "Smith",
... email: "jiggy@zzxxyy3.com",
... created: new Date()
... }
... );
> bulk.insert(
... { firstname: "Jane",
... lastname: "Smothers",
... email: "janes@zzxxyy3.com",
... created: new Date()
... }
... );
> bulk.execute()
BulkWriteResult({
  "writeErrors" : [ ],
  "writeConcernErrors" : [ ],
  "nInserted" : 2,
  "nUpserted" : 0,
  "nMatched" : 0,
  "nModified" : 0,
  "nRemoved" : 0,
  "upserted" : [ ]
})
```

In the first line, we opened up an unordered bulk operation on users and assigned it to the variable called `bulk`. We could also have made that an ordered operation, but we don't currently care about the order in which the inserts are executed.

We then add two `insert` commands to the bulk operation, one for John Smith, and another for Jane Smothers. We can then call execute on the `bulk` operation. The returned value tells us that there were no errors and that two documents were inserted.

Let's have a look at our collection now:

```
> db.users.find().pretty()
{
  "_id" : ObjectId("566dd0cb1c09d090fd36ba83"),
  "firstName" : "Mark",
  "lastName" : "Smith",
  "email" : "msmith@xyzzymail.org",
  "created" : ISODate("2015-12-13T20:10:51.336Z")
}
```

```
{
  "_id" : ObjectId("566dd0cb1c09d090fd36ba84"),
  "firstName" : "Sally",
  "lastName" : "Jones",
  "email" : "sjones@xyzzymail.org",
  "created" : ISODate("2015-12-13T20:10:51.336Z")
}
{
  "_id" : ObjectId("566dff161c09d090fd36ba85"),
  "firstname" : "John",
  "lastname" : "Smith",
  "email" : "jiggy@zzxxyy3.com",
  "created" : ISODate("2015-12-13T23:26:42.165Z")
}
{
  "_id" : ObjectId("566dff161c09d090fd36ba86"),
  "firstname" : "Jane",
  "lastname" : "Smothers",
  "email" : "janes@zzxxyy3.com",
  "created" : ISODate("2015-12-13T23:28:00.383Z")
}
```

I added the `pretty` method to the end of the `find` method in order to tidy up our output and make it a bit more readable. As you can see, `John` and `Jane` have been added to our collection.

Finding, modifying, and removing data

Queries are how we search for and return data out of our database. We've been using queries all along every time we have used the `find` method. We know that find, on its own, will return every single document in a collection. That's not exactly useful.

Specific results

Generally, we want to query a collection and return specific results. We want only those states that export peanuts, or we want a list of customers who live in France.

To specify that we want documents where a specific field matches a specific value, we do this:

```
> db.users.find({lastname:"Smith"}).pretty()
{
  "_id" : ObjectId("566dff161c09d090fd36ba85"),
  "firstname" : "John",
```

```
      "lastname" : "Smith",
      "email" : "jiggy@zzxxyy3.com",
      "created" : ISODate("2015-12-13T23:26:42.165Z")
}
```

Here, I've called the find operation and passed it an object with a single field: `lastname`. This is called the criteria. The value of that field is `Smith`. As you can see this returned the record for `John Smith`. For more than one field, you would separate the fields by commas.

Wait a minute, shouldn't I also see the document for `Mark Smith`? If you look carefully, the documents for `Mark Smith` and `Sally Jones` camelcase `firstName` and `lastName`. That is, the `N` is a capital letter. Therefore, MongoDB doesn't see this as the same field.

This is a good illustration of one of the dangers of schemaless databases, and something to keep in mind. We will fix this in the section on updates.

Let's say that we want to get documents for users with `lastName` fields matching `Smith` or `Jones`. There are a couple of ways you could write this query, but the best way when comparing the same field is to use the `$in` operator, as shown in the following commands:

```
> db.users.find({lastName: { $in: ['Jones', 'Smith']}}).pretty()
{
  "_id" : ObjectId("566dd0cb1c09d090fd36ba83"),
  "firstName" : "Mark",
  "lastName" : "Smith",
  "email" : "msmith@xyzzymail.org",
  "created" : ISODate("2015-12-13T20:10:51.336Z")
}
{
  "_id" : ObjectId("566dd0cb1c09d090fd36ba84"),
  "firstName" : "Sally",
  "lastName" : "Jones",
  "email" : "sjones@xyzzymail.org",
  "created" : ISODate("2015-12-13T20:10:51.336Z")
}
```

Query operators

MongoDB comes with a number of operators that all begin with the dollar sign. They are used for modifying and comparing within query criteria.

There are a number of types of query operators that include comparison operators such as `$eq`: equal to, `$gt`: greater than, and `$lte`: less than or equal to. Here's an example:

```
> db.users.find({payrate: {$gt: 45}})
```

This would return all documents in the `users` collection that had a `payrate` field with a value greater than `45`.

Logical operators include `$or`, `$and`, `$not`, and `$nor`. Each of these behaves like you'd expect if you're used to logical operators. Here's an example:

```
db.find({$and: [{firstName: "Steve"},{lastName: "Smith"}]})
```

This query returns all documents that have a `firstName` field equal to `Steve` and a `lastName` field equal to `Smith`.

MongoDB includes two element operators: `$exists`: to check if a field exists, and `$type`: to check the type of a specified file. Take a look at the following command:

```
> db.users.find({car: { $exists: true })
```

This query returns all documents in the `users` collection that have a `car` field.

MongoDB includes a number of other operators. These include things such as `regex` matching and geospatial comparison. There are also operators comparing arrays.

For a more complete list of operators, see the MongoDB documentation on operators at `https://docs.mongodb.org/v3.0/reference/operator/query/`.

Projections

We covered projections briefly in the previous chapter but, to refresh your memory, a projection specifies the fields returned in a query. We don't always want all of the fields in the documents that we return, so a projection lets us limit the data to the fields we are interested in.

Projections will be the second argument to the find method, as shown in the following commands:

```
> db.users.find({},{ email: 1 })
{ "_id" : ObjectId("566dd0cb1c09d090fd36ba83"), "email" :
  "msmith@xyzzymail.org" }
{ "_id" : ObjectId("566dd0cb1c09d090fd36ba84"), "email" :
  "sjones@xyzzymail.org" }
{ "_id" : ObjectId("566dff161c09d090fd36ba85"), "email" :
  "jiggy@zzxxyy3.com" }
{ "_id" : ObjectId("566dff161c09d090fd36ba86"), "email" :
"janes@zzxxyy3.com"
  }
```

We specified that we wanted all documents in the collection by passing an empty object as the first argument to find. Then, we used a projection to tell MongoDB that we wanted to see the `email` field.

You'll notice that the `_id` field is returned in the results. This is a default. To suppress that, we give it a value of `0` in the find in the projection as shown in the following command:

```
> db.users.find({},{ email: 1, _id: 0 })
{ "email" : "msmith@xyzzymail.org" }
{ "email" : "sjones@xyzzymail.org" }
{ "email" : "jiggy@zzxxyy3.com" }
{ "email" : "janes@zzxxyy3.com" }
```

In this query, `email` is included, while `_id` is excluded.

There are also a number of projection operators. You can find the details for those in the MongoDB documentation at `https://docs.mongodb.org/v3.0/reference/operator/query/`.

Query modifiers

As the name implies, query modifiers are used to modify the data coming back from a query. This includes doing things such as sorting, or returning a maximum number of results.

There are two forms of modifiers in Mongo DB (I prefer the first). Take a look at the following commands:

```
db.collection.find( { <query> } )._addSpecial( <option> )
db.collection.find( { $query: { <query> }, <option> } )
```

Let me illustrate with an example:

```
> db.users.find({},{ email:1, _id:0 }).sort({ email:1 })
{ "email" : "janes@zzxxyy3.com" }
{ "email" : "jiggy@zzxxyy3.com" }
{ "email" : "msmith@xyzzymail.org" }
{ "email" : "sjones@xyzzymail.org" }
```

Here, I am selecting all documents in the users collection. I am returning only the `email` field (and suppressing the `_id` field). I am then sorting by ascending order by `email`. If we wanted to sort the documents by the `email` field in descending order, we would make the value in the modifier `-1`, as shown in the following commands:

```
> db.users.find({},{ email:1, _id:0 }).sort({ email:-1 })
```

```
{ "email" : "sjones@xyzzymail.org" }
{ "email" : "msmith@xyzzymail.org" }
{ "email" : "jiggy@zzxxyy3.com" }
{ "email" : "janes@zzxxyy3.com" }
```

Modifying data

To modify MongoDB documents, you generally use the update method.

Take a look at following commands:

```
> db.users.find({lastname:"Smothers"}).pretty()
{
   "_id" : ObjectId("566dff161c09d090fd36ba86"),
   "firstname" : "Jane",
   "lastname" : "Smothers",
   "email" : "janes@zzxxyy3.com",
   "created" : ISODate("2015-12-13T23:28:00.383Z")
}
> db.users.update({lastname:"Smothers"},{$set:{
  email:"jsmothers@xxaayy4.com"}})
WriteResult({ "nMatched" : 1, "nUpserted" : 0, "nModified" : 1 })
> db.users.find({lastname:"Smothers"}).pretty()
{
   "_id" : ObjectId("566dff161c09d090fd36ba86"),
   "firstname" : "Jane",
   "lastname" : "Smothers",
   "email" : "jsmothers@xxaayy4.com",
   "created" : ISODate("2015-12-13T23:28:00.383Z")
}
```

Here, we do a find just to display the document for Jane Smothers. We want to change the e-mail address of Jane, so we use the update method. The first argument to the update method is the same criteria used in the find method to select a document or set of documents. The second argument is the instruction for the update.

Here, we've used the $set operator to change the e-mail address. If there wasn't an email field in the document, the $set operator would create a new field.

It's important to note that update, by default, will only update a single document. To update multiple documents, you set a multi option as part of a third option to update.

Let's fix our users collection to make the fields for `firstname` and `lastname` into camelcase:

```
> db.users.update({ lastname: { $exists: true }}, {$rename:
  {'lastname':'lastName','firstname':'firstName'}}, { multi: true })
WriteResult({ "nMatched" : 2, "nUpserted" : 0, "nModified" : 2 })
> db.users.find().pretty()
{
  "_id" : ObjectId("566dd0cb1c09d090fd36ba83"),
  "firstName" : "Mark",
  "lastName" : "Smith",
  "email" : "msmith@xyzzymail.org",
  "created" : ISODate("2015-12-13T20:10:51.336Z")
}
{
  "_id" : ObjectId("566dd0cb1c09d090fd36ba84"),
  "firstName" : "Sally",
  "lastName" : "Jones",
  "email" : "sjones@xyzzymail.org",
  "created" : ISODate("2015-12-13T20:10:51.336Z")
}
{
  "_id" : ObjectId("566dff161c09d090fd36ba85"),
  "email" : "jiggy@zzxxyy3.com",
  "created" : ISODate("2015-12-13T23:26:42.165Z"),
  "lastName" : "Smith",
  "firstName" : "John"
}
{
  "_id" : ObjectId("566dff161c09d090fd36ba86"),
  "email" : "jsmothers@xxaayy4.com",
  "created" : ISODate("2015-12-13T23:28:00.383Z"),
 "lastName" : "Smothers",
  "firstName" : "Jane"
}
```

The first argument to the `update` method uses the `$exists` operator to select any documents without the camelcase `lastname` field. The second argument uses the `$rename` operator to change both `firstname` and `lastname` field names to camelcase. The final argument sets the multi option to `true`, telling MongoDB to update all of the matched documents.

The result shows us that two documents were matched and two documents were updated. Running the `find` method shows us that all documents now have the same field names.

By default, if the query part of the `update` method doesn't match any documents, MongoDB doesn't do anything. We can tell MongoDB to create a new document if none are matched using the `upsert` option:

```
> db.users.update(
... { email: "johnny5@fbz22.com"},
... {
...     firstName: "Johnny",
...     lastName: "Fiverton",
...     email: "johnny5@zfb22.com",
...     created: new Date()
... },
... { upsert: true })
WriteResult({
  "nMatched" : 0,
  "nUpserted" : 1,
  "nModified" : 0,
  "_id" : ObjectId("566eaec7fa55252158538298")
})
> db.users.find().pretty()
{
  "_id" : ObjectId("566dd0cb1c09d090fd36ba83"),
  "firstName" : "Mark",
  "lastName" : "Smith",
  "email" : "msmith@xyzzymail.org",
  "created" : ISODate("2015-12-13T20:10:51.336Z")
}
{
  "_id" : ObjectId("566dd0cb1c09d090fd36ba84"),
  "firstName" : "Sally",
  "lastName" : "Jones",
  "email" : "sjones@xyzzymail.org",
  "created" : ISODate("2015-12-13T20:10:51.336Z")
}
{
  "_id" : ObjectId("566dff161c09d090fd36ba85"),
  "email" : "jiggy@zzxxyy3.com",
  "created" : ISODate("2015-12-13T23:26:42.165Z"),
  "lastName" : "Smith",
  "firstName" : "John"
}
{
  "_id" : ObjectId("566dff161c09d090fd36ba86"),
  "email" : "jsmothers@xxaayy4.com",
  "created" : ISODate("2015-12-13T23:28:00.383Z"),
  "lastName" : "Smothers",
  "firstName" : "Jane"
}
```

```
{
    "_id" : ObjectId("566eaec7fa55252158538298"),
    "firstName" : "Johnny",
    "lastName" : "Fiverton",
    "email" : "johnny5@zfb22.com",
    "created" : ISODate("2015-12-14T11:57:59.196Z")
}
```

Here, we select documents where an `email` field matches `johnny5@fbz22.com`. As we know, there are no documents matching this query. The second argument to `update` lists the data we want to change. Finally, we set the `upsert` option to `true`.

The write result shows us that no documents were matched or modified, but that a single document was upserted.

Invoking find shows us that the record for `Johnny Fiverton` has been added.

You may have noticed that we did not use the `$set` operator this time around. If the second argument in update uses no operators, MongoDB will replace the entire document with the data in the second argument. This is something to be careful of; use `$set` when you don't want to replace the entire documents.

A list of `update` operators is available in the MongoDB documentation: `https://docs.mongodb.org/v3.0/reference/operator/update/`.

Removing data

So far, we have covered the: create, read, and update components of CRUD (create, read, update, delete). The remaining part is deleting documents. For deletion, MongoDB has the `remove` method.

Remove has a somewhat familiar signature.

Take a look at the following commands:

```
> db.users.remove({ email: "johnny5@zfb22.com" })
WriteResult({ "nRemoved" : 1 })
> db.users.find().pretty()
{
    "_id" : ObjectId("566dd0cb1c09d090fd36ba83"),
    "firstName" : "Mark",
    "lastName" : "Smith",
    "email" : "msmith@xyzzymail.org",
    "created" : ISODate("2015-12-13T20:10:51.336Z")
}
```

```
{
    "_id" : ObjectId("566dd0cb1c09d090fd36ba84"),
    "firstName" : "Sally",
    "lastName" : "Jones",
    "email" : "sjones@xyzzymail.org",
    "created" : ISODate("2015-12-13T20:10:51.336Z")
}
{
    "_id" : ObjectId("566dff161c09d090fd36ba85"),
    "email" : "jiggy@zzxxyy3.com",
    "created" : ISODate("2015-12-13T23:26:42.165Z"),
    "lastName" : "Smith",
    "firstName" : "John"
}
{
    "_id" : ObjectId("566dff161c09d090fd36ba86"),
    "email" : "jsmothers@xxaayy4.com",
    "created" : ISODate("2015-12-13T23:28:00.383Z"),
    "lastName" : "Smothers",
    "firstName" : "Jane"
}
```

And it's goodbye `Johnny`.

You can probably surmise that the first argument to remove is the query. Here, we have selected all documents with an `email` field matching `johnny5@zfb22.com`. In this case, there is only one. The write result tells us that the number of documents removed is one.

A word of caution: by default, remove will delete all matched documents. If the query is an empty object, remove will delete everything in the collection. The indexes, however, will stay intact. To ensure that you are only removing a single document, you set the `justOne` parameter, the second optional argument to remove, to `1`, as shown in the following command:

```
db.users.remove( { lastName: "Smith" }, 1 )
```

This would remove a single `Smith` from our users collection.

The cursor

In MongoDB, the result of invoking `db.collection.find()` is actually a `cursor`. A `cursor` is a pointer to the results of a query. In the MongoDB shell, if you do not assign a `cursor` to a variable, the cursor is automatically iterated and output. This is what we have been doing so far:

```
> var cursor = db.users.find({},{ email:1, _id: 0 })
> cursor
{ "email" : "msmith@xyzzymail.org" }
{ "email" : "sjones@xyzzymail.org" }
{ "email" : "jiggy@zzxxyy3.com" }
{ "email" : "janes@zzxxyy3.com" }
> cursor
>
```

Here, we create a variable called `cursor` and assign to it the `cursor` returned by the `find` method. We then manually iterate the `cursor` simply by typing its name and hitting *Enter*. Typing the `cursor` name again and hitting *Enter* does nothing because the `cursor` has already been iterated.

This, in itself, isn't very useful, but we can do all kinds of things with the cursor. For example, if we wanted to put all of our documents into an array we could do this:

```
> var cursor = db.users.find({},{ email:1, _id: 0 })
> var myDocs = cursor.toArray()
> myDocs
[
  {
    "email" : "msmith@xyzzymail.org"
  },
  {
    "email" : "sjones@xyzzymail.org"
  },
  {
    "email" : "jiggy@zzxxyy3.com"
  },
  {
    "email" : "janes@zzxxyy3.com"
  }
]
```

MongoDB offers a ton of built-in cursor methods. Documentation for MongoDB JavaScript cursor methods can be found at: `https://docs.mongodb.org/manual/reference/method/#js-query-cursor-methods`.

Incorporating MongoDB into the SPA

All this command-line stuff is great, but we need to start incorporating our MongoDB database into our SPA. In a future chapter, we will introduce the `mongoose` plugin for node, which will allow us to do data modeling, and which will perform a lot of heavy lifting for us.

For now, we're going to add a connection to MongoDB into our SPA in a simple way, which will highlight how to incorporate our database and display some dynamic data.

Adding the NPM modules

For this chapter, we need two modules to connect and easily access our MongoDB database inside our Express application. Those modules are `mongodb` and `monk`.

In your terminal, navigate to your `giftapp` directory and type the following (remember to lead with `sudo` if you're on a Mac or Linux):

```
npm install mongodb --save
...
npm install monk -save
```

The dependencies section of your `package.json` file should now look something like this:

```
"dependencies": {
    "body-parser": "~1.13.2",
    "cookie-parser": "~1.3.5",
    "debug": "~2.2.0",
    "ejs": "~2.3.3",
    "express": "~4.13.1",
    "mongodb": "^2.1.1",
    "monk": "^1.0.1",
    "morgan": "~1.6.1",
    "serve-favicon": "~2.3.0"
}
```

Adding MongoDB into the main application

Next, we need to make our MongoDB database accessible inside the main application. We're going to add a few lines to our `app.js` file:

```
var express = require('express');
var path = require('path');
```

```
var favicon = require('serve-favicon');
var logger = require('morgan');
var cookieParser = require('cookie-parser');
var bodyParser = require('body-parser');

//Database stuffvar mongodb = require('mongodb');var monk =
require('monk');var db = monk('localhost:27017/giftapp')

var routes = require('./routes/index');
var users = require('./routes/users');

var app = express();

// view engine setup
app.set('views', path.join(__dirname, 'views'));
app.set('view engine', 'ejs');

// uncomment after placing your favicon in /public
//app.use(favicon(path.join(__dirname, 'public', 'favicon.ico')));
app.use(logger('dev'));
app.use(bodyParser.json());
app.use(bodyParser.urlencoded({ extended: false }));
app.use(cookieParser());
app.use(express.static(path.join(__dirname, 'public')));

//Database middlewareapp.use(function(req,res,next){     req.db = db;
next();});

app.use('/', routes);
app.use('/users', users);

// catch 404 and forward to error handler
app.use(function(req, res, next) {
  var err = new Error('Not Found');
  err.status = 404;
  next(err);
});

// error handlers

// development error handler
// will print stacktrace
if (app.get('env') === 'development') {
  app.use(function(err, req, res, next) {
    res.status(err.status || 500);
    res.render('error', {
      message: err.message,
      error: err
```

```
      });
    });
  }

  // production error handler
  // no stacktraces leaked to user
  app.use(function(err, req, res, next) {
    res.status(err.status || 500);
    res.render('error', {
      message: err.message,
      error: {}
    });
  });

  module.exports = app;
```

In the first highlighted section, we load the `mongodb` and `monk` modules using the require method. We then instantiate the database connection by invoking `monk` and assigning the connection to the variable `db`.

Next, we write a small piece of middleware. Note that it's important that this middleware shows up before the routing middleware. The middleware attaches the database connection to the request object and then passes it on to the next middleware by invoking the next function.

Writing a query

Now let's get some data out of your database and displayed onto the browser. For that, we need to add a new route. Open up your `routes/users.js` file and we'll add a few lines:

```
var express = require('express');
var router = express.Router();

/* GET users listing. */
router.get('/', function(req, res, next) {
  res.send('respond with a resource');
});

router.get('/show', function(req, res, next)
  {
    var db = req.db;
    var collection = db.get('users');
    collection.find({},{},function(err,docs)
  {
```

```
if(!err)
{
            res.json(docs);
        }
else
{
            res.send('error');
        }
    });
});

module.exports = router;
```

We will cover Express routing in depth in a later chapter, but what we've done here is create a new router for the /show path after /users. We've aliased the database from the request object and set the collection we're interested in using the monk get method.

We then call the monk find method on the collection, passing an empty query. We know from our command-line experiments that an empty query should return all records in the collection.

The last argument to find here is a callback function, which is executed when the query returns. The first argument to this function receives an error if the query results in an error. The second argument receives the documents returned from the query.

We check to make sure there's no error, and if there isn't, we output the documents using the response object's json function. As the name implies, the output is returned to the browser as JSON.

Ensure that your MongoDB daemon is still running, or restart it in a terminal window. In another terminal window, navigate to your giftapp directory and type npm start to start up your server.

Navigating to localhost:3000/users/show in your browser will display something like this:

```
[{"_id":"566dd0cb1c09d090fd36ba83","firstName":"Mark","lastName":"Smith","e
mail":"msmith@xyzzymail.org","created":"2015-12-13T20:10:51.336Z"},{"_id":"
566dd0cb1c09d090fd36ba84","firstName":"Sally","lastName":"Jones","email":"s
jones@xyzzymail.org","created":"2015-12-13T20:10:51.336Z"},{"_id":"566dff16
1c09d090fd36ba85","email":"jiggy@zzxxyy3.com","created":"2015-12-13T23:26:4
2.165Z","lastName":"Smith","firstName":"John"},{"_id":"566dff161c09d090fd36
ba86","email":"jsmothers@xxaayy4.com","created":"2015-12-13T23:28:00.383Z",
"lastName":"Smothers","firstName":"Jane"}]
```

It's not pretty, but it is an array that contains all of our documents in JSON format. We could already consume this as a web service, but let's do something a little prettier with it.

Displaying data in a page

Let's format our data and put it into an HTML page to make it a little nicer to look at. Inside your `views` folder, create a new folder called `users`. Inside there, create a new file called `show.ejs` with the following code in it:

```
<!DOCTYPE html>
<html>
<head>
    <title>Show Users</title>
    <link rel='stylesheet' href='/stylesheets/style.css' />
</head>
<body>
<h1>User List</h1>

<table>
    <thead>
        <tr>

            <th>First Name</th>
            <th>Last Name</th>
            <th>Email Address</th>
        </tr>
    </thead>
    <tbody>
    <% users.forEach(function(user, index){ -%>
        <tr>
            <td><%= user.firstName %></td>
            <td><%= user.lastName %></td>
            <td><%= user.email %></td>
        </tr>
    <% }); %>
    </tbody>
</table>


</body>
</html>
```

We've created an embedded JavaScript document here that takes a collection of items called users. We iterate over that using the forEach function, assigning each instance to a variable called user.

For each pass through we create a table row. That table row contains table data elements for the user's first name, last name, and e-mail address.

This alone won't work; we have to query the database and pass the data to the page. To do that we need to change up the route we just created to render this template and pass the docs we retrieve to it.

Here are the changes to the users router file:

```
var express = require('express');
var router = express.Router();

/* GET users listing. */
router.get('/', function(req, res, next) {
  res.send('respond with a resource');
});

router.get('/show', function(req, res, next) {
    var db = req.db;
    var collection = db.get('users');
    collection.find({}, {}, function(err,docs){
        if(!err){
            //res.json(docs);            res.render('users/show', { users:
docs });
        }else{
            res.send('error');
        }
    });
});

module.exports = router;
```

The only real change here is that we've commented out the line that sent the results as JSON back to the browser using the response's json method. Instead, we use the response's render function to choose the users/show.ejs template, and pass the retrieved docs as a property called users.

Now, if you restart the `giftapp` server and navigate to `localhost:3000/users/show`, you should see this:

User List

First Name	Last Name	Email Address
Mark	Smith	msmith@xyzzymail.org
Sally	Jones	sjones@xyzzymail.org
John	Smith	jiggy@zzxxyy3.com
Jane	Smothers	jsmothers@xxaayy4.com

You can see how using Express with MongoDB gives us a lot of ease and flexibility in sending data to the browser. It's a simple thing to send JSON formatted data, and it is also simple to render pages dynamically.

As we continue to build our SPA, we will rely more on building out web services which will return JSON data.

MongoDB database performance

Topics such as replication and sharding are beyond the scope of this book. However, there are a number of things developers can do to optimize the performance of your MongoDB database.

Mainly, we'll talk about cover indexing and tuning queries for performance.

Indexing

In many database systems, adding an `index` in a field when appropriate can speed up querying. Queries are optimized when performed on indexed fields. MongoDB is no different.

The downside to indexes is that they add some extra time to write operations. They also take up extra space in the database. It makes sense to index wisely. When considering adding indexes, you want to think about whether you expect more read than write operations. This would be a plus for adding additional indexes.

Let's add an index to our user collection. We'll say that we want to frequently look up our users by their last names. It makes sense to add an `index` on the `lastname` field, as shown in the following commands:

```
> db.users.createIndex({lastname:1})
{
  "createdCollectionAutomatically" : false,
  "numIndexesBefore" : 1,
  "numIndexesAfter" : 2,
  "ok" : 1
}
```

We use the collection's `createIndex` method command passing it an object containing a single field. That field has the key of `lastname` with a value of 1. This tells MongoDB that we want to create an index where we store the `lastname` fields in the collection in ascending order.

Internally, this creates a list of all the last names in ascending order, with pointers to the documents. Read operations keyed to the `lastname` field are efficient because the MongoDB engine doesn't have to search through every single document in the collection to find matching values, it can just search the list of last names.

Write operations will be slightly slower, because they will also have to update the `index`.

Optimizing queries

Web application performance can be impacted by slow data read operations. Optimizing database operations can help in scaling operations, but also in perceived performance, enhancing user satisfaction.

One of the ways developers can significantly impact performance is by optimizing queries. The main methods for reducing the amount of time taken for queries revolve around reducing the amount of data returned and by using indexes to make the lookup more efficient.

Using limit

The `limit()` method, when added to a query, limits the number of records returned in the query. Limiting the number of records returned means less data transfer and thus faster performance and less use of resources.

Take a look at the following commands:

```
> db.users.find().limit(2).pretty()
{
  "_id" : ObjectId("566dd0cb1c09d090fd36ba83"),
  "firstName" : "Mark",
  "lastName" : "Smith",
  "email" : "msmith@xyzzymail.org",
  "created" : ISODate("2015-12-13T20:10:51.336Z")
}
{
  "_id" : ObjectId("566dd0cb1c09d090fd36ba84"),
  "firstName" : "Sally",
  "lastName" : "Jones",
  "email" : "sjones@xyzzymail.org",
  "created" : ISODate("2015-12-13T20:10:51.336Z")
}
```

We've added the `limit` function here to find with no query, giving it an argument of 2. This tells MongoDB to return two documents, which you can see here.

Note that we can still add the `pretty()` function onto the end by chaining.

Using projections

We've already discussed projections as a way to limit the number of fields returned per document. Projections are another tool that reduce data transfer, as shown in the following commands:

```
> db.users.find({},{email:1,_id:0}).limit(2)
{ "email" : "msmith@xyzzymail.org" }
{ "email" : "sjones@xyzzymail.org" }
```

In this query, we've added a projection to show `email` and suppress `_id`. We've kept the `limit` function. The result is two documents each containing only the `email` field.

Using hint()

Using the `hint()` function forces MongoDB to use a particular `index` for a query.

If you remember, we created an `index` on the `lastname` field of the `users` collection earlier. However, this isn't going to help us, since we changed our documents to use the camelCased field name `lastName`. Let's have a look:

```
db.users.getIndexes()
[
    {
        "v" : 1,
        "key" : {
            "_id" : 1
        },
        "name" : "_id_",
        "ns" : "giftapp.users"
    },
    {
        "v" : 1,
        "key" : {
            "lastname" : 1
        },
        "name" : "lastname_1",
        "ns" : "giftapp.users"
    }
]
```

You can see that both `_id` and `lastname` are indexes. Let's drop `lastname` and add `lastName`:

```
> db.users.dropIndex({ 'lastname':1})
{ "nIndexesWas" : 2, "ok" : 1 }
> db.users.createIndex({ lastName:1 })
{
    "createdCollectionAutomatically" : false,
    "numIndexesBefore" : 1,
    "numIndexesAfter" : 2,
    "ok" : 1
}
> db.users.getIndexes()
[
    {
        "v" : 1,
        "key" : {
            "_id" : 1
        },
```

```
      "name" : "_id_",
      "ns" : "giftapp.users"
    },
    {
      "v" : 1,
      "key" : {
        "lastName" : 1
      },
      "name" : "lastName_1",
      "ns" : "giftapp.users"
    }
  ]
```

Now we can execute our query ensuring we use the `lastName` index:

```
> db.users.find({ lastName: "Smith" }).hint({ lastName:1 }).pretty()
{
  "_id" : ObjectId("566dd0cb1c09d090fd36ba83"),
  "firstName" : "Mark",
  "lastName" : "Smith",
  "email" : "msmith@xyzzymail.org",
  "created" : ISODate("2015-12-13T20:10:51.336Z")
}
{
  "_id" : ObjectId("566dff161c09d090fd36ba85"),
  "email" : "jiggy@zzxxyy3.com",
  "created" : ISODate("2015-12-13T23:26:42.165Z"),
  "lastName" : "Smith",
  "firstName" : "John"
}
```

Analyzing performance

If you'd like to get into the nitty-gritty of a query, you can use the `explain()` method tacked onto a query.

Take a look at the following commands:

```
> db.users.find({},{email:1,_id:0}).limit(2).explain()
{
  "queryPlanner" : {
    "plannerVersion" : 1,
    "namespace" : "giftapp.users",
    "indexFilterSet" : false,
    "parsedQuery" : {
      "$and" : [ ]
    },
```

```
      "winningPlan" : {
        "stage" : "LIMIT",
        "limitAmount" : 2,
        "inputStage" : {
          "stage" : "PROJECTION",
          "transformBy" : {
            "email" : 1,
            "_id" : 0
          },
          "inputStage" : {
            "stage" : "COLLSCAN",
            "filter" : {
              "$and" : [ ]
            },
            "direction" : "forward"
          }
        }
      },
      "rejectedPlans" : [ ]
    },
    "serverInfo" : {
      "host" : "Mac-695b35ca77e.local",
      "port" : 27017,
      "version" : "3.0.4",
      "gitVersion" : "nogitversion"
    },
    "ok" : 1
}
```

To make sense of the output, consult the MongoDB documentation at `https://docs.mongo db.org/v3.0/reference/explain-results/`.

Summary

MongoDB is a flexible and scalable NoSQL database. It's non-relational, maintaining its records as documents in collections as opposed to rows in tables. MongoDB is schemaless; its collections are flexible and do not enforce a particular data structure.

MongoDB documents are stored as binary encoded JSON, or BSON. The object-oriented nature of its documents makes MongoDB well suited for use with object-oriented languages such as JavaScript.

As with all databases, MongoDB offers CRUD operations. Operations on MongoDB are carried out using JavaScript-like syntax.

Optimizing MongoDB performance as a developer involves reducing the amount of data returned by queries and using indexes well.

In the next chapter, you will begin handling web requests for your SPA using the Express web application framework.

9
Handling Web Requests with Express

Express is a powerful, unopinionated web application framework built on top of Node.js. It provides a highly pluggable interface and a few basic objects to handle the HTTP request response life cycle.

We have already begun working with Express, beginning our SPA with the Express generator. It's time to build things out further and learn more about the power of Express.

Express's true power comes from its minimal and unopinionated nature. It's highly flexible and extensible, making it a good tool for a number of web applications, single page, hybrid, even socket-based.

This chapter covers Express in more detail, starting with built-in objects. We will build out a number of routes, organizing the code of our application into logical modules. We will learn about the request and response objects in Express in detail, and develop our own middleware functionality to handle AJAX requests.

We will conclude by stubbing out a RESTful API for our SPA, configuring it to respond using different data formats.

This chapter covers the following topics:

- Configuring Express
- Express request and response objects
- Passing variables in GET and POST request
- Developing Express middleware
- Building RESTful services
- Organizing routes into logical modules

Examining Express in detail

Express represents a very thin layer on top of Node's HTTP server, but it has a few built-in objects that are important to become familiar with. These include the App, Request, Response, and Router objects. These objects, and a couple of plugins, provide all of the core functionality of the Express framework.

App object

In Express, the app object typically refers to the Express application. This is by convention and is the result of calling the express() function. Open up your app.js file and see the line that reads varapp=express(). This is where we create our application and assign it to the variable app. We could have used any variable name, but the convention is to use app. We'll stick to convention and refer to this object as app.

Let's take a closer look at our app.js file and look at how we're already using the app object:

```
var express = require('express');
var path = require('path');
var favicon = require('serve-favicon');
var logger = require('morgan');
var cookieParser = require('cookie-parser');
var bodyParser = require('body-parser');

//Database stuff
var mongodb = require('mongodb');
var monk = require('monk');
var db = monk('localhost:27017/giftapp')

var routes = require('./routes/index');
```

```
var users = require('./routes/users');

var app = express();

// view engine setup
app.set('views', path.join(__dirname, 'views'));
app.set('view engine', 'ejs');

// uncomment after placing your favicon in /public
//app.use(favicon(path.join(__dirname, 'public', 'favicon.ico')));
app.use(logger('dev'));
app.use(bodyParser.json());
app.use(bodyParser.urlencoded({ extended: false }));
app.use(cookieParser());
app.use(express.static(path.join(__dirname, 'public')));

//Database middlewear
app.use(function(req,res,next){
    req.db = db;
    next();
});

app.use('/', routes);
app.use('/users', users);

// catch 404 and forward to error handler
app.use(function(req, res, next) {
  var err = new Error('Not Found');
  err.status = 404;
  next(err);
});

// error handlers

// development error handler
// will print stacktrace
if (app.get('env') === 'development') {
  app.use(function(err, req, res, next) {
    res.status(err.status || 500);
    res.render('error', {
      message: err.message,
      error: err
    });
  });
}

// production error handler
// no stacktraces leaked to user
```

```
app.use(function(err, req, res, next) {
  res.status(err.status || 500);
  res.render('error', {
    message: err.message,
    error: {}
  });
});

module.exports = app;
```

The `app` API includes an important property, event, and a number of methods. To see a full list of functionality in the Express application API, you can view the documentation at `http://expressjs.com/en/api.html`, but we'll cover some of the most important features here.

app.locals

`app.locals` is a JavaScript object that persists within the application itself. Any properties or functions added to the object will be available throughout the `app`. This is useful for creating helper functions or app level values.

The `app.locals` objects are available in middleware through the request object through `req.app.locals`.

Add the following line in your `app.js` file after the calls to `app.set();`:`app.locals.appName="MyGiftApp";`

Now open up your `routes/users.js` file and modify it like so:

```
var express = require('express');
var router = express.Router();

/* GET users listing. */
router.get('/', function(req, res, next) {
  res.send('respond with a resource');
});

router.get('/show', function(req, res, next) {
    var db = req.db;
    var collection = db.get('users');
    collection.find({}, {}, function(err,docs){
        if(!err){
            //res.json(docs);
            res.render('users/show',
  {

            users: docs,
```

```
                    appName: req.app.locals.appName
            }
    );
        }else{
            res.send('error');
        }
    });
});
module.exports = router;
```

Inside the route for show, we added a bit of data to the second argument to res.render(). We mapped req.app.locals.appname to the property appName. This makes it available to our template.

Now open your views/users/show.ejs template file and modify it:

```
<!DOCTYPE html>
<html>
<head>
    <title>Show Users</title>
    <link rel='stylesheet' href='/stylesheets/style.css' />
</head>
<body>
<h1>User List: <%= appName %></h1>

<table>
    <thead>
        <tr>

            <th>First Name</th>
            <th>Last Name</th>
            <th>Email Address</th>
        </tr>
    </thead>
    <tbody>
    <% users.forEach(function(user, index){ -%>
        <tr>
            <td><%= user.firstName %></td>
            <td><%= user.lastName %></td>
            <td><%= user.email %></td>
        </tr>
    <% }); %>
    </tbody>
</table>
</body>
</html>
```

We've added an output tag for the `appName` property.

Now, make sure that the Mongo daemon is running and start or restart your application. In your browser, navigate to: `localhost:3000/users/show` and you should see something like the following:

User List: My Gift App

First Name	Last Name	Email Address
Mark	Smith	msmith@xyzzymail.org
Sally	Jones	sjones@xyzzymail.org
John	Smith	jiggy@zzxxyy3.com
Jane	Smothers	jsmothers@xxaayy4.com

We've successfully added an application level local property and displayed it in one of our templates.

app.set()

After we create the application by calling the express function, we see a couple of calls to `app.set()` setting the path to the views directory and the view engine. The set function takes two arguments. The first argument is a string containing the name of one of the application settings for Express. Some application settings include the following:

- `casesensitiverouting`: A Boolean, disabled by default. When enabled, it ignores the case of routes. `/route` and `/Route` would be treated as the same route.
- `env`: A string setting for the environment mode. The default is `development` or whatever the `NODE_ENV` environment variable is set to.
- `etag`: A setting for the `ETag` response header. It has a sensible default, but if you want to change it, I suggest referring to the documentation.
- `jsonpcallbackname`: A string, specifying a default callback function for JSONP responses.
- `jsonspaces`: Numeric, when specified, it sends JSON responses back prettified and indented by the specified number of spaces.
- `queryparser`: By default, this is set to `extended`, but you can use it to disable query parsing or to set a simpler or customized query parsing function.
- `strictrouting`: A Boolean, disabled by default treating `/route` the same as `/route/`.

- `views`: A string or array telling Express where to look up display templates. If the value is an array, Express will look them up in the order they occur in the array.
- `viewcache`: A Boolean, true in production, this tells Express to cache the view templates. This is usually undesired in development.
- `viewengine`: A string – the default engine extension (such as `ejs`).
- `x-powered-by`: A Boolean, true by default, sends a `X-Powered-By:Express` HTTP header. I think it's normally a good idea to shut this off, giving less information to potential hackers. Go ahead and add `app.set('x-powered-by',false);` to your `app.js` file after the line setting the view engine.

app.enable()

Any of the `app` settings that take Booleans can be turned on with `app.enable();` for example, to enable view caching, you can use `app.enable('viewcache');`.

app.disable()

If you have an enable function, you should have a disable function as well, right? `app.disable()` sets any `app` settings that are Boolean to false, turning them off.

app.listen()

Under the covers, the app object returned by the call to `express()` is a JavaScript function. Remember that functions in JavaScript are objects and can be passed around like any other objects. When we call `app.listen()`, it essentially invokes Node's native `http.createServer()` function passing itself, the `app` function, as a callback.

If we want to use HTTPS, it's a little different, and we'll cover that in a later chapter.

For our purposes, we would use `app.listen()` passing the port we wish to listen to as the argument. However, the Express generator has set up our code for us in `bin/www`, as shown in the following code:

```
/**
 * Module dependencies.
 */

var app = require('../app');
var debug = require('debug')('giftapp:server');
```

```
var http = require('http');

/**
 * Get port from environment and store in Express.
 */

var port = normalizePort(process.env.PORT || '3000');
app.set('port', port);

/**
 * Create HTTP server.
 */

var server = http.createServer(app);

/**
 * Listen on provided port, on all network interfaces.
 */

server.listen(port);
server.on('error', onError);
server.on('listening', onListening);
```

Instead of simply calling `app.listen()`, the Express generator has set up this method, which is essentially doing the same thing, but adding some event listeners to the server object for error handling, and more.

app.METHOD()

`app.METHOD()` routes requests that come into the server using an actual method. There isn't a `METHOD` function, the actual functions are the lowercase of specific HTTP request methods. In other words, you would use `app.get()` or `app.post()` methods.

There can be small point of confusion here because `app.get('somevalue')` can also be used to return an `app` setting.

In general, we are going to hand off requests to the Express router and handle routing in a more modular manner.

app.all()

`app.all()` is similar to `app.METHOD()`, but it matches all HTTP request methods. It's often used to easily add global functionality via middleware to a path or part of an application.

For example, if you want to add authentication to a part of your `app` without the bother of adding it to each individual route or method, you might do something like this:

```
app.all('/protected/', authenticationRequired);
```

This would pass all requests, regardless of method, which began with the path `/protected/` through the `authenticationRequired` middleware.

Request object

The request object in Express holds data related to the HTTP request. By default, it will contain properties for things such as the query string, parameters, headers, post parameters, and more. It is the first argument in callback functions provided by middleware, like routing, and, by convention, is usually called `req`:

```
router.get('/show', function(req, res, next) {
    var db = req.db;
    var collection = db.get('users');
    collection.find({}, {}, function(err,docs){
        if(!err){
            //res.json(docs);
            res.render('users/show', {
                users: docs,
                appName: req.app.locals.appName
            });
        }else{
            res.send('error');
        }
    });
});
```

In our routes/`users` file, here is our one route for a get request for the URI /`show`. You can see that the first argument to the callback function is `req`. This is the request object. We get a reference to the database from the request object, as well as a reference to the `app.locals.appName` property.

req.params

The params property of the request object gives us access to parameters passed to the server through the URL.

Let's modify our routes/users file to add a new route:

```
var express = require('express');
var router = express.Router();

/* GET users listing. */
router.get('/', function(req, res, next) {
  res.send('respond with a resource');
});

router.get ('/show/:id', function(req, res, next)
 {
    var db = req.db;
    var collection = db.get('users');
    collection.findOne({ "_id": req.params.id },{}, function(err,User)
{
if(!err)
{
            res.render('users/user',
 {
                user: User,
                appName: req.app.locals.appName
            }
);
        }
else
{
            res.send('error');
        }
    });
});

router.get('/show', function(req, res, next) {
    var db = req.db;
    var collection = db.get('users');
    collection.find({}, {}, function(err,docs){
        if(!err){
            //res.json(docs);
            res.render('users/show', {
                users: docs,
                appName: req.app.locals.appName
            });
        }else{
```

```
                res.send('error');
            }
        });
    });

    module.exports = router;
```

We've added a new route that matches /show/:id. The :id portion will match a variable part of the URL; in this case we are expecting an ID, and place that on the req.params object as a property named id.

We issue a findOne query to our database on the users collection. findOne returns a single object (the first match), where find returns an array with all matches. In this case, we are only interested in a single match; we are looking for a user with a specific _id.

Then we render the users/user template passing our values. We don't have a user template yet, so let's create user.ejs in our views/users directory:

```
<!DOCTYPE html>
<html>
<head>
    <title><%= appName %>: <%= user.firstName %> <%= user.lastName
%></title>
    <link rel='stylesheet' href='/stylesheets/style.css' />
</head>
<body>
<h1><%= user.firstName %> <%= user.lastName %></h1>
<ul>
    <li>Email: <%= user.email %></li>
    <li>Id: <%= user._id %></li>
</ul>

<p><a href="/users/show">&lt; Back</a></p>


</body>
</html>
```

The object passed into the template containing our user data is called user. Here, we can access all its properties, firstName, lastName, email, and _id. To make life a little easier, we've added a link to go back to the show route.

Let's modify `show.ejs` a little to add navigation:

```html
<!DOCTYPE html>
<html>
<head>
    <title>Show Users</title>
    <link rel='stylesheet' href='/stylesheets/style.css' />
</head>
<body>
<h1>User List: <%= appName %></h1>

<table>
    <thead>
        <tr>

            <th>First Name</th>
            <th>Last Name</th>
            <th>Email Address</th>
        </tr>
    </thead>
    <tbody>
    <% users.forEach(function(user, index){ -%>
        <tr>
            <td><a href="""show/<%= user._id%>"""><%= user.firstName
%></a></td>
            <td><%= user.lastName %></td>
            <td><%= user.email %></td>
        </tr>
    <% }); %>
    </tbody>
</table>


</body>
</html>
```

We've added a link to `show/<%=user._id%>`, which will create the URL we need to navigate to the individual user's show route.

Start or restart your server. A restart is required any time you change a route or the main application, but not for simple template changes.

Navigate to `localhost:3000/users/show` and click on one of your user's first names. You should see something like this:

Sally Jones

- Email: sjones@xyzzymail.org
- Id: 566dd0cb1c09d090fd36ba84

≤ Back

Of course, because Mongo generates the `_id` field, yours will not match mine. Well, they might, but it would be an astronomical coincidence.

req.body

The `body` property on the request object contains name value pairs typically sent as part of a post request. In order to get access to this, you need to add `body` parsing middleware to your `app`.

The Express generator has already set this up for us by requiring a `body` parser and then adding the middleware in these two lines:

```
app.use(bodyParser.json());
app.use(bodyParser.urlencoded({ extended: false }));
```

These two lines allow us to parse data sent back as `application/json or application/x-www-form-urlencoded`.

In our routes, we would have access to parameters passed in through `req.body`. We'll be doing a lot of that when we start to build resourceful routes later. Here's an example (there's no need to add it to our code):

```
router.post('/user', function(req, res, next) {
    var db = req.db;
    var collection = db.get('users');
    collection.insert({ firstName: req.body.firstName,
                        lastName: req.body.lastName,
                        email: req.body.email},
                        function(err){
        if(!err){
            res.redirect('/users/show');
        }else{
            res.send('error');
        }
    });
```

```
});
```

Here, we accept a post to `users/user`. We use `monk` to do an insert (adding a record to our MongoDB database). The first argument to the insert function is an object, and we are using the `firstName`, `lastName`, and `email` fields from `req.body` to populate the same properties of the document to be inserted. Assuming there's no error, we redirect to `users/show`, which displays a list of users including our new user.

req.query

Another way we can get data from a request is using the query string appended to a URL. If you are unfamiliar with this, the query string is data that is appended as name value pairs after a question mark on the URL.

For example, in `http:www.mymadeupdomain.org/foo?name=john+smith&q=foo`, the query string part is the `name=john+smith&q=foo`. To access this inside our `app`, we would use `req.query.name` and `req.query.q`. This would give us back `johnsmith` and `foo` respectively with no plus sign between `john` and `smith`. The plus sign is part of URL encoding that happens because spaces don't translate in URLs.

If there is no query string, `req.query` will contain an empty object.

When should I use a query string instead of parameters?
There's no best answer for this. In general, you want to use route parameters when you want multiple routes to handle different types of operations. We're going to take this approach most of the time. Query strings are good if you want a single `GET` request route that's going to be flexible with the type of data it receives, and you want users to be able to bookmark it. Google uses query strings for searches: `https://www.google.com/search?q=things`.

req.cookies

`req.cookies` requires the use of the cookie parser middleware, conveniently already installed for us by the Express generator, and gives us access to the cookies in the request. If there are no cookies, the value of `req.cookies` will be an empty object.

Cookies are accessed by name: `req.cookies.userID` would give us a cookie named `userID`.

We will delve into cookies in more detail later, but the cookie parser is required for things such as authentication and security. It's best to leave it in place whether you are going to use cookies directly or not.

req.xhr

This is a simple Boolean value that is true if the X-Requested-With request header is XMLHttpRequest. Most commonly, this happens with AJAX requests issued by libraries such as jQuery.

This is useful for SPAs because we may want to respond with an HTML page when the request comes from a change in location from the browser, but with data when subsequent requests come from client-side code issuing requests through AJAX.

Let's look at our /show/:id route from /routes/users.js:

```
router.get('/show/:id', function(req, res, next) {
    var db = req.db;
    var collection = db.get('users');
    collection.findOne({ ""_id"": req.params.id }, {}, function(err,User){
        if(!err){
            if(req.xhr){
                User.appName = req.app.locals.appName;
                res.json(User);
            } else {
                res.render('users/user',
    {
                    user: User,
                    appName: req.app.locals.appName
                });
            }
        }else{
            res.send('error');
        }
    });
});
```

So we check to see if the request has come in through XMLHTTPRequest, AJAX. If it has, we add the appName to the User object and then return it as JSON. If it didn't, we render and return the page as normal.

This is quite handy, and we'll use this mechanism later.

req.accepts()

`req.accepts` is a function which checks a request's `Accept` header and returns `true` if there's a match. It can accept a string or array or extensions or MIME types, and returns either the best match or `false` (`undefined`, which is a falsy value in JavaScript), if there's nothing matching.

For example, let's say the browser sends back the header: `Accept:text/*`. `application/json`: `req.accepts('html')` would match the `text/*` part and return `html`. `req.accepts(['image/png','application/json'])` would return `json`.

As with `req.xhr`, this can be very useful for responding flexibly to different types of requests on the same route.

req.get()

`req.get()` is a function that returns the value of an HTTP header sent in the request. The function takes a string which does case-insensitive matching. An alias of this function is `req.header()`.

For example, `req.get('content-type')` returns the content type header from the HTTP request as a string, such as `application/json` or `text/html`.

Response object

The Express response object is a JavaScript object that represents the response that we are going to send back from the server to the client. We see it paired with the request object and, like using `req` for request, the convention is to use `res`.

res.app

The `res.app` object is identical to the `req.app` property. It's a reference to the application, but attached to the response object in this case. This offers some flexibility in accessing the app properties.

res.cookie()

This is a response object method that allows us to set a cookie and send it back with the response. It takes a name, value, and an optional object containing parameters.

Here's an example:

```
res.cookie('userName', 'Joe', { maxage: 900000, secure: true, signed:true
});
```

This sets a userName cookie with a value of Joe. The cookie expires 900,000 seconds from the response. The cookie is to be used with HTTPS only, and it is to be signed. Other options that can be set are the domain and path for the cookie, and an actual expiration date.

This method clears the named cookie:

```
res.clearCookie()
```

This would clear the cookie we set previously:

```
res.clearCooke('userName');
```

res.download()

res.download transfers a file at a given path as an attachment. It takes the path, an optional filename, and an option callback function once the file transfer completes:

```
res.download('/reports/TPS-coversheet.pdf', 'coversheet.pdf, function(err){
  if(err){
    //handle error here
  } else {
    //do something appropriate
  }
});
```

We initiate a download of the file at /reports/TPS-coversheet, but transfer it as coversheet.pdf. Once complete, we check if there was an error, doing something appropriate in any case.

res.json()

This method sends a JSON response, it's that straightforward. It can take any JavaScript object. The nice thing about using a MongoDB database is that often we can just pass out raw database responses using `res.json()`:

```
res.json({dog: 'Fido', breed: 'Sheltie' commands: {sit: true, stay:
false});
```

Here, we respond with JSON passing an object with properties for our `Sheltie` named `Fido` and the commands that she knows.

res.jsonp()

This method returns JSON data wrapped in a callback function, otherwise known as JSONP. By default the function will be called callback. But this can be overridden using `app.set('jsonpcallbackname', 'someFunction');`. In this case, we get the following:

```
res.jsonp({dog: 'Fido');
//returns someFunction({""dog"": ""Fido""})
```

Of course, the appropriate client-side code would have to be in place to handle the response.

res.redirect()

We've already used this one. This sends a redirect back to the requester with an appropriate HTTP status code. If no status code is specified, a `302` is used.

Here's something we looked at earlier:

```
router.post('/user', function(req, res, next) {
    var db = req.db;
    var collection = db.get('users');
    collection.insert({ firstName: req.body.firstName,
                        lastName: req.body.lastName,
                        email: req.body.email},
                        function(err){
        if(!err){
            res.redirect('/users/show');
        }else{
            res.send('error');
        }
    });
```

```
});
```

After an insert operation, adding a new document to our database, we send a redirect back to the browser to go to `/users/show`. Because no status was specified, a `302` will be returned.

The path is quite flexible and can be anything from a fully formed URL: `res.redirect('https://www.google.com/search?q=food');` to a relative path: `res.redirect('../dashboard/show');`.

```
res.redirect(301, 'http://www.whitehouse.gov');
```

This sends a permanently moved redirect to `whitehouse.gov`, consequently confusing Google and ruining your SEO. For more information about various redirect codes, check out the official HTTP specification, paying attention to the `3xx` status codes: `http://www.w3.org/Protocols/rfc2616/rfc2616-sec10.html`.

res.render()

This is another method we've already used, which sends back rendered HTML which has been compiled from a `view` template. The arguments to the method are the template view, an optional object containing local variables, and an optional callback function.

Let's take a peek at our `/show` route inside our `routes/users.js` file:

```
router.get('/show', function(req, res, next) {
    var db = req.db;
    var collection = db.get('users');
    collection.find({}, {}, function(err,docs){
        if(!err){
            //res.json(docs);
            res.render('users/show',
  {

            users: docs,
            appName: req.app.locals.appName
            }
);
        }else{
            res.send('error');
        }
    });
});
```

As we've seen, this call to `res.render()` renders the template at `/views/users/show`. It makes the local object with users and `appName` available to the template.

If we you add a callback method to the render method, you need to call `res.send()` explicitly:

```
res.render('users/show', {
    users: docs,
    appName: req.app.locals.appName
}, function(err, html){
    if(!err){
    res.cookie('rendered':""someValue"")
        res.send(html);
    } else {
        res.send(""There's been a horrible error."");
    }
});
```

Here, we've added a callback function which has two arguments, an error, if any, and the rendered `html`. This allows us to add an error handler, set a cookie on the response object, and then send the response.

res.send()

We've seen that `res.send()` is a method that is used to send the HTTP response. `res.send()` is pretty flexible and can give a number of different types of arguments, including a `Buffer`, an object, array, or a string.

`res.send()` will adjust the HTTP `Content-Type` header appropriately for the argument. When the argument is a string the `Content-Type` will be `text/html`, when an object or array it will be `application/json`, and when it's a `Buffer` object it will be set to `application/octet-stream`. These defaults can be overridden by calling `res.set()` with a different `Content-Type`.

We can also chain a call to `status()` to pass an HTTP status:

```
router.get('/show', function(req, res, next) {
    var db = req.db;
    var collection = db.get('users');
    collection.find({}, {}, function(err,docs){
        if(!err){
            //res.json(docs);
            res.render('users/show', {
                users: docs,
```

```
                appName: req.app.locals.appName
        });
    }else{
        res.status(500).send(""There has been a major error"");
    }
    });
});
```

By chaining the status with a 500 HTTP status, we can send a message that there's been an internal server error along with our message.

Router object

The router object is described in the Express documentation as a mini-application that only provides middleware and routing functionality. The router acts as middleware so it can be used as an argument in app.use() or in another router's use() method, making nesting and organizing routes easy.

We create a router object by calling the express.Router() function:

```
var router = express.Router();
```

In our router files, we always export the router using module.exports=router. This allows us to load the router as a module through require() and then use it like any other middleware.

Let's review our app.js file again:

```
var express = require('express');
var path = require('path');
var favicon = require('serve-favicon');
var logger = require('morgan');
var cookieParser = require('cookie-parser');
var bodyParser = require('body-parser');

//Database stuff
var mongodb = require('mongodb');
var monk = require('monk');
var db = monk('localhost:27017/giftapp')

var routes = require('./routes/index');var users =
require('./routes/users');

var app = express();
```

```
// view engine setup
app.set('views', path.join(__dirname, 'views'));
app.set('view engine', 'ejs');

app.set('x-powered-by', false);

app.locals.appName = "My Gift App";

// uncomment after placing your favicon in /public
//app.use(favicon(path.join(__dirname, 'public', 'favicon.ico')));
app.use(logger('dev'));
app.use(bodyParser.json());
app.use(bodyParser.urlencoded({ extended: false }));
app.use(cookieParser());
app.use(express.static(path.join(__dirname, 'public')));

//Database middlewear
app.use(function(req,res,next){
    req.db = db;
    next();
});

app.use('/', routes);app.use('/users', users);

// catch 404 and forward to error handler
app.use(function(req, res, next) {
  var err = new Error('Not Found');
  err.status = 404;
  next(err);
});

// error handlers

// development error handler
// will print stacktrace
if (app.get('env') === 'development') {
  app.use(function(err, req, res, next) {
    res.status(err.status || 500);
    res.render('error', {
      message: err.message,
      error: err
    });
  });
}

// production error handler
// no stacktraces leaked to user
app.use(function(err, req, res, next) {
```

```
    res.status(err.status || 500);
    res.render('error', {
      message: err.message,
      error: {}
    });
  });

  module.exports = app
```

We require the index route, assigning it to the variable routes, and then we require the users route, assigning it to the variable users. Then we add the routes to the app using the app.use function, matching the root path and the /users path.

Note that Express will try to match routes in order. Since every route will match the root path, it will look there first, and if it finds no match to anything starting with /users, Express will then match to the next route. Inside our /users route, we know we have a route for show, so /users/show will be matched there.

router.METHOD()

This works the same exact way as app.METHOD(). We add lowercase HTTP verbs as functions, passing in a route to match and a callback function. We've seen this pattern already:

```
router.get('/something', function(req, res, next) {
    res.send(""something loaded"");
});
```

One thing to note here is that res.send(), res.render(), and res.end() will all terminate the response. This means that whatever is in next() will not be called. Think of it as returning out of a JavaScript function. There's no more you can do after that. However, you can call multiple routes in succession by not terminating:

```
router.get('/something', function(req, res, next) {
    res.locals.foo = ""bar"";
    next()
});

router.get('/something', function(req, res, next) {
    res.send(res.locals.foo);
    //send s 'bar'
});
```

Both routes match /something, so the first one would get called, and it adds foo to the locals property on the response object. Then it makes a call to next which calls the next matching route, sending the value of res.locals, foo.

router.all()

router.all() works like router.METHOD() except that it matches all HTTP verbs, get, post, and so on. It's incredibly useful for adding global functionality to a series of routes. For example, let's say that you have an api route and want to make sure that every call to any route in api is authenticated:

```
router.all('/api/*', someAuthenticationMiddleware);
```

Placing this at the top of your routes file would make all calls to any URL starting with /api/ to go through the someAuthenticationMiddleware middleware.

router.param()

router.param() is a powerful way to add callback functionality based on route parameters. Let's say, for example, that in our users route file, every time we get an id parameter.

Let's dive back into our routes/users.js file:

```
var express = require('express');
var router = express.Router();

/* GET users listing. */
router.get('/', function(req, res, next) {
  res.send('respond with a resource');
});

router.param('id', function(req, res, next, id)
  {
     var db = req.db;
     var collection = db.get('users');
     collection.findOne({ ""_id"": id }, {}, function(err,User)
{
        if(err)
{
           res.send(err);
        }else if(User){
           req.user = User;
           next();
```

```
            }
    else
    {
                res.send(new Error('User not found.')
    );
            }
        });
    });
    router.get('/show/:id', function(req, res, next)
    {
            if(req.xhr)
    {
                User.appName = req.app.locals.appName;
                res.json(req.user);
            }
    else
    {
                res.render('users/user',
    {
                    user: req.user,
                    appName: req.app.locals.appName
                });
            }}));

    router.get('/show', function(req, res, next) {
        var db = req.db;
        var collection = db.get('users');
        collection.find({}, {}, function(err,docs){
            if(!err){
                //res.json(docs);
                res.render('users/show', {
                    users: docs,
                    appName: req.app.locals.appName
                });
            }else{
                res.send('error');
            }
        });
    });

    module.exports = router;
```

We use `router.param()` to look for calls to any route that has an `id` parameter. The callback function does a database lookup on user. If there's an error, we terminate by sending the error. The user, if one is found, is added to the request object. We then call `next()` to pass the request to the matching route.

Writing our own middleware

As we've seen, Express is designed to rely heavily on pluggable middleware for adding functionality to our application. Let's roll our own piece of middleware that will give us an easy way to switch our responses to JSON format anywhere in our app.

Add a `utils` directory to your `giftapp` project folder and create a file called `json.js` inside that folder:

```
var isJSON = function(req, res, next){
    if(req.xhr || req.headers['accepts'] == 'application/json'){
        req.isJSON = true;
    }
    next();
}

module.exports = isJSON;
```

The `isJSON` function we create takes the three arguments that all Express middleware accepts – the request object, the response object, and the reference to next. We check to see if the request object's `xhr` value is `true` or if the accepts header on the request is `application/json`. If either condition is true, we can assume that the client is requesting JSON rather than HTML.

We add an `isJSON` property to the request object, setting it to `true`.

Now, let's modify our `app.js` file to include this middleware anywhere in the application where we need it:

```
var express = require('express');
var path = require('path');
var favicon = require('serve-favicon');
var logger = require('morgan');
var cookieParser = require('cookie-parser');
var bodyParser = require('body-parser');
var isJSON = require('./utils/json');

//Database stuff
var mongodb = require('mongodb');
var monk = require('monk');
var db = monk('localhost:27017/giftapp')

var routes = require('./routes/index');
var users = require('./routes/users');

var app = express();
```

```
// view engine setup
app.set('views', path.join(__dirname, 'views'));
app.set('view engine', 'ejs');

app.set('x-powered-by', false);

app.locals.appName = ""My Gift App"";

// uncomment after placing your favicon in /public
//app.use(favicon(path.join(__dirname, 'public', 'favicon.ico')));
app.use(logger('dev'));
app.use(bodyParser.json());
app.use(bodyParser.urlencoded({ extended: false }));
app.use(cookieParser());
app.use(express.static(path.join(__dirname, 'public')));
app.use(isJSON);

//Database middlewear
app.use(function(req,res,next){
    req.db = db;
    next();
});

app.use('/', routes);
app.use('/users', users);

// catch 404 and forward to error handler
app.use(function(req, res, next) {
  var err = new Error('Not Found');
  err.status = 404;
  next(err);
});

// error handlers

// development error handler
// will print stacktrace
if (app.get('env') === 'development') {
  app.use(function(err, req, res, next) {
    res.status(err.status || 500);
    res.render('error', {
      message: err.message,
      error: err
    });
  });
}

// production error handler
```

```
// no stacktraces leaked to user
app.use(function(err, req, res, next) {
  res.status(err.status || 500);
  res.render('error', {
    message: err.message,
    error: {}
  });
});

module.exports = app;
```

First, we require in our module, assigning it to the variable isJSON. Note that we need to use an explicit path here. If we simply used a module name, Node will try to look for it in the node_modules directory.

Then we add our middleware to the application using app.use(isJSON). Where we place this in the file is important as middleware is called sequentially. In our case, this can be anywhere as long as it appears before the routes that use it:

```
Next, we'll modify our routes/users.js file to use the middleware:var
express = require('express');
var router = express.Router();

/* GET users listing. */
router.get('/', function(req, res, next) {
  res.send('respond with a resource');
});

router.param('id', function(req, res, next, id) {
    var db = req.db;
    var collection = db.get('users');
    collection.findOne({ ""_id"": id }, {}, function(err,User){
        if(err){
            res.send(err);
        }else if(User){
            req.user = User;
            next();
        } else {
            res.send(new Error('User not found.'));
        }
    });
});

router.get('/show/:id', function(req, res, next) {
        if(req.isJSON){              User.appName = req.app.locals.appName;
res.json(req.user);         } else {              res.render('users/user', {
user: req.user,                      appName: req.app.locals.appName
```

```
    });          }
});

router.get('/show', function(req, res, next) {
    var db = req.db;
    var collection = db.get('users');
    collection.find({}, {}, function(err,docs){
        if(!err){
            if(req.isJSON)
{
                res.send(docs);
            }
  else
  {
                res.render('users/show',
  {
                    users: docs,
                    appName: req.app.locals.appName
                });
            }
        }else{
            res.send('error');
        }
    });
});

module.exports = router;
```

We modify our two routes to conditionally send JSON or HTML depending on our new
isJSON flag. Restarting your server and then browsing to either route should show no
difference, since you're not actually requesting JSON.

If you'd like to test this, you can use a browser plugin such as Postman or a terminal
request such as curl to issue an xhr request and see the data come back as JSON.

Developing a RESTful API

Let's do a little more work setting up our SPA by building out some resourceful routing as
part of a RESTFul API that we can connect later to our database and our client-side code.
We're lucky that Express has such a vibrant community of developers building many add-
ons, and we're going to use one for resourceful routing.

Installing resourceful routing

The first thing we need to do is to install our module, which will provide us with some resourceful routing:

```
npm install resource-routing –save
```

This installs the resourceful routing plugin we're going to use, and saves a reference to the `package.json` file.

Next, we need to do some setup in our `app.js` file:

```
var express = require('express');
var path = require('path');
var favicon = require('serve-favicon');
var logger = require('morgan');
var cookieParser = require('cookie-parser');
var bodyParser = require('body-parser');
var isJSON = require('./utils/json');
var routing = require('resource-routing');var controllers =
path.resolve('./controllers');

//Database stuff
var mongodb = require('mongodb');
var monk = require('monk');
var db = monk('localhost:27017/giftapp')

var routes = require('./routes/index');
var users = require('./routes/users');

var app = express();
routing.expose_routing_table(app, { at: ""/my-routes"" });

// view engine setup
app.set('views', path.join(__dirname, 'views'));
app.set('view engine', 'ejs');

app.set('x-powered-by', false);

app.locals.appName = ""My Gift App"";

// uncomment after placing your favicon in /public
//app.use(favicon(path.join(__dirname, 'public', 'favicon.ico')));
app.use(logger('dev'));
app.use(bodyParser.json());
app.use(bodyParser.urlencoded({ extended: false }));
app.use(cookieParser());
```

```
app.use(express.static(path.join(__dirname, 'public')));
app.use(isJSON);

//Database middlewear
app.use(function(req,res,next){
    req.db = db;
    next();
});

app.use('/', routes);
app.use('/users', users);

routing.resources(app, controllers, ""giftlist"");

// catch 404 and forward to error handler
app.use(function(req, res, next) {
  var err = new Error('Not Found');
  err.status = 404;
  next(err);
});

// error handlers

// development error handler
// will print stacktrace
if (app.get('env') === 'development') {
  app.use(function(err, req, res, next) {
    res.status(err.status || 500);
    res.render('error', {
      message: err.message,
      error: err
    });
  });
}

// production error handler
// no stacktraces leaked to user
app.use(function(err, req, res, next) {
  res.status(err.status || 500);
  res.render('error', {
    message: err.message,
    error: {}
  });
});

module.exports = app;
```

We pull in the resource routing module using `require()` and assign it to the variable `routing`. Then we create a shortcut variable to a controllers directory, which we will be building next.

We add the following code, `routing.expose_routing_table(app,{at:""/my-routes""});` which allows us to view our routing table at the URL `my-routes`. Obviously, this is not something we'd leave intact in production, but it's a useful debugging tool.

Finally, we set up our resourceful routing for `giftlists` with `routing.resources(app,controllers,""giftlist"");`. This won't do anything yet because we haven't set up our controller.

Building out giftlist controller

By default, our resourceful router will build a number of standard restful routes for us, including:

```
GET      /giftlist                giftlist_controller.index
GET      /giftlist.format          giftlist_controller.index
GET      /giftlist/new             giftlist_controller.new
GET      /giftlist/new.format      giftlist_controller.new
POST     /giftlist                giftlist_controller.create
POST     /giftlist:format          giftlist_controller.create
GET      /giftlist/:id             giftlist_controller.show
GET      /giftlist/:id.format      giftlist_controller.show
GET      /giftlist/:id/edit        giftlist_controller.edit
GET      /giftlist/:id/edit.format giftlist_controller.edit
PUT      /giftlist/:id             giftlist_controler.update
PUT      /giftlist/:id.format      giftlist_controller.update
DELETE   /giftlist/:id             giftlist_controller.destroy
DELETE   /giftlist/:id.format      giftlist_controller.destroy
```

As you can see, these routes provide use with basic CRUD (create, read, update, delete) functionality.

However, these routes will only be created if the controller and routes actually exist, so we need to build them. Create a controllers directory in your `giftapp` folder with a file called `giftlist_controller.js`. Our plugin will add the `_controller` part when it goes to load our controller, so be sure to name it correctly. For now, we are going to stub out our routes to make sure they are working:

```
exports.index = function(req, res){
    res.send('giftlist index');
};
```

```
exports.new = function(req, res){
    res.send('new giftlist');
};

exports.create = function(req, res){
    res.send('create giftlist');
};

exports.show = function(req, res){
    res.send('show giftlist'+ req.params.id);
};

exports.edit = function(req, res){
    res.send('edit giftlist');
};

exports.update = function(req, res){
    res.send('update giftlist');
};

exports.destroy = function(req, res){
    res.send('destroy giftlist');
};
```

As you can see, each of our route handlers is a function that receives the request and response objects.

Restart your server and navigate to `localhost:3000/giftlist/17`, where you should see:

```
show giftlist 17
```

Responding with different data formats

Our resourceful routes can also support different data formats, so let's stub those out as well, and we'll also use our isJSON property in our giftlist_controller.js:

```
exports.index = function(req, res){
    if(req.params.format == ""json"" || req.isJSON){
        res.json({""title"":""giftlist index""})
    }else{
        res.send('<h1>giftlist index</h1>');
    }

};
```

```
exports.new = function(req, res){
    exports.index = function(req, res){
        if(req.params.format == ""json"" || req.isJSON){
            res.json({""title"":""new giftlist""})
        }else{
            res.send('<h1>new giftlist</h1>');
        }

    };

};

exports.create = function(req, res){
    exports.index = function(req, res){
        if(req.params.format == ""json"" || req.isJSON){
            res.json({""title"":""create giftlist""})
        }else{
            res.send('<h1>create giftlist</h1>');
        }

    };

};

exports.show = function(req, res){
    exports.index = function(req, res){
        if(req.params.format == ""json"" || req.isJSON){
            res.json({ ""title"":""show giftlist"",
""giftlist"":req.params.id })
        }else{
            res.send('<h1>show giftlist' + req.params.id + '</h1>');
        }

    };

};

exports.edit = function(req, res){
    exports.index = function(req, res){
        if(req.params.format == ""json"" || req.isJSON){
            res.json({ ""title"":""edit giftlist"",
""giftlist"":req.params.id })
        }else{
            res.send('<h1>edit giftlist' + req.params.id + '</h1>');
        }

    };
```

```
};

exports.update = function(req, res){
    exports.index = function(req, res){
        if(req.params.format == ""json"" || req.isJSON){
            res.json({ ""title"":""update giftlist"",
""giftlist"":req.params.id })
        }else{
            res.send('<h1>update giftlist' + req.params.id + '</h1>');
        }

    };

};

exports.destroy = function(req, res){
    exports.index = function(req, res){
        if(req.params.format == ""json"" || req.isJSON){
            res.json({ ""title"":""delete giftlist"",
""giftlist"":req.params.id })
        }else{
            res.send('<h1>delete giftlist' + req.params.id + '</h1>');
        }

    };

};
```

Here, we added tests to each of our routes to see if the client is requesting JSON data. If they are, we return JSON. Otherwise, we return HTML.

We check to see if the client is expecting JSON in two ways.

First, we look to see if the `req.params.format` is `json`. Using this resourceful routing middleware, appending a .:format to the URL adds that format to the `req.params` object as the value of the format. In other words, entering the URL `localhost:3000/giftlist.json` triggers the `giftlist_controller.index` route, setting the format parameter to `json`.

The second method is to rely on the `req.isJSON` parameter set by our middleware.

In the next chapter, we will connect these resourceful routes to CRUD operations on our database, and start to render data to a page as we flesh out our SPA.

Summary

In this chapter, we looked at Express, a Node.js web application framework, in greater detail. You learned that Express is an extremely flexible and unopinionated web framework built on top of Node.js HTTP services.

At its core, Express provides access to a request, response, application, and router objects. Using these objects, we can manipulate web requests and respond in a sophisticated manner.

Using Express predominantly means writing or using middleware plugins, through which requests flow. We learned to use these plugins, and we wrote some utility middleware of our own. We examined routing in detail, and used a resourceful routing plugin to start to build a RESTful API for our SPA. We made the API flexible, capable of responding with either JSON or HTML data depending on the request.

The next chapter will cover the frontend. Specifically, you will be learning about view templates, as well as AngularJS.

10
Displaying Views

The heart and soul of most SPAs is a dynamic frontend. SPAs move a lot of the heavy lifting, related to display logic, onto the browser. Modern browsers have fast and powerful JavaScript engines that can handle a lot more computation than just a few years ago. In fact, Node.js is built on top of the VB engine, which is a standard part of the Chrome browser.

Most importantly, however, the main idea of an SPA is to give the user an experience approaching that of a desktop application. Complete page loads are a thing of the past, replaced by snappy changes in state.

In this chapter, we will build out the heart of our own SPA. This will be a dashboard where users can build `giftlists` and share them with other users. We will have to build out a couple more routes and data structures on the backend, but we will focus on the frontend. We will build an Express view that will load AngularJS – a JavaScript toolkit designed specifically for rapid creation of SPAs.

We will build AngularJS routes, views, services, and controllers that will implement the core functionality of the SPA. Using the AngularJS plugin, UI-router, we will manage the state of our application. We will also implement services to communicate to the end so that data can flow freely in our application.

In this chapter we will cover the following topics:

- Developing the initial dashboard view in Express
- Implementing AngularJS
- AngularJS routing
- Using AngularJS `$resource` to access RESTful endpoints

Setting up our dashboard

Since this is a SPA, we need to set up a single page to contain our application. In our case, we are going to build a user dashboard. That dashboard will allow a user to create `giftlists` (such as birthday wish lists), choose who they want to share them with, and see lists that have been shared with them. In the next chapter, we're going to build authentication so that individual users will only be able to see their own dashboards, but for now we need to mock things up without authentication a bit.

We'll need a couple of routes, and a view. We're also going to use `Bootstrap` to style our view a little.

Building the view

We need to create a view for our dashboard. Create a new folder in your views directory called `dash`. Inside that folder, create a file called `dashboard.ejs`:

```
<!DOCTYPE html>
<html>
<head>
    <title>Dashboard for <%= user.firstName %> <%= user.lastName %>
</title>
</head>
<body>
<h1><%= user.firstName %> <%= user.lastName %> Dashboard</h1>
<div>
    <h2>My Lists</h2>
</div>

<div>
    <h2>Lists Shared With Me</h2>
</div>

</body>
</html>
```

So there's nothing too exciting here yet. We have set up some placeholders, and we are assuming that we'll have a `user` object to display. We can't see our view yet – for that we need a `route` which will render the view.

Let's set up the `route` to display our dashboard. In your `routes` directory, create a new file called `dashboard.js`:

```
var express = require('express');
var router = express.Router();


router.get('/', function(req, res, next) {
    res.send('respond with a resource');
});

router.param('id', function(req, res, next, id) {
    var db = req.db;
    var collection = db.get('users');
    collection.findOne({ "_id": id }, {}, function(err,User){
        if(err){
            res.send(err);
        }else if(User){
            req.user = User;
            next();
        } else {
            res.send(new Error('User not found.'));
        }
    });
});

router.get('/:id', function(req, res, next){
    res.render('dash/dashboard', {user: req.user});
});

module.exports = router;
```

We have done a couple of things here. First, we set up our middleware to respond to routes with an id parameter as we did with our users' routes. Next, we set up a route for displaying our dashboard.

Unless you have the ID for a user memorized, it's going to be hard to test our new view. Let's make it a little easier by modifying the view that lists our users. Open up `views/users/show.ejs`:

```
<!DOCTYPE html>
<html>
<head>
    <title>Show Users</title>
    <link rel='stylesheet' href='/stylesheets/style.css' />
</head>
<body>
```

```
<h1>User List: <%= appName %></h1>

<table>
    <thead>
        <tr>

            <th>First Name</th>
            <th>Last Name</th>
            <th>Email Address</th>
            <th>Dashboard</th>
        </tr>
    </thead>
    <tbody>
    <% users.forEach(function(user, index){ -%>
        <tr>
            <td><a href="show/<%= user._id%> "><%= user.firstName
%></a></td>
            <td><%= user.lastName %></td>
            <td><%= user.email %></td>
            <td><a href="/dash/<%= user._id %>">View</a></td>
        </tr>
    <% }); %>
    </tbody>
</table>


</body>
</html>
```

We added a new column in our users table with a link to the dashboard for each user. We still can't display our dashboard yet. We have to make a change to our app.js file:

```
var express = require('express');
var path = require('path');
var favicon = require('serve-favicon');
var logger = require('morgan');
var cookieParser = require('cookie-parser');
var bodyParser = require('body-parser');
var isJSON = require('./utils/json');
var routing = require('resource-routing');
var controllers = path.resolve('./controllers');

//Database stuff
var mongodb = require('mongodb');
var monk = require('monk');
var db = monk('localhost:27017/giftapp')

var routes = require('./routes/index');
```

```
var users = require('./routes/users');
var dashboard = require('./routes/dashboard');

var app = express();

// view engine setup
app.set('views', path.join(__dirname, 'views'));
app.set('view engine', 'ejs');

app.set('x-powered-by', false);

app.locals.appName = "My Gift App";

// uncomment after placing your favicon in /public
//app.use(favicon(path.join(__dirname, 'public', 'favicon.ico')));
app.use(logger('dev'));
app.use(bodyParser.json());
app.use(bodyParser.urlencoded({ extended: false }));
app.use(cookieParser());
app.use(express.static(path.join(__dirname, 'public')));
app.use(isJSON);

//Database middleware
app.use(function(req,res,next){
    req.db = db;
    next();
});

app.use('/', routes);
app.use('/users', users);
app.use('/dash', dashboard);

routing.resources(app, controllers, "giftlist");
routing.expose_routing_table(app, { at: "/my-routes" });

// catch 404 and forward to error handler
app.use(function(req, res, next) {
  var err = new Error('Not Found');
  err.status = 404;
  next(err);
});

// error handlers

// development error handler
// will print stacktrace
if (app.get('env') === 'development') {
  app.use(function(err, req, res, next) {
```

```
        res.status(err.status || 500);
        res.render('error', {
          message: err.message,
          error: err
        });
      });
    }

    // production error handler
    // no stacktraces leaked to user
    app.use(function(err, req, res, next) {
      res.status(err.status || 500);
      res.render('error', {
        message: err.message,
        error: {}
      });
    });
```

```
    module.exports = app;
```

The two key changes here are that we import the dashboard router, we then map any requests to `/dash` to that `router`.

Make sure your MongoDB daemon is still running, and restart it if it isn't. Start or restart your server. Navigate to your list of users at `http://localhost:3000/users/show` and then click on one of the `view` links in the right of the table:

User List: My Gift App

First Name	Last Name	Email Address	Dashboard
Mark	Smith	msmith@xyzzymail.org	View
Sally	Jones	sjones@xyzzymail.org	View
John	Smith	jiggy@zzxxyy3.com	View
Jane	Smothers	jsmothers@xxaayy4.com	View

The URL should look something like this:
`http://localhost:3000/dash/566dd0cb1c09d090fd36ba83`. You should see a page that looks like this:

Mark Smith Dashboard

My Lists

Lists Shared With Me

Now we have a `view` template and routing set up to display the page. The next thing we need to do is to build out some data.

Connecting to initial data

Our application is going to allow users to build `giftlists` and share them with other users. We want to think a little bit about how we want to represent our data. A good data model will serve us, even as we add and change features.

As we have learned, MongoDB is very flexible, and we could just embed documents inside documents. This might work; we could just have each user with an array of lists. The issue with that is that our individual user documents would be highly mutable, and could grow to an enormous size easily. It also doesn't offer a lot of flexibility down the road if we want to do something like having shared lists.

The type of relationship that we want to have for now is a one-to-many relationship. One user can have many lists. The way we'll accomplish this is to store a reference to the user who owns the list on the list itself. Later, if we want to have more than one user *own* a list, the change would be pretty straightforward.

We want to use our `giftapp` database, and we are going to be creating a new collection of `giftlists`. Start up the MongoDB command-line tool in a new terminal window. Note that you'll want to copy the exact `ID` of one of your users since it will differ from mine:

```
>use giftapp
switched to db giftapp
> db.giftlist.insert({'name':'Birthday List', 'gifts':[{'name':'ball'},
 {'name':'pony'},{'name':'gift card'}], 'owner_id':
   566dff161c09d090fd36ba85"})
WriteResult({ "nInserted" : 1 })
> db.giftlist.insert({'name':'Christmas  List', 'gifts':[{'name':'TV'},
   {'name':'Corvette'},{'name':'gift card'}], 'owner_id':
   566dff161c09d090fd36ba85"})
WriteResult({ "nInserted" : 1 })
```

The important part here is the format of the insert statement. Let's break it apart a little bit.

```
db.giftlist.insert({
    'name':'Christmas  List',
    'gifts':[{'name':'TV'},{'name':'Corvette'},{'name':'gift card'}],
    'owner_id': 566dff161c09d090fd36ba85")
    }
})
```

We insert this object into the `giftlist` collection, which will be created if it doesn't already exist. The object has a name property and a `gifts` property. The `gifts` property is an array of objects, each containing a name property.

We also have an `owner_id` property. This property is a reference to the user to whom the `giftlist` belongs. It's just the string of the user's `_id`. Since MongoDB is a non-relational database, we will just stash this in here to do lookups in the `users` collection.

We know we're going to be looking things up by the owner, so let's add an `index`:

```
> db.giftlist.ensureIndex({'owner_id':1})
{
    "createdCollectionAutomatically" : false,
    "numIndexesBefore" : 1,
    "numIndexesAfter" : 2,
    "ok" : 1
}
```

Now, let's see what we have got by running a query on the command line:

```
>db.giftlist.find({'owner':{'$ref':'users','$id':ObjectId('566dff161c09d090
fd36ba85')}}).pretty()
    {
        "_id" : ObjectId("569bd08d94b6b374a00e8b49"),
        "name" : "Birthday List",
        "gifts" : [
            {
                "name" : "ball"
            },
            {
                "name" : "pony"
            },
            {
                "name" : "gift card"
            }
        ],
        "owner_id" : 566dff161c09d090fd36ba85"
    }
    {
        "_id" : ObjectId("569bd0d794b6b374a00e8b4a"),
        "name" : "Christmas  List",
        "gifts" : [
            {
                "name" : "TV"
            },
            {
                "name" : "Corvette"
```

```
    },
    {
        "name" : "gift card"
    }
  ],
  "owner_id" : "566dff161c09d090fd36ba85"
}
```

Just what we would expect.

Now, let's modify our `dashboard.js` route:

```
var express = require('express');
var router = express.Router();


router.get('/', function(req, res, next) {
    res.send('respond with a resource');
});

router.param('id', function(req, res, next, id)
 {
    var db = req.db;
    var collection = db.get('giftlist');
    collection.find({'owner_id':id}, {}, function(err,giftlists)
{         if(err){
            res.send(err);
         }else if(giftlists)
{
            req.giftlists = giftlists;
            collection = db.get('users');
collection.findOne({"_id":id}, function(err, user)
{
                if(err){
                    res.send(err);
                } else
 {
                    req.user = user;
                    next();
                }
            });
        } else {
            res.send(new Error('User not found.'));
        }
    });
});

router.get('/:id', function(req, res, next){
```

```
    res.render('dash/dashboard', {user: req.user, giftlists:
req.giftlists});
});

module.exports = router;
```

We have modified the call to `router.param()` to search the `giftlists` collection based on the user `id` passed in. If we get a `giftlist` back, we then search the `users` collection to get the user data.

Yes, there are two calls to the database here. This is a bit of a trade-off in performance for flexibility. Remember that we decided earlier not to embed `giftlists` in the user document. This trade-off is something you will want to think through in your own applications.

Let's also modify our `dashboard.ejs` view template:

```
<!DOCTYPE html>
<html>
<head>
    <title>Dashboard for <%= user.firstName %> <%= user.lastName %>
</title>
</head>
<body>
<h1><%= user.firstName %> <%= user.lastName %> Dashboard</h1>
<div>
    <h2>My Lists</h2>

    <ul>    <% giftlists.forEach(function(giftlist, index){ -%>
<li><%= giftlist.name %></li>    <% }); %>    </ul>
</div>

<div>
    <h2>Lists Shared With Me</h2>
</div>

</body>
</html>
```

Now we have an unordered list that renders the name of each of our `giftlists`. When we start adding AngularJS, we'll link each of these to a state that displays the lists. Navigating to the `user dashboard` page, you should see this:

Mark Smith Dashboard

My Lists

- Birthday List
- Christmas List

Lists Shared With Me

We now have a list of our user's `giftlists` and a placeholder for lists that have been shared with them. In a little bit, when we add AngularJS, we will also add the code for adding, editing, and sharing lists.

Right now, our dashboard is somewhat ugly. Let's fix that a little bit.

Implementing Bootstrap

If you haven't heard of `Bootstrap` before, it is an extremely popular CSS framework. Plugging in `Bootstrap` helps frontend developers do things such as layout, painting buttons, and implementing controls without writing a lot of code by hand.

You can get `Bootstrap`, and see its documentation at `https://getbootstrap.com`.

Let's sweeten up our `dashboard.ejs` template a little:

```
<!DOCTYPE html>
<html>
<head>
    <title>Dashboard for <%= user.firstName %> <%= user.lastName %>
</title>

    <meta name="viewport" content="width=device-width, initial-scale=1">

    <link rel="stylesheet"
href="https://maxcdn.bootstrapcdn.com/bootstrap/3.3.6/css/bootstrap.min.css
">
    <link rel="stylesheet"
href="https://maxcdn.bootstrapcdn.com/bootstrap/3.3.6/css/bootstrap-theme.m
in.css">

</head>
<body>
<nav class="nav navbar-default">
    <div class="container-fluid">
        <div class="navbar-header">
            <a class="navbar-brand" href="#"><%= user.firstName %> <%=
```

```
user.lastName %> Dashboard</a>
        </div>
    </div>
</nav>


<div class="container">
    <div class="row">
        <div class="col-xs-12 col-md-6">
            <h2>My Lists</h2>

            <ul class="list-unstyled">
            <% giftlists.forEach(function(giftlist, index){ -%>
                <li><a class="btn btn-link" href="#" role="button"><%=
giftlist.name %></a></li>
            <% }); %>
            </ul>
        </div>

        <div class="col-xs-12 col-md-6">
            <h2>Lists Shared With Me</h2>
        </div>
    </div>
</div>

</body>
</html>
```

In the head of our document, you'll see three new lines. The first is a meta tag, which sets the viewport for mobile devices. The next two load Bootstrap and a Bootstrap theme from a CDN.

We then place what we had inside an H1 tag into a number of elements, which will paint a nav bar at the top of the page.

The next section is a div element with a class of container. This is necessary for the Bootstrap layout to work. Bootstrap uses a grid system for a layout with rows and columns. Basically, there are 12 columns of equal width in a row.

Classes such as col-xs-12 tell Bootstrap that, when the view port is extra small (like on a phone), that particular element should take up the entire width of the container. The col-md-6 class, makes the element half the width (six columns) when the screen is medium width or greater. By combining these classes, we can have a variable layout that makes sense based upon screen width. This is a main component of what's referred to as responsive design.

Looking at our dashboard in full width, we see this:

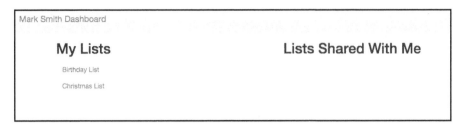

In full size, our dashboard is divided into two equal width columns. You can also see our top `nav` bar is with **Mark Smith Dashboard** is rendering. Now, if you drag the side of your browser to make it narrow like a mobile phone screen, you'll see this:

Our columns are now stacked one on top of each other, which makes a lot more sense for a mobile form factor. Let's add a button element to add new lists, which we'll actually connect later:

```
<!DOCTYPE html>
<html>
<head>
    <title>Dashboard for <%= user.firstName %> <%= user.lastName %>
</title>

    <meta name="viewport" content="width=device-width, initial-scale=1">

    <link rel="stylesheet"
href="https://maxcdn.bootstrapcdn.com/bootstrap/3.3.6/css/bootstrap.min.css
">
    <link rel="stylesheet"
href="https://maxcdn.bootstrapcdn.com/bootstrap/3.3.6/css/bootstrap-theme.m
in.css">

</head>
```

```
<body>
<nav class="nav navbar-default">
    <div class="container-fluid">
        <div class="navbar-header">
            <a class="navbar-brand" href="#"><%= user.firstName %> <%=
user.lastName %> Dashboard</a>
        </div>
    </div>
</nav>


<div class="container">
    <div class="row">
        <div class="col-xs-12 col-md-6">
            <h2>My Lists</h2>
            <button class="btn btn-primary">                 <span
class="glyphicon glyphicon-plus" aria-hidden="true"></span>
Add List</button>
            <ul class="list-unstyled">
            <% giftlists.forEach(function(giftlist, index){ -%>
                <li><a class="btn btn-link" href="#" role="button"><%=
giftlist.name %></a></li>
            <% }); %>
            </ul>
        </div>

        <div class="col-xs-12 col-md-6">
            <h2>Lists Shared With Me</h2>
        </div>
    </div>
</div>

<script
src="https://ajax.googleapis.com/ajax/libs/jquery/1.11.3/jquery.min.js"></s
cript>
<script
src="https://maxcdn.bootstrapcdn.com/bootstrap/3.3.6/js/bootstrap.min.js"
></script>
</body>
</html>
```

We added a button with a class of `btn-primary`. Inside that button we have a span with a couple of `glyphicon` classes. These classes actually use a font to paint different types of common symbols.

Viewing our page now, we'll see a pretty blue button with a plus sign:

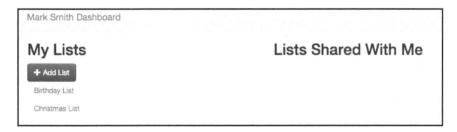

We'll be developing further visual components as AngularJS views.

Implementing AngularJS

Now it's time to implement most of our view logic by implementing a more robust AngularJS application. The first thing we need to do is to add AngularJS code to our `dashboard.ejs` view template:

```
<!DOCTYPE html>
<html ng-app>
<head>
    <title>Dashboard for <%= user.firstName %> <%= user.lastName %>
</title>

    <meta name="viewport" content="width=device-width, initial-scale=1">

    <link rel="stylesheet"
href="https://maxcdn.bootstrapcdn.com/bootstrap/3.3.6/css/bootstrap.min.css
">
    <link rel="stylesheet"
href="https://maxcdn.bootstrapcdn.com/bootstrap/3.3.6/css/bootstrap-theme.m
in.css">
    <script
src="https://ajax.googleapis.com/ajax/libs/angularjs/1.4.8/angular.min.js">
</script>    <script
src="https://cdnjs.cloudflare.com/ajax/libs/angular-ui-router/0.2.15/angula
r-ui-router.min.js"></script>


</head>
<body>
<nav class="nav navbar-default">
    <div class="container-fluid">
        <div class="navbar-header">
```

```
                    <a class="navbar-brand" href="#"><%= user.firstName %> <%=
    user.lastName %> Dashboard</a>
            </div>
        </div>
    </nav>


    <div class="container">
        <div class="row">
            <div class="col-xs-12 col-md-6">
                <h2>My Lists</h2>
                <button class="btn btn-primary">
                    <span class="glyphicon glyphicon-plus" aria-
    hidden="true"></span>
                    Add List</button>
                <ul class="list-unstyled">
                <% giftlists.forEach(function(giftlist, index){ -%>
                    <li><a class="btn btn-link" href="#" role="button"><%=
    giftlist.name %></a></li>
                <% }); %>
                </ul>
            </div>

            <div class="col-xs-12 col-md-6">
                <h2>Lists Shared With Me</h2>
            </div>
        </div>
    </div>

    </body>
    </html>
```

We linked to AngularJS version 1.4.8 on a CDN, as well as a plugin called UI-router. We'll be talking about UI-router in depth. We also added the AngularJS directive ng-app to the opening html tag. When AngularJS loads, it looks for this directive to see what part of the document it should manage. Most applications will have Angular manage from the top level by doing this, though one could Bootstrap AngularJS into any part of the document.

Our AngularJS module

AngularJS packages applications, parts of applications, and dependencies using modules. Everything we're going to do with AngularJS is going to be done by using modules or using code, such as controllers, which have been added to modules.

This is a core part of AngularJS architecture. Modules are containers for the parts of your application, and allow AngularJS to properly `Bootstrap` your application.

For now, our module is going to be simple, then we'll add to it as we go on. Create a new file called `giftapp.js` inside `public/javascripts`:

```
var giftAppModule = angular.module('giftAppModule', ['ui.router']);
```

We create our module by invoking the `angular.module()` function. The first argument is the name of the module. The second argument is an array containing a list of dependencies we want to inject into our module. In this case, the only one we're injecting at the moment is UI-router.

Now, we need to add our module to our `dashboard.ejs` template:

```
<!DOCTYPE html>
<html ng-app="giftAppModule">
<head>
    <title>Dashboard for <%= user.firstName %> <%= user.lastName %>
</title>

    <meta name="viewport" content="width=device-width, initial-scale=1">

    <link rel="stylesheet"
href="https://maxcdn.bootstrapcdn.com/bootstrap/3.3.6/css/bootstrap.min.css
">
    <link rel="stylesheet"
href="https://maxcdn.bootstrapcdn.com/bootstrap/3.3.6/css/bootstrap-theme.m
in.css">
    <script
src="https://ajax.googleapis.com/ajax/libs/angularjs/1.4.8/angular.min.js">
</script>
    <script
src="https://cdnjs.cloudflare.com/ajax/libs/angular-ui-router/0.2.15/angula
r-ui-router.min.js"></script>


</head>
<body>
<nav class="nav navbar-default">
    <div class="container-fluid">
        <div class="navbar-header">
            <a class="navbar-brand" href="#"><%= user.firstName %> <%=
user.lastName %> Dashboard</a>
        </div>
    </div>
</nav>
```

```
<div class="container">
    <div class="row">
        <div class="col-xs-12 col-md-6">
            <h2>My Lists</h2>
            <button class="btn btn-primary">
                <span class="glyphicon glyphicon-plus" aria-
hidden="true"></span>
                Add List</button>
            <ul class="list-unstyled">
            <% giftlists.forEach(function(giftlist, index){ -%>
                <li><a class="btn btn-link" href="#" role="button"><%=
giftlist.name %></a></li>
            <% }); %>
            </ul>
        </div>

        <div class="col-xs-12 col-md-6">
            <h2>Lists Shared With Me</h2>
        </div>
    </div>
</div>

<script src="/javascripts/giftapp.js"></script>
</body>
</html>
```

We simply load our module using a normal `script` tag. Also, we change the `ng-app`
directive so that it will use our new module as the main application entry point for the
page.

Controlling state with UI-router

State can mean a lot of things in applications, but in our SPA it refers to a given set of views,
controllers, and data that can be invoked using a URL changer. By far the most popular way
for developers to handle state in their AngularJS applications is with a plugin called UI-
router.

The UI-router plugin allows us to control state rather elegantly, and is extremely flexible.

Let's implement UI-router in our application. First, we will reference UI-router from a CDN
in our `dashboard.ejs` template:

```
<!DOCTYPE html>
<html ng-app="giftapp">
<head >
```

```
    <title>Dashboard for <%= user.firstName %> <%= user.lastName %>
</title>

    <meta name="viewport" content="width=device-width, initial-scale=1">

    <link rel="stylesheet"
href="https://maxcdn.bootstrapcdn.com/bootstrap/3.3.6/css/bootstrap.min.css
">
    <link rel="stylesheet"
href="https://maxcdn.bootstrapcdn.com/bootstrap/3.3.6/css/bootstrap-theme.m
in.css">
    <script
src="https://ajax.googleapis.com/ajax/libs/angularjs/1.4.8/angular.min.js">
</script>
    <script
src="https://cdnjs.cloudflare.com/ajax/libs/angular-ui-router/0.2.15/angula
r-ui-router.min.js"></script>


</head>
<body>
<nav class="nav navbar-default">
    <div class="container-fluid">
        <div class="navbar-header">
            <a class="navbar-brand" href="#"><%= user.firstName %> <%=
user.lastName %> Dashboard</a>
        </div>
    </div>
</nav>


<div class="container">

    <div ui-view></div>


</div>


<script src="/javascripts/giftapp.js"></script>
</body>
</html>
```

We linked to UI-router on a CDN and loaded it using a normal `script` tag. The other major change in our template is the addition of a `ui-view` directive implemented as an attribute on a `div` element. The `ui-view` directive tells UI-router where to load the views that it's going to be painting.

The next step is to edit our `giftapp.js` application file to add routing:

```
angular.module('giftapp', ['ui.router'])

  .config(
    ['$stateProvider', '$urlRouterProvider',
      function ($stateProvider,   $urlRouterProvider) {

        $urlRouterProvider
          .otherwise('/dash');

        $stateProvider

          .state('dash', {
            url:'/dash',
            templateUrl: '/templates/dash-main.tpl.html'
          })
          .state('add', {
            url:'/add',
            templateUrl: '/templates/dash-add.tpl.html'
          });

  }]);
```

First, we make sure to inject the `ui.router` module into our module. We chain a `config` function onto our module declaration. Using an array notation, we inject `$stateProvider` and `$urlRouteprovider` into the `config` function.

Inside that function, the magic happens. First, we invoke `$urlRouterProvider.otherwise('/dash');`, which sets the default route. When we load our page, unless another route is triggered with a URL fragment, `#/dash` will be appended to the URL.

Next, we set up two states on `$stateProvider`. For now, each is named and has a URL and `templateURL` property. The template URL points to a URL for a visual template to load.

Let's mock up our two templates. Create a new directory at `public/templates`.

Here's our `dash-main.tpl.html`:

```
<div class="row">
    <div class="col-xs-12 col-md-6">
        <h2>My Lists</h2>
        <a class="btn btn-primary" role="button" ui-sref="add"
href="#/add">
```

```
            <span class="glyphicon glyphicon-plus" aria-
hidden="true"></span>
            Add List</a>
        <ul class="list-unstyled">

            <li><a class="btn btn-link" href="#" role="button">Angular
Router List</a></li>
            <li><a class="btn btn-link" href="#" role="button">Angular
Router List 2</a></li>
        </ul>
    </div>

    <div class="col-xs-12 col-md-6">
        <h2>Lists Shared With Me</h2>
    </div>
</div>
```

And this is our `dash-add.tpl.html` file:

```
<div class="row">
    <div class="col-md-12">
        <h2>Add a new list</h2>
        <form class="form-horizontal">
            <div class="form-group">
                <label for="listname" class="col-sm-2 control-label">List
Name</label>
                <div class="col-sm-10">
                    <input type="text" class="form-control" id="listname"
placeholder="Name">
                </div>
            </div>
            <div class="form-group">
                <label for="item[]" class="col-sm-2 control-label">Item
1</label>
                <div class="col-sm-10">
                    <input type="text" class="form-control" id="Item[]">
                </div>
            </div>
            <div class="form-group">
                <label for="item[]" class="col-sm-2 control-label">Item
1</label>
                <div class="col-sm-10">
                    <input type="text" class="form-control" id="Item[]">
                </div>
            </div>
            <div class="form-group">
                <label for="item[]" class="col-sm-2 control-label">Item
1</label>
```

```
            <div class="col-sm-10">
                <input type="text" class="form-control" id="Item[]">
            </div>
        </div>
        <div class="form-group">
            <div class="col-sm-offset-2 col-sm-10">
                <a href="#/dash" class="btn btn-default">
                Save
                </a>
            </div>
        </div>
    </form>

</div>

</div>
```

Here, we've mocked up a form that could be used to add a new list. We'll flesh it out later, and actually connect it to the backend to store data.

AngularJS controllers

Right now, our templates are basically just dumb HTML, the AngularJS method of linking our DOM to data and functionality. Controllers contain business logic, but should not be used to manipulate the DOM directly.

In using UI-router, we can easily attach controllers to states, making their $scope available to our views.

Create a new controllers folder inside public/javascripts. Create a new JavaScript file called dashMainController.js:

```
angular.module('giftappControllers',[])
    .controller('DashMainController', ['$scope', function($scope) {
        $scope.lists = [{'name':'Christmas List'}, {'name':'Birthday
List'}];
    }]);
```

We create a new module called giftAppControllers that takes no dependencies. Then, we build a controller called DashMainController. Using an array notation, we inject $scope and then declare a constructor function.

Inside that function we attach a lists array to $scope, which will make it available to any view that references this controller.

Next, we need to load that file into the `dashboard.ejs` view template:

```
<!DOCTYPE html>
<html ng-app="giftapp">
<head >
    <title>Dashboard for <%= user.firstName %> <%= user.lastName %>
</title>

    <meta name="viewport" content="width=device-width, initial-scale=1">

    <link rel="stylesheet"
href="https://maxcdn.bootstrapcdn.com/bootstrap/3.3.6/css/bootstrap.min.css
">
    <link rel="stylesheet"
href="https://maxcdn.bootstrapcdn.com/bootstrap/3.3.6/css/bootstrap-theme.m
in.css">
    <script
src="https://ajax.googleapis.com/ajax/libs/angularjs/1.4.8/angular.min.js">
</script>
    <script
src="https://cdnjs.cloudflare.com/ajax/libs/angular-ui-router/0.2.15/angula
r-ui-router.min.js"></script>


</head>
<body>
<nav class="nav navbar-default">
    <div class="container-fluid">
        <div class="navbar-header">
            <a class="navbar-brand" href="#"><%= user.firstName %> <%=
user.lastName %> Dashboard</a>
        </div>
    </div>
</nav>


<div class="container">

    <div ui-view></div>

    <!-- div class="row">
        <div class="col-xs-12 col-md-6">
            <h2>My Lists</h2>
            <a class="btn btn-primary" role="button" ui-sref="add">
                <span class="glyphicon glyphicon-plus" aria-
hidden="true"></span>
                Add List</a>
            <a class="btn btn-primary" role="button" ui-sref="dash">
```

```
                    <span class="glyphicon glyphicon-plus" aria-
hidden="true"></span>
                    Add List</a>
            <ul class="list-unstyled">
            <% giftlists.forEach(function(giftlist, index){ -%>
                <li><a class="btn btn-link" role="button"><%= giftlist.name
%>></a></li>
            <% }); %>
            </ul>
        </div>

        <div class="col-xs-12 col-md-6">
            <h2>Lists Shared With Me</h2>
        </div>
    </div -->

</div>


<script src="/javascripts/giftapp.js"></script>
<script src="/javascripts/controllers/dashMainController.js"></script>
</body>
</html>
```

You'll note that you can load the controller module after your main module.

Next, we need to edit our main `giftapp.js` module to use the new controller as part of a route:

```
angular.module('giftapp', ['ui.router', 'giftappControllers' ])

    .config(
        ['$stateProvider', '$urlRouterProvider',
            function ($stateProvider, $urlRouterProvider) {

                $urlRouterProvider
                    .otherwise('/dash');

                $stateProvider

                    .state('dash', {
                        url:'/dash',
                        templateUrl: '/templates/dash-main.tpl.html',
                        controller: 'DashMainController'
                    })
                    .state('add', {
                        url:'/add',
                        templateUrl: '/templates/dash-add.tpl.html',
```

```
                });

        }]);
```

The first thing we do is to inject our new controller module into our `giftapp` module. This makes the `DashMainController` available in the module. We then set its name, as a string, to the controller property on our `dash` state.

The last thing we should do is to modify our template to take advantage of our new controller. Any methods or properties added to `$scope` in a controller become available inside the view.

Here's our new `dash-main.tpl.html`:

```html
<div class="row">
    <div class="col-xs-12 col-md-6">
        <h2>My Lists</h2>
        <a class="btn btn-primary" role="button" ui-sref="add"
href="#/add">
            <span class="glyphicon glyphicon-plus" aria-
hidden="true"></span>
            Add List</a>
        <ul class="list-unstyled">
            <li ng-repeat="list in lists"><a class="btn btn-link" href="#"
role="button">{{ list.name }}</a></li>

        </ul>
    </div>

    <div class="col-xs-12 col-md-6">
        <h2>Lists Shared With Me</h2>
    </div>
</div>
```

Instead of canned list items, we rely on the `ng-repeat` directive (provided by AngularJS itself). The `ng-repeat` directive iterates over things that are iterable – in this case an array called list. For each member of the array, the directive will paint a `li` element, assigning the instance to the variable list (essentially creating a new scope). Since our list objects all have name properties, we can access this in a markup expression with `{{list.name}}`.

Making sure our database and server are running, refreshing our dashboard should look like this:

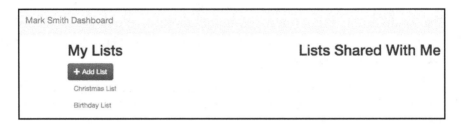

Christmas List and **Birthday List** are coming from $scope in our new controller. Clicking on the **Add List** button takes us to our add state and the page suddenly looks like this:

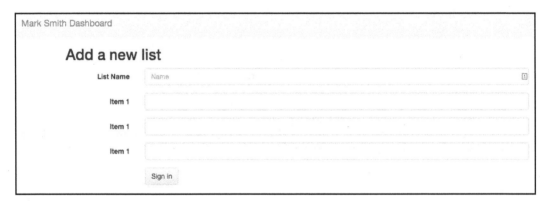

So now we have the essence of a single page web application working. We have a model, views, and a controller. We have a method of managing state.

In mocking up this functionality, we did remove the connection to the database. So let's add that back in the AngularJS way.

Talking to the backend

So now we need to connect our frontend to our backend. Instead of rendering data in our page on load, we want to use AJAX to connect and do all of our CRUD. Fortunately for us, Angular has a pretty elegant way of handling this.

Creating an AngularJS factory

Let's say that different parts of our application may need access to some of the same data endpoints, or some other functionality. A great way to handle this is with an AngularJS provider. A provider is essentially an injectable singleton, and there are a number of options available – see `https://docs.angularjs.org/guide/providers`.

The provider type we are going to use is a factory. Let's start by creating a `services` directory inside our `public/javascripts` directory. Create a new file called `giftlistFactory.js` inside that directory:

```
angular.module('giftlistServices', [])
    .factory('List', function(){
        return {}
    });
```

We've created another module for services, and then created a factory called `List` on that module. That factory doesn't do much yet, but we'll get to that.

Next, we'll load this file using a `script` tag in our `dashboard.ejs` template:

```
<!DOCTYPE html>
<html ng-app="giftapp">
<head >
    <title>Dashboard for <%= user.firstName %> <%= user.lastName %>
</title>

    <meta name="viewport" content="width=device-width, initial-scale=1">

    <link rel="stylesheet"
href="https://maxcdn.bootstrapcdn.com/bootstrap/3.3.6/css/bootstrap.min.css
">
    <link rel="stylesheet"
href="https://maxcdn.bootstrapcdn.com/bootstrap/3.3.6/css/bootstrap-theme.m
in.css">
    <script
src="https://ajax.googleapis.com/ajax/libs/angularjs/1.4.8/angular.min.js">
</script>
    <script
src="https://cdnjs.cloudflare.com/ajax/libs/angular-ui-router/0.2.15/angula
r-ui-router.min.js"></script>

</head>
<body>
<nav class="nav navbar-default">
    <div class="container-fluid">
```

```
        <div class="navbar-header">
            <a class="navbar-brand" href="#"><%= user.firstName %> <%=
user.lastName %> Dashboard</a>
        </div>
    </div>
</nav>


<div class="container">

    <div ui-view></div>


</div>


<script src="/javascripts/giftapp.js"></script>
<script src="/javascripts/controllers/dashMainController.js"></script>
<script src="/javascripts/services/giftlistFactory.js"></script>
</body>
</html>
```

Now that we're loading this module, we can inject it into our controller. Open up `dashMainController.js` and edit the following:

```
angular.module('giftappControllers',['giftlistServices'])
.controller('DashMainController', ['$scope','List', function($scope,List) {
        $scope.lists = [{'name':'Christmas List'}, {'name':'Birthday
List'}];
    }]);
```

We inject the `giftlistServices` module into our `giftappControllers` module. In our `DashMainController`, we inject the `List` factory. Currently, `List` only returns an empty object, but anything we place in there going forward becomes available to our controller.

Using AngularJS $resource

The smart people who develop AngularJS figured out that a lot of what people want to do in an SPA is to talk to RESTful services. They had the idea to build a factory on top of their `$http` service (which provides AJAX functionality), which would provide an easy way to interact with a RESTful interface. That's precisely what `$resource` does.

We will begin by loading the `ngResource` module, which exposes `$resource`. In our `dashboard.ejs` template, add a `script` tag to load the module from CDN:

```
<!DOCTYPE html>
<html ng-app="giftapp">
<head >
    <title>Dashboard for <%= user.firstName %> <%= user.lastName %>
</title>

    <meta name="viewport" content="width=device-width, initial-scale=1">

    <link rel="stylesheet"
href="https://maxcdn.bootstrapcdn.com/bootstrap/3.3.6/css/bootstrap.min.css
">
    <link rel="stylesheet"
href="https://maxcdn.bootstrapcdn.com/bootstrap/3.3.6/css/bootstrap-theme.m
in.css">
    <script
src="https://ajax.googleapis.com/ajax/libs/angularjs/1.4.8/angular.min.js">
</script>
    <script
src="https://cdnjs.cloudflare.com/ajax/libs/angular-ui-router/0.2.15/angula
r-ui-router.min.js"></script>
    <script
src="https://ajax.googleapis.com/ajax/libs/angularjs/1.4.8/angular-resource
.js"></script>


</head>
<body>
<nav class="nav navbar-default">
    <div class="container-fluid">
        <div class="navbar-header">
            <a class="navbar-brand" href="#"><%= user.firstName %> <%=
user.lastName %> Dashboard</a>
        </div>
    </div>
</nav>


<div class="container">

    <div ui-view></div>


</div>
```

```
<script src="/javascripts/giftapp.js"></script>
<script src="/javascripts/controllers/dashMainController.js"></script>
<script src="/javascripts/services/giftlistFactory.js"></script>
</body>
</html>
```

Now we have the module loaded, let's edit our factory to utilize $resource. Open giftlistFactory and make the following edits:

```
angular.module('giftlistServices', ['ngResource'])
    .factory('List', function($resource){
        return $resource('/giftlist/:id',{id: '@_id'})
    });
```

You can see that we inject the ngResource module in our module. This allows us to inject $resource into our List factory. Lastly, we return the result of invoking $resouce with the path /giftlist/:id. This, combined with the second argument, sets up a number of functions that optionally include an id.

Remember the resourceful controller we built earlier? We're going to make an edit with some hardcoded data, for now. Opencontrollers/giftlist_controller.js:

```
exports.index = function(req, res){

        var db = req.db;
        var collection = db.get('giftlist');

        collection.find({'owner_id':'566dd0cb1c09d090fd36ba83'}, {},
function(err,giftlists){
            if(err){
                res.send(err);
            }else if(giftlists){
                res.json(giftlists);

        };
    });


};
```

For now, only edit the index. You can see that I've hardcoded the owner_id for the query to match the user in the database I've been working with. You should match your user id accordingly as it will differ from mine.

Now, edit your dashMainController.js file:

```
angular.module('giftappControllers',['giftlistServices'])
    .controller('DashMainController', ['$scope','List',
function($scope,List) {
        $scope.lists = List.query();
    }]);
```

We set the value of $scope.lists to the result of running a query on our List resource. In this case, the result is an array of objects. If you restart your server and then reload the page, you'll see this:

Summary

In this chapter, you built out the major parts of the UI side of your SPA. You started by building a view in Express. You included Bootstrap for some easy styling, layout, and responsiveness. Then you refactored the page to utilize AngularJS.

You set up modules, routes, templates, and a controller using AngularJS. You then built a factory and injected $resource into it. You started to access data from a RESTful endpoint and then displayed that data in your application by mapping it to $scope in your controller.

11
Adding Security and Authentication

In previous chapters, we mocked up users so that we could test various functions, but obviously this isn't how we want our application to work going forward. We want only authorized users to be able to add and edit their lists and share them with others. Our application is currently not very secure.

Authentication is a basic functionality of almost every web application. We have a great option for managing users signing up, logging in, and accessing privileged routes. We will install Passport authentication middleware for Node.js, configure it for local authentication, and set up session management. We will secure our dashboard route so that only authenticated users see their own dashboard.

In this chapter, we will use Node.js and Express middleware to secure our SPA by preventing common exploits such as **Cross-Site Request Forgery** (**CSRF**). We'll also talk about additional security concerns that we'll handle during deployment.

Here are the topics that would be covered in this chapter:

- Setting up **Passport** to authenticate users
- Creating local authentication strategies for signing up and logging in
- Modeling users with **Mongoose**
- Securing routes
- Adding security headers and preventing CSRF attacks on our application

Adding authentication with Passport

Passport is a Node.js plugin that has the singular purpose of authenticating requests. That is, making sure only people who are logged in and who should be able to make certain requests are able to do so. Authentication is a basic security feature of every web application, including SPAs.

Passport is extremely flexible, allowing authentication through a number of different means, called strategies. Strategies include logging in with a simple username and password, or using **OAuth** to log in with Facebook or Twitter. Passport provides over 100 different strategies we should use for authentication. This chapter will focus on a local authentication strategy, while the following chapter will integrate social media strategies.

Like most plugins used with Express, Passport is middleware and so its use will be familiar to us. This is a great architecture as well, because it keeps concerns separated in our application.

Installing Passport

The first thing we need to do is to install Passport. Getting the actual Passport module couldn't be easier, we just use npm to install it:

```
$ npm install passport --save
passport@0.3.2 node_modules/passport
|- pause@0.0.1
|_ passport-strategy@1.0.0
```

We also need to install each strategy we're going to use for Passport separately:

```
$ npm install passport-local -save
passport-local@1.0.0 node_modules/passport-local
|_ passport-strategy@1.0.0
```

The last thing we need is some middleware to manage user sessions. For that, we'll install the express-session package:

```
$ npm install express-session -save
express-session@1.13.0 node_modules/express-session
|- utils-merge@1.0.0
|- cookie-signature@1.0.6
|- parseurl@1.3.1
|- cookie@0.2.3
|- on-headers@1.0.1
|- depd@1.1.0
```

```
|- crc@3.4.0
|- uid-safe@2.0.0 (base64-url@1.2.1)
```

Next, we need to add Passport into our app. Open up our main `app.js` file and make the following modifications:

```
var express = require('express');
var path = require('path');
var favicon = require('serve-favicon');
var logger = require('morgan');
var cookieParser = require('cookie-parser');
var bodyParser = require('body-parser');
var isJSON = require('./utils/json');
var routing = require('resource-routing');
var controllers = path.resolve('./controllers');

//Database stuff
var mongodb = require('mongodb');
var monk = require('monk');
var db = monk('localhost:27017/giftapp');

var routes = require('./routes/index');
var users = require('./routes/users');
var dashboard = require('./routes/dashboard');

var app = express();

// view engine setup
app.set('views', path.join(__dirname, 'views'));
app.set('view engine', 'ejs');

app.set('x-powered-by', false);

app.locals.appName = "My Gift App";

// uncomment after placing your favicon in /public
//app.use(favicon(path.join(__dirname, 'public', 'favicon.ico')));
app.use(logger('dev'));
app.use(bodyParser.json());
app.use(bodyParser.urlencoded({ extended: false }));
app.use(cookieParser());
app.use(express.static(path.join(__dirname, 'public')));
app.use(isJSON);

var passport = require('passport');var expressSession = require('express-
session');app.use(expressSession({secret:
'someKeyYouPick'}));app.use(passport.initialize());app.use(passport.session
());
```

```
//Database middleware
app.use(function(req,res,next){
    req.db = db;
    next();
});

app.use('/', routes);
app.use('/users', users);
app.use('/dash', dashboard);

routing.resources(app, controllers, "giftlist");
routing.expose_routing_table(app, { at: "/my-routes" });

// catch 404 and forward to error handler
app.use(function(req, res, next) {
  var err = new Error('Not Found');
  err.status = 404;
  next(err);
});

// error handlers

// development error handler
// will print stacktrace
if (app.get('env') === 'development') {
  app.use(function(err, req, res, next) {
    res.status(err.status || 500);
    res.render('error', {
      message: err.message,
      error: err
    });
  });
}

// production error handler
// no stacktraces leaked to user
app.use(function(err, req, res, next) {
  res.status(err.status || 500);
  res.render('error', {
    message: err.message,
    error: {}
  });
});


module.exports = app;
```

It's important that we require and initialize Passport before any of the routing, to make sure our authentication is available to our routes. In initializing `expressSession`, set a secret key that's something different than what I've given you here. It can be any string, really.

We are almost ready. Express local strategy assumes users stored in a MongoDB database. We already have a MongoDB database with a users' table, but we really need to enforce some consistency, and it would be nice to have an easy way to model our data.

Using Mongoose to configure the database

We're going to use a package called Mongoose. Mongoose is a data modeling tool for Node.js, used widely in Express packages. Where we accessed our database directly before, we are now going to let Mongoose do a lot of the heavy lifting for us.

Installing and configuring Mongoose

As with other modules, we will use npm to install mongoose:

```
$ npm install mongoose -save
mongoose@4.3.7 node_modules/mongoose
|- ms@0.7.1
|- regexp-clone@0.0.1
|- hooks-fixed@1.1.0
|- async@0.9.0
|- mpromise@0.5.4
|- mpath@0.1.1
|- muri@1.0.0
|- sliced@0.0.5
|- kareem@1.0.1
|- bson@0.4.21
|- mquery@1.6.3 (bluebird@2.9.26)
|_ mongodb@2.1.4 (es6-promise@3.0.2, readable-stream@1.0.31,
kerberos@0.0.18, mongodb-core@1.2.32)
```

Now we will add the code to initialize Mongoose in our app.js file:

```
var express = require('express');
var path = require('path');
var favicon = require('serve-favicon');
var logger = require('morgan');
var cookieParser = require('cookie-parser');
var bodyParser = require('body-parser');
var isJSON = require('./utils/json');
var routing = require('resource-routing');
```

```
var controllers = path.resolve('./controllers');

//Database stuff
var mongodb = require('mongodb');
var monk = require('monk');
var db = monk('localhost:27017/giftapp');

var mongoose =
require('mongoose');mongoose.connect('localhost:27017/giftapp');

var routes = require('./routes/index');
var users = require('./routes/users');
var dashboard = require('./routes/dashboard');

var app = express();

// view engine setup
app.set('views', path.join(__dirname, 'views'));
app.set('view engine', 'ejs');

app.set('x-powered-by', false);

app.locals.appName = "My Gift App";

// uncomment after placing your favicon in /public
//app.use(favicon(path.join(__dirname, 'public', 'favicon.ico')));
app.use(logger('dev'));
app.use(bodyParser.json());
app.use(bodyParser.urlencoded({ extended: false }));
app.use(cookieParser());
app.use(express.static(path.join(__dirname, 'public')));
app.use(isJSON);

var passport = require('passport');
var expressSession = require('express-session');
app.use(expressSession({secret: 'mySecretKey'}));
app.use(passport.initialize());
app.use(passport.session());

//Database middleware
app.use(function(req,res,next){
    req.db = db;
    next();
});

app.use('/', routes);
app.use('/users', users);
app.use('/dash', dashboard);
```

```
routing.resources(app, controllers, "giftlist");
routing.expose_routing_table(app, { at: "/my-routes" });

// catch 404 and forward to error handler
app.use(function(req, res, next) {
  var err = new Error('Not Found');
  err.status = 404;
  next(err);
});

// error handlers

// development error handler
// will print stacktrace
if (app.get('env') === 'development') {
  app.use(function(err, req, res, next) {
    res.status(err.status || 500);
    res.render('error', {
      message: err.message,
      error: err
    });
  });
}

// production error handler
// no stacktraces leaked to user
app.use(function(err, req, res, next) {
  res.status(err.status || 500);
  res.render('error', {
    message: err.message,
    error: {}
  });
});


module.exports = app;
```

Here, we require in the Mongoose library and initialize it with the URL of our local database.

Creating the user model

Mongoose uses predefined data models to validate, store, and access MongoDB databases. We need to create a model that will represent our user documents. We already have a `users` collection in our `db`, so let's blow that away to avoid any conflicts or confusion.

Make sure you have a terminal window open with the Mongo daemon running. If not, just open a new terminal and type `mongod` to start it. In a second terminal window, start the MongoDB command-line tool by typing `mongo`.

Once that's running, type the following:

```
> use giftapp
switched to db giftapp
> show collections
giftapp
giftlist
system.indexes
test
users
> db.users.drop()
true
> show collections
giftapp
giftlist
system.indexes
test
```

We make sure we're using the Gift App database. We then run `showcollections` to list the collections, and see there's a `users` collection. We run the `db.users.drop()` collection method to drop the collection. Then we show the collections again to check that the users collection has been removed.

With that complete, create a new folder called models. Inside that folder, create a file called `user.js`:

```
var mongoose = require('mongoose');
var Schema = mongoose.Schema;
module.exports = mongoose.model('User', new Schema({
    id: String,
    username: String,
    email: String,
    password: String,
    firstName: String,
    lastName: String
}));
```

We require mongoose at the top of the file and then create a model called User with the mongoose.model() function. That function takes a string, which becomes the model name, and an object, which represents the actual model. In our case, we have an id, username, email, password, firstName, and lastName, which are each defined as strings. Mongoose will ensure that every User document stored in our database matches this format definition.

> The default for the Passport local strategy is for there to be a username and password field. This could be changed if you wanted to just use email and password or some other scheme.

Setting up Passport strategies

Now we have to set up a local Passport strategy. We need to extend this strategy to handle users logging in and signing up.

Initializing Passport

Create a new directory called passport. Create a file called init.js:

```
var User = require('../models/user');

module.exports = function(passport){
  passport.serializeUser(function(user, done) {
      done(null, user._id);
    });

    passport.deserializeUser(function(id, done) {
      User.findById(id, function(err, user) {

          done(err, user);
      });
    });
}
```

This code gives Passport access to our User model. The serialize and deserialize functions are used to look up a user from the database (deserialize) and to store user information to the session of User (serialize).

Now let's initialize Passport using our `init` function in our main `app.js` file:

```javascript
var express = require('express');
var path = require('path');
var favicon = require('serve-favicon');
var logger = require('morgan');
var cookieParser = require('cookie-parser');
var bodyParser = require('body-parser');
var isJSON = require('./utils/json');
var routing = require('resource-routing');
var controllers = path.resolve('./controllers');

//Database stuff
var mongodb = require('mongodb');

var mongoose = require('mongoose');
mongoose.connect('localhost:27017/giftapp');

var routes = require('./routes/index');
var users = require('./routes/users');
var dashboard = require('./routes/dashboard');

var app = express();

// view engine setup
app.set('views', path.join(__dirname, 'views'));
app.set('view engine', 'ejs');

app.set('x-powered-by', false);

app.locals.appName = "My Gift App";

// uncomment after placing your favicon in /public
//app.use(favicon(path.join(__dirname, 'public', 'favicon.ico')));
app.use(logger('dev'));
app.use(bodyParser.json());
app.use(bodyParser.urlencoded({ extended: false }));
app.use(cookieParser());
app.use(express.static(path.join(__dirname, 'public')));
app.use(isJSON);

var flash = require('connect-flash');app.use(flash());

var passport = require('passport');
var expressSession = require('express-session');
app.use(expressSession({secret: 'mySecretKey'}));
app.use(passport.initialize());
app.use(passport.session());
```

```
var initializePassport =
require('./passport/init');initializePassport(passport);

//Database middleware
app.use(function(req,res,next){
    req.db = db;
    next();
});

app.use('/', routes);
app.use('/users', users);
app.use('/dash', dashboard);

routing.resources(app, controllers, "giftlist");
routing.expose_routing_table(app, { at: "/my-routes" });

// catch 404 and forward to error handler
app.use(function(req, res, next) {
  var err = new Error('Not Found');
  err.status = 404;
  next(err);
});

// error handlers

// development error handler
// will print stacktrace
if (app.get('env') === 'development') {
  app.use(function(err, req, res, next) {
    res.status(err.status || 500);
    res.render('error', {
      message: err.message,
      error: err
    });
  });
}

// production error handler
// no stacktraces leaked to user
app.use(function(err, req, res, next) {
  res.status(err.status || 500);
  res.render('error', {
    message: err.message,
    error: {}
  });
});
module.exports = app;
```

We require in our `init` file, assigning the exported function to the variable name `initializePassport`, then we invoke that function passing an instance of Passport into it.

We also added a new library before the Passport code, `connect-flash`. This allows us to store flash messages in session such as *invalid password* and pass them back to display to a view. We need to install this software with `npm`:

```
$ npm install connect-flash --save
connect-flash@0.1.1 node_modules/connect-flash
```

Creating the signup strategy

Now let's build out and require the strategy for signing users up.

First things first, we need to add a library for hashing the user password so we don't store unencrypted passwords in our database, that's bad news. We're going to use a module called `bycrypt-nodejs`, which is easily installed using `npm`:

```
$ npm install bcrypt-nodejs --save
bcrypt-nodejs@0.0.3 node_modules/bcrypt-nodejs
```

In your `passport` directory, create a new file called `signup.js`:

```
var LocalStrategy   = require('passport-local').Strategy;
var User = require('../models/user');
var bCrypt = require('bcrypt-nodejs');

module.exports = function(passport){

    passport.use('signup', new LocalStrategy({
            passReqToCallback : true
        },
        function(req, username, password, done) {
            //this is asynchronous
            process.nextTick(function () {
                console.log('inside signup');
                // see if user already exists
                User.findOne({'username': username}, function (err, user) {
                    if (err) {
                        console.log('Error in SignUp: ' + err);
                        return done(err);
                    }
                    // user exists
                    if (user) {
                        console.log('User already exists');
                        return done(null, false, req.flash('message', 'User
```

```
                        Already Exists'));
                } else {
                    //create a new User and store to the
                    database
                    var user = new User();

                    user.username = username;
                    user.email = req.param('email');
                    user.password =
                    bCrypt.hashSync(password,
                    bCrypt.genSaltSync(10), null);
                    user.firstName =
                    req.param('firstName');
                    user.lastName = req.param('lastName');


                    user.save(function (err) {
                        if (err) {
                            console.log('save error ' +
                                        err);
                            throw err;
                        }
                        console.log("saving")
                        return done(null, user);
                    });
                }
            });
        });

    })
);


}
```

We require the modules we need, which includes a reference to the Mongoose `User` module. We set up the strategy with a call to `passport.use()`. The first argument is the name of the strategy, in this case, `signup`. The next argument is a call to construct a new `LocalStrategy`.

That call receives an object, in this case containing `passReqToCallback = true`. This makes the request object available to the callback function, which is next. This is important so that we have the info for the signup.

The callback function sets up a new function called `newSignup`, which does the bulk of the work. We first search to see if there is a user with the specified username. If there is, we exit and set a flash message that the user already exists. If the user doesn't exist, we create a new one. Finally, we pass the function to the next tick of the Node.js event loop to be executed.

You'll note that the actual callback functionality executes inside a call to `process.nextTick()` due to the asynchronous nature of this call.

Now let's edit our `init.js` file to include and initialize our signup strategy:

```
var signup = require('./signup');
var User = require('../models/user');

module.exports = function(passport){

  passport.serializeUser(function(user, done) {

      done(null, user._id);
  });

    passport.deserializeUser(function(id, done) {
        User.findById(id, function(err, user) {

            done(err, user);
      });
  });

    signup(passport);

}
```

We simply require our signup module and then invoke the exported function inside our `init` function.

Creating the login strategy

So, now we have the signup strategy to create users, we need a strategy for users to log in. Create a new file in the `passport` directory, called `signin.js`:

```
var LocalStrategy   = require('passport-local').Strategy;
var User = require('../models/user');
var bCrypt = require('bcrypt-nodejs');

module.exports = function(passport){

    passport.use('login', new LocalStrategy({
```

```
            passReqToCallback : true
        },
        function(req, username, password, done) {
            User.findOne({ 'username' :  username },
                function(err, user) {
                    if (err)
                        return done(err);
                    if (!user){
                        // username not found
                        return done(null, false, req.flash('message',
'Username
                        or password incorrect.'));
                    }

                    if (!bCrypt.compareSync(password, user.password)){
                        //password is invalid
                        return done(null, false, req.flash('message',
'Username
                        or password incorrect.'));
                    }
                    //success condition
                    return done(null, user);
                }
            );

        })
    );
}
```

Once again, we require in our dependencies. We then create and export a function that, when invoked, creates a new Passport strategy for login.

The first thing we do is query the database to see if a user with our username exists. If the user doesn't exist, we set an error message in the flash and return the result of the done function, with the second argument being false.

The next step, assuming we matched on a username, is to use the bCrypt.compareSync() function to check that the password passed in matches the hashed password for the user from the database. If it doesn't, we again set an error message on the flash and then return done, with the second argument being false.

Finally, assuming the username returns a user, and the password matches, we authenticate merely by returning done, with the second argument being the user.

Now, we'll load and initialize the login strategy in our `init.js` file:

```
var signup = require('./signup');
var login = require('./login');
var User = require('../models/user');

module.exports = function(passport){


    passport.serializeUser(function(user, done) {

        done(null, user._id);
    });

    passport.deserializeUser(function(id, done) {
        User.findById(id, function(err, user) {

            done(err, user);
        });
    });

    signup(passport);
    login(passport);


}
```

Just like with the signup strategy, we simply require the login strategy module then invoke the exported function.

Creating routes for authentication

Now we've set up Passport, we can't quite sign up or log in users yet. We need to set up routes and views to render the signup and login experience.

Create a new file called `login.js` in your routes folder:

```
var express = require('express');
var router = express.Router();


module.exports = function(passport){


    router.get('/', function(req, res) {
        res.render('login/login', { message: req.flash('message') });
    });
```

```
router.post('/', passport.authenticate('login', {
    successRedirect: '/dash',
    failureRedirect: '/login',
    failureFlash : true
}));


router.get('/signup', function(req, res){
    res.render('login/signup',{message: req.flash('message')});
});


router.post('/signup', passport.authenticate('signup', {
    successRedirect: '/dash',
    failureRedirect: '/login/signup',
    failureFlash : true
}));



router.get('/signout', function(req, res) {
    req.logout();
    res.redirect('/login');
});

    return router;
}
```

As you can see, we export a function that sets up routes for logging in, signing up, and logging out. We expect an instance of passport to be passed when the function is invoked. When a user logs in successfully, they will be redirected to the /dash path.

Now let's add the routes to our main app.js file:

```
var express = require('express');
var path = require('path');
var favicon = require('serve-favicon');
var logger = require('morgan');
var cookieParser = require('cookie-parser');
var bodyParser = require('body-parser');
var isJSON = require('./utils/json');
var routing = require('resource-routing');
var controllers = path.resolve('./controllers');

//Database stuff
var mongodb = require('mongodb');

var mongoose = require('mongoose');
```

```
mongoose.connect('localhost:27017/giftapp');

var routes = require('./routes/index');
var users = require('./routes/users');
var dashboard = require('./routes/dashboard');

var app = express();

// view engine setup
app.set('views', path.join(__dirname, 'views'));
app.set('view engine', 'ejs');

app.set('x-powered-by', false);

app.locals.appName = "My Gift App";

// uncomment after placing your favicon in /public
//app.use(favicon(path.join(__dirname, 'public', 'favicon.ico')));
app.use(logger('dev'));
app.use(bodyParser.json());
app.use(bodyParser.urlencoded({ extended: false }));
app.use(cookieParser());
app.use(express.static(path.join(__dirname, 'public')));
app.use(isJSON);

var flash = require('connect-flash');
app.use(flash());

var passport = require('passport');
var expressSession = require('express-session');
app.use(expressSession({secret: 'mySecretKey'}));
app.use(passport.initialize());
app.use(passport.session());

var initializePassport = require('./passport/init');
initializePassport(passport);

//Database middleware
app.use(function(req,res,next){
    req.db = db;
    next();
});

app.use('/', routes);
app.use('/users', users);
app.use('/dash', dashboard);

var login = require('./routes/login')(passport);app.use('/login', login);
```

```
routing.resources(app, controllers, "giftlist");
routing.expose_routing_table(app, { at: "/my-routes" });

// catch 404 and forward to error handler
app.use(function(req, res, next) {
  var err = new Error('Not Found');
  err.status = 404;
  next(err);
});

// error handlers

// development error handler
// will print stacktrace
if (app.get('env') === 'development') {
  app.use(function(err, req, res, next) {
    res.status(err.status || 500);
    res.render('error', {
      message: err.message,
      error: err
    });
  });
}

// production error handler
// no stacktraces leaked to user
app.use(function(err, req, res, next) {
  res.status(err.status || 500);
  res.render('error', {
    message: err.message,
    error: {}
  });
});


module.exports = app;
```

You'll notice that we necessarily pass a reference to Passport to the route.

Creating views for authentication

Now that we have the routes to sign up and log in, we need views to render and show the user.

Create a login folder in your views directory. In that folder, create a new template called `signup.ejs`:

```
<!DOCTYPE html>
<html>
<head >
    <title>Signup</title>

    <meta name="viewport" content="width=device-width, initial-scale=1">

    <link rel="stylesheet"
href="https://maxcdn.bootstrapcdn.com/bootstrap/3.3.6/css/bootstrap.min.css
">
    <link rel="stylesheet"
href="https://maxcdn.bootstrapcdn.com/bootstrap/3.3.6/css/bootstrap-theme.m
in.css">

</head>
<body>

<nav class="nav navbar-default">
    <div class="container-fluid">
        <div class="navbar-header">
            <a class="navbar-brand" href="#"> Giftapp Signup</a>
        </div>
    </div>
</nav>

<div class="container">
    <% if(message){ %>
    <div class="row">
        <div class="col-md-4 col-md-offset-4" role="alert">
            <%= message %>
        </div>
    </div>
    <% } %>

    <div class="row">
        <div class="col-md-6 col-md-offset-3">
            <form method="post" action="/login/register">
                <div class="form-group">
                    <label for="username">Username</label>
                    <input type="text" class="form-control" id="username"
```

```
                    name="username" placeholder="username">
                </div>
                <div class="form-group">
                    <label for="password">Password</label>
                    <input type="password" class="form-control"
id="password"
                     name="password" placeholder="Password">
                </div>
                <div class="form-group">
                    <label for="email">Email address</label>
                    <input type="email" class="form-control" id="email"
                      name="email" placeholder="Email">
                </div>
                <div class="form-group">
                    <label for="firstName">First Name</label>
                    <input type="text" class="form-control" id="firstName"
                      name="firstName" placeholder="First Name">
                </div>

                <div class="form-group">
                    <label for="lastName">Last Name</label>
                    <input type="text" class="form-control" id="lastName"
                      name="lastName" placeholder="Last Name">
                </div>
                <button type="submit" class="btn btn-
default">Submit</button>
            </form>
        </div>
    </div>


</div>

</body>
</html>
```

This is a pretty standard form for signup, and we've used some `Bootstrap` classes to pretty things up a bit. If you start up your server and navigate to `http://localhost:3000/login/signup`, you'll see the following:

If you fill out the form—making sure to have at least a `username` and `password`–you should create a `user` and be redirected to the `/dash` URL. It's not impressive yet, but it looks as follows:

respond with a resource

Now, if you start up your MongoDB command line and look, you'll see a `users` collection once again. Mongoose created that automatically for us. If you create a couple of users, you can see them here:

```
> db.users.find({}).pretty()
{
  "_id" : ObjectId("56ae11990d7ca83f048f3c2a"),
  "lastName" : "Moore",
  "firstName" : "John",
  "password" :
  "$2a$10$OFhNNsA5MKrWCyFG9nATq.CIpTYZ5DH.jr8FnJYYFzgH7P4qM5QZy",
  "email" : "john@johnmoore.ninja",
  "username" : "ninja",
  "__v" : 0
```

```
  }
  {
    "_id" : ObjectId("56ae18d10d7ca83f048f3c2b"),
    "lastName" : "Blanks",
    "firstName" : "Billy",
    "password" :
    "$2a$10$NZQz8Nq4hBjSuU5yvO1Lnen.sy.sxEWwhtOnPrIlP3aKC0jUrgSTq",
    "email" : "billy@fakeemailaddress.com",
    "username" : "billy",
    "__v" : 0
  }
```

You see that we have two users. I created each of these using the signup form. Only the hash of their passwords is stored in the database. To round out signup in production, you would want to at least validate users' email addresses, but for development purposes, it's easier for us to be able to create fake accounts at will.

Now we need a form for logging in. Create a new login.ejs template in your views/login directory:

```
<!DOCTYPE html>
<html>
<head >
    <title>Signup</title>

    <meta name="viewport" content="width=device-width, initial-scale=1">

    <link rel="stylesheet"
href="https://maxcdn.bootstrapcdn.com/bootstrap/3.3.6/css/bootstrap.min.css
">
    <link rel="stylesheet"
      href="https://maxcdn.bootstrapcdn.com/bootstrap/3.3.6/css/bootstrap-
      theme.min.css">

</head>
<body>

<nav class="nav navbar-default">
    <div class="container-fluid">
        <div class="navbar-header">
            <a class="navbar-brand" href="#"> Giftapp Login</a>
        </div>
    </div>
</nav>

<div class="container">
    <% if(message){ %>
```

```
            <div class="row">
                <div class="col-md-4 col-md-offset-4" role="alert">
                    <%= message %>
                </div>
            </div>
            <% } %>

            <div class="row">
                <div class="col-md-6 col-md-offset-3">
                    <form method="post" action="/login">
                        <div class="form-group">
                            <label for="username">Username</label>
                            <input type="text" class="form-control" id="username"
                             name="username" placeholder="username">
                        </div>
                        <div class="form-group">
                            <label for="password">Password</label>
                            <input type="password" class="form-control"
    id="password"
                             name="password" placeholder="Password">
                        </div>

                        <button type="submit" class="btn btn-
    default">Submit</button>
                    </form>
                </div>
            </div>


        </div>

        </body>
        </html>
```

Going to `http://localhost:3000/login` gives us a page that looks like the following:

Logging in with a correct set of user credentials will take you to our still-boring /dash route. Logging in with incorrect credentials returns us to the login route and populates the flash message:

Authenticating requests

The main part of our application is our user dashboard, where our user will be able to create giftlists. Previously, we would access a user's dashboard by passing the user id in the dashboard URL. Obviously, there is no authentication here, and it's not a secure way of doing it.

Now we want users to log in before viewing only their own dashboard. If they go to the dashboard URL directly, they should be redirected to a login page.

We are going to handle this in stereotypical Express fashion by writing a piece of middleware to handle adding authentication for routes.

Adding authentication-check middleware

Passport gives us in-session access to check if a user is currently authenticated. We can use this to easily protect whole sections of an application, or add authentication on a route-by-route basis.

Create a new file called authenticated.js in your utils directory:

```
var authenticated = function (req, res, next) {

    if (req.isAuthenticated()){
        return next();
```

```
    } else {
        res.redirect('/login');
    }

}

module.exports = authenticated;
```

Our authenticated function is set up with the signature of all Express middleware—with arguments for request, response, and next. We check the return value of a call to the request object's isAuthenticed() function—this is something Passport provides to us.

If we are authenticated, we merely pass the request forward by calling next(). If we aren't authenticated, we will redirect the request to the /login route, rendering our login page.

Inserting middleware into routes

Next, we want to insert our new middleware where we want to use it, in our dashboard route file:

```
var express = require('express');
var router = express.Router();
var isAuthenticated = require('../utils/authenticated');router.get('/',
isAuthenticated, function(req, res, next) {     res.send('respond with a
resource');});

router.param('id', function(req, res, next, id) {
    var db = req.db;
    var collection = db.get('giftlist');

    collection.find({'owner_id':id}, {}, function(err,giftlists){
        if(err){
            res.send(err);
        }else if(giftlists){
            req.giftlists = giftlists;
            collection = db.get('users');
            collection.findOne({"_id":id}, function(err, user){
                if(err){
                    res.send(err);
                } else {

                    req.user = user;
                    next();
                }

            });
```

```
        } else {
            res.send(new Error('User not found.'));
        }
    });
});


router.get('/:id', function(req, res, next){
    res.render('dash/dashboard', {user: req.user, giftlists:
req.giftlists});
});

module.exports = router;
```

We require our new module into the router file, assigning it to the `isAuthenticated` variable. Next, we add the middleware to the main route.

Restarting your server should log you out. If you want to log out without restarting your server, you can access the sign-out route at `http://localhost:3000/login/signout`. You can then try to access `/dash`, and you'll be redirected back to login. Signing back in as a valid user will redirect you to dash, which will render properly.

Changing the dashboard route

Before, we set up our `dash/:id` route to look up the user using a `param` function. That's no longer going to suit our purposes. What we want is to show an authenticated user their own dashboard after logging in. Fortunately, Passport has already cached the user data we need in-session for us so we don't have to look the user up every time we render the dashboard.

Let's make some changes to our `dashboard` router:

```
var express = require('express');
var router = express.Router();
var isAuthenticated = require('../utils/authenticated');

router.get('/', isAuthenticated, function(req, res, next) {

    var db = req.db;
    var collection = db.get('giftlist');

    collection.find({'owner_id':req.user._id}, {}, function(err,giftlists){
        if(err){
```

```
            res.send(err);
        }else {
            giftlists = giftlists || [];
            res.render('dash/dashboard', {user: req.user, giftlists:
giftlists});
        }
    });
});

module.exports = router;
```

Now we've simplified the code a bit. Our /:id route is now gone and the only route remaining is the main route, which gets triggered by get requests to /dash.

We already have user data cached in the request thanks to Passport, so it saves us one database lookup, helping our code perform better. We still look up the gift lists owned by this user, then we render the dashboard template we built earlier, which contains our single-page application frontend.

We get the following:

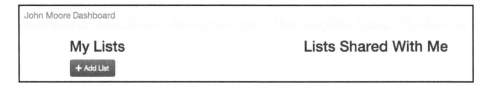

So we have authenticated the user and stashed the user object in the session, making it available during the request.

Securing Express

Authentication is perhaps the most important and one of the trickier topics with regard to securing a web application from the front. Certainly, there are lots of different threat vectors.

Helmet

One of the easiest things we can do to secure our Express application is to install and use the security middleware called Helmet. Helmet adds a number of security headers and policies, as well as preventing some attacks, such as clickjacking.

It does most of this under the covers, without the need for configuration on our part. For more detailed information, and to find alternative ways to `congigure` it.

To get started with Helmet, first install it using `npm`:

```
$ npm install helmet --save
helmet@1.1.0 node_modules/helmet
|- nocache@1.0.0
|- hide-powered-by@1.0.0
|- dont-sniff-mimetype@1.0.0
|- dns-prefetch-control@0.1.0
|- ienoopen@1.0.0
|- hpkp@1.0.0
|- x-xss-protection@1.0.0
|- hsts@1.0.0 (core-util-is@1.0.2)
|- frameguard@1.0.0 (lodash.isstring@3.0.1)
|- connect@3.4.0 (parseurl@1.3.1, utils-merge@1.0.0,
finalhandler@0.4.0)
   |_ helmet-csp@1.0.3 (lodash.isfunction@3.0.6, platform@1.3.0,
camelize@1.0.0, lodash.assign@3.2.0, content-security-policy-builder@1.0.0,
lodash.reduce@3.1.2, lodash.some@3.2.3)
```

You can actually see by the names of the submodules what some of the protections include.

Next, we simply need to add the module to our main `app.js` file:

```
var express = require('express');
var path = require('path');
var favicon = require('serve-favicon');
var logger = require('morgan');
var cookieParser = require('cookie-parser');
var bodyParser = require('body-parser');
var isJSON = require('./utils/json');
var routing = require('resource-routing');
var controllers = path.resolve('./controllers');
var helmet = require('helmet');

//Database stuff
var mongodb = require('mongodb');
var monk = require('monk');
var db = monk('localhost:27017/giftapp');

var mongoose = require('mongoose');
mongoose.connect('localhost:27017/giftapp');

var routes = require('./routes/index');
var users = require('./routes/users');
var dashboard = require('./routes/dashboard');
```

```
var app = express();

// view engine setup
app.set('views', path.join(__dirname, 'views'));
app.set('view engine', 'ejs');

app.set('x-powered-by', false);

app.locals.appName = "My Gift App";

// uncomment after placing your favicon in /public
//app.use(favicon(path.join(__dirname, 'public', 'favicon.ico')));
app.use(logger('dev'));
app.use(bodyParser.json());
app.use(bodyParser.urlencoded({ extended: false }));
app.use(cookieParser());
app.use(express.static(path.join(__dirname, 'public')));
app.use(isJSON);

var flash = require('connect-flash');
app.use(flash());

var passport = require('passport');
var expressSession = require('express-session');
app.use(expressSession({secret: 'mySecretKey'}));
app.use(passport.initialize());
app.use(passport.session());

var initializePassport = require('./passport/init');
initializePassport(passport);

//Database middleware
app.use(function(req,res,next){
    req.db = db;
    next();
});

app.use('helmet');

app.use('/', routes);
app.use('/users', users);
app.use('/dash', dashboard);

var login = require('./routes/login')(passport);
app.use('/login', login);

routing.resources(app, controllers, "giftlist");
routing.expose_routing_table(app, { at: "/my-routes" });
```

```
// catch 404 and forward to error handler
app.use(function(req, res, next) {
  var err = new Error('Not Found');
  err.status = 404;
  next(err);
});

// error handlers

// development error handler
// will print stacktrace
if (app.get('env') === 'development') {
  app.use(function(err, req, res, next) {
    res.status(err.status || 500);
    res.render('error', {
      message: err.message,
      error: err
    });
  });
}

// production error handler
// no stacktraces leaked to user
app.use(function(err, req, res, next) {
  res.status(err.status || 500);
  res.render('error', {
    message: err.message,
    error: {}
  });
});


module.exports = app;
```

And there you have it. We've mitigated a pile of common web security vulnerabilities.

Please note that `app.use('helmet')` must come before any of the routes or the protection will not be in place for those routes.

CSRF

One of the most common web attack vectors is the **Cross-Site Request Forgery** (**CSRF**). CSRF is an attack where some untrusted source, such as another website or even an e-mail, takes advantage of a user's authenticated status to execute privileged code on another application. You can find more detailed information about CSRF at https://www.owasp.or g/index.php/Cross-Site_Request_Forgery_(CSRF).

Once again, middleware to the rescue:

```
$ npm install csurf --save
csurf@1.8.3 node_modules/csurf
|- cookie@0.1.3
|- cookie-signature@1.0.6
|- http-errors@1.3.1 (inherits@2.0.1, statuses@1.2.1)
|_ csrf@3.0.1 (rndm@1.2.0, base64-url@1.2.1, scmp@1.0.0, uid-
safe@2.1.0)
```

The csurf middleware is then plugged into our app.js the same way, with Helmet required in and then used. Please note that the app.use('csurf') must come after the cookie parser and express-session middleware, since it uses both.

Next, we edit our login routes file:

```
var express = require('express');
var router = express.Router();


module.exports = function(passport){


    router.get('/', function(req, res) {
        res.render('login/login', { message: req.flash('message'),
csrfToken:
        req.csrfToken() });
    });


    router.post('/', passport.authenticate('login', {
        successRedirect: '/dash',
        failureRedirect: '/login',
        failureFlash : true
    }));


    router.get('/signup', function(req, res){
        console.log('signing up');
```

```
        res.render('login/signup',{message: req.flash('message'),
csrfToken:
        req.csrfToken()});
    });


    router.post('/register', passport.authenticate('signup', {
        successRedirect: '/dash',
        failureRedirect: '/login/signup',
        failureFlash : true
    }));

    router.get('/signout', function(req, res) {
        req.logout();
        res.redirect('/login');
    });

    return router;
}
```

We add a CSRF token to the data we pass to the login and signup pages.

Next, we add a hidden field to our login and signup pages:

```
<!DOCTYPE html>
<html>
<head >
    <title>Signup</title>

    <meta name="viewport" content="width=device-width, initial-scale=1">

    <link rel="stylesheet"
href="https://maxcdn.bootstrapcdn.com/bootstrap/3.3.6/css/bootstrap.min.css
">
    <link rel="stylesheet"
href="https://maxcdn.bootstrapcdn.com/bootstrap/3.3.6/css/bootstrap-theme.m
in.css">

</head>
<body>

<nav class="nav navbar-default">
    <div class="container-fluid">
        <div class="navbar-header">
            <a class="navbar-brand" href="#"> Giftapp Signup</a>
        </div>
    </div>
</nav>
```

```
<div class="container">
    <% if(message){ %>
    <div class="row">
        <div class="col-md-4 col-md-offset-4" role="alert">
            <%= message %>
        </div>
    </div>
    <% } %>

    <div class="row">
        <div class="col-md-6 col-md-offset-3">
            <form method="post" action="/login/register">
                <div class="form-group">
                    <label for="username">Username</label>
                    <input type="text" class="form-control"
                     id="username" name="username" placeholder="username">
                </div>
                <div class="form-group">
                    <label for="passwordd">Password</label>
                    <input type="password" class="form-control"
    id="password"
                        name="password" placeholder="Password">
                </div>
                <div class="form-group">
                    <label for="email">Email address</label>
                    <input type="email" class="form-control" id="email"
                     name="email" placeholder="Email">
                </div>
                <div class="form-group">
                    <label for="firstName">First Name</label>
                    <input type="text" class="form-control"
                     id="firstName" name="firstName" placeholder="First
    Name">
                </div>

                <div class="form-group">
                    <label for="lastName">Last Name</label>
                    <input type="text" class="form-control" id="lastName"
                     name="lastName" placeholder="Last Name">
                </div>
                <input type="hidden" name="_csrf" value="<% csrfToken %>">
<button type="submit" class="btn btn-default">Submit</button>

            </form>
        </div>
    </div
```

```
</div>

</body>

</html>
```

Restarting our server, reloading our login or `signup` page, and viewing source, you'll see a hidden input tag like the following:

```
<input type="hidden" name="_csrf" value="UBDtLOuZ-
emrxDagDmIjxxsomxFS2pSeXKb4">
```

That hidden field gets passed back with our request and checked for validity.

Taking additional security measures

We've taken some basic, yet powerful, steps to secure our application against some of the biggest threats. A full exploration of the possible threats and security measures is beyond the scope of this book, but there are a few considerations worth mentioning.

Implementing HTTPS

Implementing HTTPS when you deploy to production prevents a number of different man-in-the-middle attacks, and prevents data from being intercepted and modified along the way. We'll explore this in the chapter on deploying to production.

Furthermore, you can set your cookies to be secure. Again, we'll cover this when we talk about deployment.

Avoiding running as root

One of the reasons we use port 3000 locally is that in many environments, running on port 80 (the standard HTTP port) requires running as root. A well-known security policy is that all processes should be run with as few privileges as possible. Again, this is something we'll take of when we deploy—mostly by using a PaaS provider.

Validating user input

Right now, our application does very little input validation—except that `username` and `password` are required for signup and login. But we can and should check user input on both the client and server side.

We will add some input validation in the next chapter.

Summary

We started this chapter by installing and configuring the Passport middleware for Node.js. Passport provides us with a framework for authentication, including creating new users, logging in, and securing specific routes. We then built out local authentication strategies for logging in and signing up.

We created routes and view templates for logging in and signing up, and redirected successful attempts to our main dashboard URL. We were able to reduce database lookups by relying on Passport caching our user in-session.

Finally, we enhanced the security of our application by using Helmet to add security headers to requests, and using `csurf` to mitigate CSRF attempts. We closed by discussing a few additional security concerns when moving the application into a production environment.

12
Connecting the App to Social Media

Many web applications use third-party authentication for registering and logging in. In particular, using popular social media sites such as Facebook and Twitter to authenticate users has become very popular. Since these sites have already done some work to validate users, sites using them to authenticate users save a some time.

In this chapter, we are going to set up Passport strategies to sign up and authenticate users using their Facebook and Twitter accounts. We're going to be using a popular protocol called OAuth 2.

Additionally, we're going to finish building out the functionality for users to create and share gift lists. In this chapter, we will cover the following:

- Authenticating users with Facebook
- Authenticating users with Twitter
- Handling gift list creation in the dashboard
- Adding share buttons

Connecting to Facebook

We are going to begin integration with social media by allowing users to create accounts and log in using their Facebook accounts. The first things we need to do are to set up a Facebook developer account and build a Facebook app.

Setting up your Facebook developer account and app

In order to authenticate users using Facebook, you have to have a Facebook app. Fortunately, Facebook makes setting this up really easy.

If you do not have a Facebook developer account, head over to `https://developers.faceb ook.com/` right now and sign up for a developer account. Just follow the instructions and agree to the terms of service. Next, we need to set up an app. From the developers' dashboard, select **Add New App** from the **My Apps** dropdown. You'll get a modal window that looks like the following screenshot:

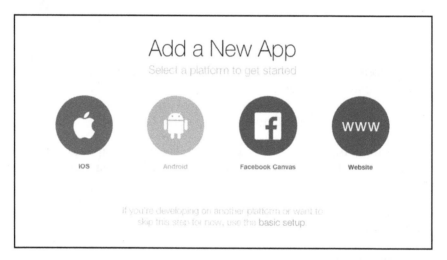

Select **Website**:

Give your new app a name and select **Create New Facebook App ID**:

Choose a category for your new app (any one will do, really). Make sure to leave off the selection for **Is this a test version of another app?** Then click **Create App ID**:

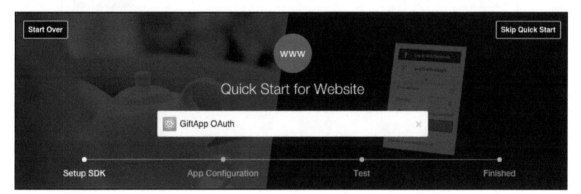

From here, I suggest you select **Skip Quick Start** and we'll set up your application manually. On the next screen, select **Settings**:

You'll need to enter your e-mail address here and click **Save Changes**. Next, click on **App Review**:

Select **Yes** for **Do you want to make this app and all its live features available to the general public?** Next, go back to your dashboard:

You're going to need your App ID and App Secret values. Facebook will force you to enter your password to show your App Secret.

App Secret is exactly that – secret. You should protect it and not do anything like check it into public source control.

Setting up the Passport strategy

The next thing we need to do is to set up the strategy in Passport. Open up your terminal and navigate to your `giftapp` root directory:

```
$ npm install passport-facebook --save
passport-facebook@2.1.0 node_modules/passport-facebook
|__ passport-oauth2@1.1.2 (uid2@0.0.3, passport-strategy@1.0.0,
oauth@0.9.14)
```

Here, we've installed the Passport Facebook module, which allows us to log in with Facebook using OAuth 2.

> OAuth is an open protocol to allow secure authorization in a simple and standard method from web, mobile and desktop applications. You can find more information about OAuth 2, the latest version of the protocol, at `http://oauth.net/2/`.

Configuring for Facebook

Now we need to set up our strategy. Inside your giftapp directory, make a new directory called `config`, and add a new file called `authorization.js`:

```
module.exports = {
    facebookAuth : {
        clientID: '695605423876152', // App ID
        clientSecret: 'd8591aa38e06a07b040f20569a', // App secret
        callbackURL: 'http://localhost:3000/login/FBcallback'
    }
}
```

We just stash an object with a few values we're going to need later. The `clientID` is our App ID. The `clientSecret` is our App Secret (no, that isn't my real secret). The last value is our `callBackURL`. This is a URL that Facebook will redirect to on authorization.

If you are using a Git repository to store your source code, it would be a good idea to add this `config` file to your `.gitignore` file.

Setting up the routes for Facebook authentication

The next thing we need to do is to set up a couple of routes. In your routes directory, open up your routes file, login.js:

```
var express = require('express');s
var router = express.Router();


module.exports = function(passport){


    router.get('/', function(req, res) {
        res.render('login/login', { message: req.flash('message'),
csrfToken:
        req.csrfToken() });
    });


    router.post('/', passport.authenticate('login', {
        successRedirect: '/dash',
        failureRedirect: '/login',
        failureFlash : true
    }));


    router.get('/signup', function(req, res){
        console.log('signing up');
        res.render('login/signup',{message: req.flash('message'),
csrfToken:
        req.csrfToken()});
    });


    router.post('/register', passport.authenticate('signup', {
        successRedirect: '/dash',
        failureRedirect: '/login/signup',
        failureFlash : true
    }));

    router.get('/signout', function(req, res) {
        req.logout();
        res.redirect('/login');
    });

    router.get('/facebook', passport.authenticate('facebook',
scope:['emails']));
    router.get('/FBcallback',          passport.authenticate('facebook',
```

```
{
successRedirect: '/dash',                    failureRedirect: '/login' }));

    return router;
}
```

The first new route is going to be used to log in using Facebook. The callback URL is used after authentication. On failure, the user is redirected to login. On success, the user is sent to the dashboard.

Note that the second argument to the call to `passport.authenticate` on the `facebook` route. This object contains a scope property, which takes an array. That array consists of strings for data fields for which Facebook requires extra permissions to access. Facebook requires extra permissions to access a user's e-mail address.

Finishing setting up the Passport strategy

Now we have a few more steps to set up the strategy. In your Passport directory, create a new file called `facebook.js`:

```
var FacebookStrategy = require('passport-facebook').Strategy;
var User = require('../models/user');
var auth = require('../config/authorization');

module.exports = function(passport){

    passport.use('facebook', new FacebookStrategy({
            clientID: auth.facebookAuth.clientID,
            clientSecret: auth.facebookAuth.clientSecret,
            callbackURL: auth.facebookAuth.callbackURL,
            profileFields: ['id', 'displayName', 'email']
        },
        function(accessToken, refreshToken, profile, cb) {
            User.findOne({ 'facebook.id': profile.id }, function (err,
user) {
                if(err){
                    return cb(err)
                } else if (user) {
                    return cb(null, user);
                } else {
                    var newUser = new User();
                    newUser.facebook.id = profile.id;
                    newUser.facebook.token = accessToken;
                    newUser.facebook.name = profile.displayName;
                    if(profile.emails){
                        newUser.email = profile.emails[0].value;
```

```
                    }
               newUser.save(function(err){
                    if(err){
                         throw err;
                    }else{
                         return cb(null, newUser);
                    }
               });
          }
     });
  }
));
}
```

We begin by requiring our dependencies, including the Strategy object provided by the `passport-facebook` module, our User model, and our authorization configuration file containing our Facebook credentials.

We then create a module that defines our Facebook authentication strategy. It receives a configuration object as its first argument, which we define using the `facebook` authorization values from our configuration file. The final property, `profileFields`, sets the fields we're expecting to receive in the profile object we get back from Facebook.

The second argument is a function that gets called when the authorization strategy is used. It receives an `accessToken`, `refreshToken`, `profile`, and `callback` as arguments from Facebook.

We use the User's `findOne` function to see if the user already exists based on the `profile.id` returned from Facebook. We first check to see if there's an error. If there is, we return it to the callback. If there's no error and the user exists, the user object is passed back to the callback with a null in the error field. Finally, if the user doesn't already exist, we create a new user, save that user to the database, then pass the new user object back to the callback.

Note that we will not always get e-mails back from Facebook, so we need to test to see if we get that property back on profile before we try to access it.

Remember that if you want to delete your `users` collection you can use the Mongo console. Enter `use giftapp` to select the database, then `db.users.drop()` to drop the collection.

Altering the User model for Facebook data

Let's make some changes to our `User` model. Our Facebook authorization will give us some data that we weren't getting before, and there's some stuff we need to store. Open up your `user.js` file in your models directory and edit the following:

```
var mongoose = require('mongoose');

var userSchema = mongoose.Schema({
    id: String,
    email: String,
    username: String,
    password: String,
    firstName: String,
    lastName: String,

    facebook: {

        id: String,
        token: String
    }

});
module.exports = mongoose.model('User',userSchema);
```

Here, we're going to use the `mongoose.Schema` function to start to build out our schema. We've added a `Facebook` object to the user which stores an ID, and a token. Note that this new ID is provided by Facebook and is different from the ID at the top level of the `User` object.

The token is a unique `id` that Facebook provides on an application-by-application basis. We need to store this for authentication to work correctly.

Finishing the connection to Facebook

We are almost good to go. We have just a couple more steps to do to complete the work for authenticating and signing up with Facebook.

Recreating our home page

Let's make life a little easier on ourselves and rewrite our `index.ejs` file inside our views directory:

```
<!DOCTYPE html>
<html>
  <head>
    <title><%= title %></title>
    <meta name="viewport" content="width=device-width, initial-scale=1">

    <link rel="stylesheet"
href="https://maxcdn.bootstrapcdn.com/bootstrap/3.3.6/css/bootstrap.min.css
">
    <link rel="stylesheet"
href="https://maxcdn.bootstrapcdn.com/bootstrap/3.3.6/css/bootstrap-theme.m
in.css">

  </head>
  <body>
    <div class="container">
      <div class="jumbotron">
        <h1 class="text-center">Welcome to Giftapp</h1>
        <hr>
        <p class="text-center">
          <a class="btn btn-default btn-lg" href="/login/"
role="button">Log in</a>
          <a class="btn btn-default btn-lg" href="/login/signup"
role="button">Sign Up</a>
          <a class="btn btn-primary btn-lg" href="/login/facebook"
role="button">Log in or sign up with Facebook</a>
        </p>
      </div>
    </div>
  </body>
</html>
```

Here, we've created a simple welcome page using the Bootstrap `jumbotron`. We have three buttons, which are actually links styled as buttons: one for login, one for signup, and one for Facebook signup/login.

The page, at `http://localhost:3000`, will look like the following:

You can test out the buttons. Unfortunately, clicking on our Facebook button gets you an error:

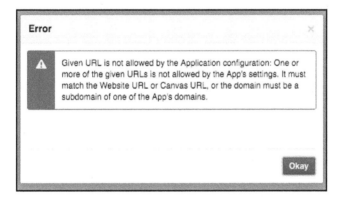

This is because we have to specifically enable URLs inside our Facebook app. Facebook enforces this security measure. Not a problem for us. Go back to **Settings** on your Facebook app dashboard:

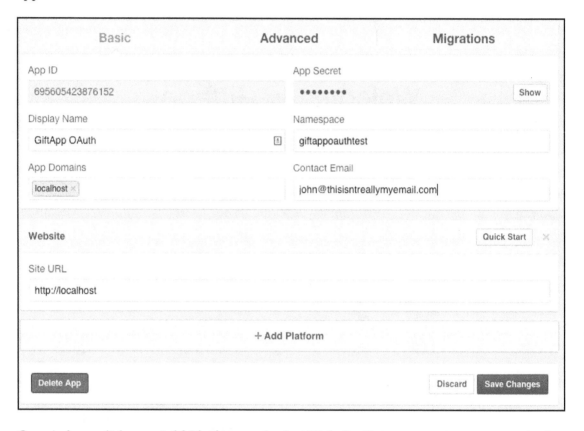

Once in here, click on **+ Add Platform** and select **Website**. Enter `http://localhost` in the URL field. Now you should be able to register and authenticate with Facebook.

One thing you may want to implement on your own is checking to see if a user already exists in the database by checking any e-mail address returned by Facebook against user e-mails already in the database. This will help to avoid duplicate accounts.

Connecting to Twitter

One of the great things about Passport, and OAuth 2, is that there are a ton of different strategies we can use to authenticate with third parties. Let's set up Twitter authentication.

Adding a Twitter app

Similar to Facebook, we need to set up an app on Twitter for our application to communicate with. Head on over to `https://apps.twitter.com` and create a new app:

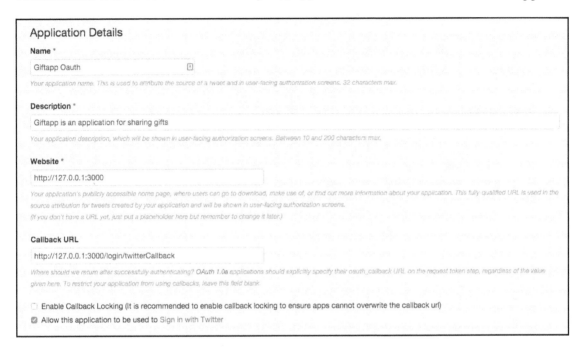

Fill in a name, description, and the two URLs. At the time of writing, Twitter does not allow `http://localhost` as a URL, so you have to use `http://127.0.0.1`.

Now click over to **Keys and Access Tokens** and grab your Consumer Key and Consumer Secret. We're going to add these to our `authorization.js` configuration file:

```
module.exports = {
    facebookAuth : {
        clientID: '695605423876152', // App ID
        clientSecret: 'd85fR1nkOz2056801c8f9a', // App secret
        callbackURL: 'http://localhost:3000/login/FBcallback'
    },

    twitterAuth : {
        'consumerKey'       : 'JksPJOz46tf10/15/16asUdgxWlJp',
        'consumerSecret'    :
'IVO95CmDyUsSOZo21GnejiShTXWzzxxybalubae82P4hfLa',
        'callbackURL'       : 'http://127.0.0.1:3000/login/twitterCallback'
    }
```

```
}
```

We add a `twitterAuth` section to our authorization `config` file that contains the keys we need as well as the callback. This all is very similar to Facebook.

Setting up our Twitter strategy

Now we need to take the steps to build our Twitter strategy.

First things first, we need to install the Passport Twitter strategy module:

```
$ npm install passport-twitter --save
passport-twitter@1.0.4 node_modules/passport-twitter
|--- passport-oauth1@1.0.1 (passport-strategy@1.0.0, utils-merge@1.0.0,
    oauth@0.9.14)
|__ xtraverse@0.1.0 (xmldom@0.1.22)
```

Now create a `twitter.js` file inside your Passport directory:

```
var TwitterStrategy = require('passport-twitter').Strategy;
var User = require('../models/user');
var auth = require('../config/authorization');

module.exports = function(passport){

    passport.use('twitter', new TwitterStrategy({
            consumerKey      : auth.twitterAuth.consumerKey,
            consumerSecret   : auth.twitterAuth.consumerSecret,
            callbackURL      : auth.twitterAuth.callbackURL
        },
        function(token, tokenSecret, profile, cb) {
            User.findOne({ 'twitter.id': profile.id }, function (err, user)
{
                if(err){
                    return cb(err)
                } else if (user) {
                    return cb(null, user);
                } else {
                    // if there is no user, create them
                    var newUser              = new User();

                    // set all of the user data that we need
                    newUser.twitter.id       = profile.id;
                    newUser.twitter.token     = token;
                    newUser.twitter.username  = profile.username;
                    newUser.twitter.displayName =
```

```
                                    profile.displayName;

                newUser.save(function(err){
                    if(err){
                        throw err;
                    }else{
                        return cb(null, newUser);
                    }
                });
            }
        });
    }
));
}
```

This strategy is very similar to our Facebook strategy. We set up our keys and callback using our authorization config. We then check if a user with the same Twitter ID is already in the database. If not, we create a new user with the data Twitter sends us and save the record to the database.

Speaking of databases, we now need to make a change to our `User` model to handle our Twitter data:

```
var mongoose = require('mongoose');

var userSchema = mongoose.Schema({
    id: String,
    email: String,
    username: String,
    password: String,
    firstName: String,
    lastName: String,

    facebook: {
        name: String,
        id: String,
        token: String
    },

    twitter: {          id: String,          token: String,          username:
String,          displayName: String     }

});
module.exports = mongoose.model('User',userSchema);
```

Just like with the Facebook section, we add a Twitter property to store the data that we get back from Twitter separately.

Next, we need to add the routes for Twitter authentication to our `routes/login.js` file:

```
var express = require('express');
var router = express.Router();


module.exports = function(passport){


    router.get('/', function(req, res) {
        res.render('login/login', { message: req.flash('message'),
csrfToken:
        req.csrfToken() });
    });


    router.post('/', passport.authenticate('login', {
        successRedirect: '/dash',
        failureRedirect: '/login',
        failureFlash : true
    }));


    router.get('/signup', function(req, res){
        console.log('signing up');
        res.render('login/signup',{message: req.flash('message'),
csrfToken:
        req.csrfToken()});
    });


    router.post('/register', passport.authenticate('signup', {
        successRedirect: '/dash',
        failureRedirect: '/login/signup',
        failureFlash : true
    }));

    router.get('/signout', function(req, res) {
        req.logout();
        res.redirect('/login');
    });

    router.get('/facebook', passport.authenticate('facebook', {scope:
['email']}));
```

```
router.get('/FBcallback',
    passport.authenticate('facebook', { successRedirect: '/dash',
        failureRedirect: '/login' }));

router.get('/twitter', passport.authenticate('twitter'));
// handle the callback after twitter has authenticated the user
    router.get('/twitterCallback',
        passport.authenticate('twitter',
{

        successRedirect : '/dash',
        failureRedirect : '/login'
    }));

    return router;
}
```

Again, the Twitter routes are very similar to the routes we use for Facebook authentication. We have the main authorization route and the route we use for callback.

Now we just need to make a couple of edits to our `passport/init.js` file to include the Twitter strategy:

```
var signup = require('./signup');
var login = require('./login');
var facebook = require('./facebook');
var twitter = require('./twitter');
var User = require('../models/user');


module.exports = function(passport){


    passport.serializeUser(function(user, done) {

        done(null, user._id);
    });

    passport.deserializeUser(function(id, done) {
        User.findById(id, function(err, user) {

            done(err, user);
        });
    });

    signup(passport);
    login(passport);
    facebook(passport);
    twitter(passport);
```

```
}
```

The only changes we need here are to import the Twitter strategy and initialize it. At this point, our Twitter strategy should work. Let's just make it a little easier for our users.

Adding Twitter authorization to our home page

As with our Facebook strategy, let's add a Twitter login button to our `index.ejs` file:

```html
<!DOCTYPE html>
<html>
  <head>
    <title><%= title %></title>
    <meta name="viewport" content="width=device-width, initial-scale=1">

    <link rel="stylesheet"
href="https://maxcdn.bootstrapcdn.com/bootstrap/3.3.6/css/bootstrap.min.css
">
    <link rel="stylesheet"
href="https://maxcdn.bootstrapcdn.com/bootstrap/3.3.6/css/bootstrap-theme.m
in.css">

  </head>
  <body>
    <div class="container">
      <div class="jumbotron">
        <h1 class="text-center">Welcome to Giftapp</h1>
        <hr>
        <p class="text-center">
          <a class="btn btn-default btn-lg" href="/login/"
role="button">Log in</a>
          <a class="btn btn-default btn-lg" href="/login/signup"
role="button">Sign Up</a>
          <a class="btn btn-primary btn-lg" href="/login/facebook"
role="button">Log in or sign up with Facebook</a>
          <a class="btn btn-primary btn-lg" href="/login/twitter"
role="button">Log in or sign up with Twitter</a>
        </p>
      </div>
    </div>
  </body>
</html>
```

We've added a Twitter login button.

Note that to test this, start at `http://127.0.0.1:3000/` and not `http://localhost:3000`. The reason for this is that you need the domain for the session cookies to match in the callback URL. When you do, you'll see the following:

Clicking on the Twitter login button will redirect you to Twitter, which will ask you to log in or authorize for your app:

Clicking on **Sign in** should bring you to your dashboard.

Now that we have logged in with both Facebook and Twitter, let's look at our `users` collection on our `giftapp` database. Fire up your MongoDB client by typing mongo on your command line:

```
> use giftapp
switched to db giftapp
```

```
> db.users.find({}).pretty()
{
  "_id" : ObjectId("56bbdc4308ca9a596f0006d8"),
  "email" : "john@thisisafakeemail.com",
  "facebook" : {
    "name" : "John Moore",
    "token" :
"CAAJ4pkIxqDgBABrsfsds345435ZAZAE73UZCjehrtjWQ8YhGWVxdoa6VA0OuydPPuQO8wJWBD
O4ZCylNX7dMPOJL4VW7WX3nZCLt1b16Mghgdfdg34543543",
    "id" : "101539512345670"
  },
  "__v" : 0
}
{
  "_id" : ObjectId("56bd252d32d162207ab35be4"),
  "twitter" : {
    "displayName" : "John Moore",
    "username" : "JohnMooreNinja",
    "token" : "4867525577-dvlIz4uEZMgMZHFd6tRjhgjhgjgf8WrGv",
    "id" : "486633445565657"
  },
  "__v" : 0
}
```

So, we have two users in our `users` collection, one with a set of Facebook credentials, and one with Twitter credentials. You'll notice that the Twitter profile does not include e-mail.

Sharing giftlists

Currently, our giftlist functionality doesn't really work. We want users to be able to create giftlists which they can then share.

Fleshing out the giftlist model

Since we're using Mongoose to model data for our users, let's also put it to use to model our `giftlists`. Inside your `models` folder, create a new file called `giftlist.js`:

```
var mongoose = require('mongoose');

var giftlistSchema = mongoose.Schema({
    id: String,
    user_id: String,
    name: String,
    gifts: [{name: String}]
```

```
        sharedWith [{user_id: String}]

});
module.exports = mongoose.model('Giftlist',giftlistSchema);
```

This model is pretty straightforward. A giftlist has an ID, a name, a list of `gift` objects, and a `user_id` field. We will populate the `user_id` with the ID of the user who owns the giftlist. In a relational database, this would be a foreign key, defining a one-to-many relationship between users and giftlists.

The gifts field is an array of objects expecting only a name property. We also have a list of users with whom we have shared the giftlist. We will leave the sharing functionality for later.

Connecting the UI

The next thing we want to do is to allow users to create new giftlists from our SPA dashboard.

Since we're going to be POSTing data back via Ajax, we need to do a little work to make the CSRF token available to our Angular application. There are two steps to do this; first, we want to pass the token in our `dashboard.js` route:

```
var express = require('express');
var router = express.Router();
var isAuthenticated = require('../utils/authenticated');

router.get('/', isAuthenticated, function(req, res, next) {


    var db = req.db;
    var collection = db.get('giftlist');
        console.log("routing dash for " + req.user._id);
    collection.find({'owner_id':req.user._id}, {}, function(err,giftlists){
        if(err){
            res.send(err);
        }else {
            giftlists = giftlists || [];
            res.render('dash/dashboard', {user: req.user, giftlists:
giftlists, csrfToken: req.csrfToken() });
        }
    });
});

module.exports = router;
```

We pass the token to the render function.

Next, we will add something to our `dashboard.ejs` template:

```
<!DOCTYPE html>
<html ng-app="giftapp">
<head >
    <title>Dashboard for <%= user.firstName %> <%= user.lastName %>
</title>

    <meta name="viewport" content="width=device-width, initial-scale=1">

    <link rel="stylesheet"
href="https://maxcdn.bootstrapcdn.com/bootstrap/3.3.6/css/bootstrap.min.css
">
    <link rel="stylesheet"
href="https://maxcdn.bootstrapcdn.com/bootstrap/3.3.6/css/bootstrap-theme.m
in.css">
    <script
src="https://ajax.googleapis.com/ajax/libs/angularjs/1.4.8/angular.min.js">
</script>
    <script
src="https://cdnjs.cloudflare.com/ajax/libs/angular-ui-router/0.2.15/angula
r-ui-router.min.js"></script>
    <script
src="https://ajax.googleapis.com/ajax/libs/angularjs/1.4.8/angular-resource
.js"></script>


</head>
<body>
<nav class="nav navbar-default">
    <div class="container-fluid">
        <div class="navbar-header">
            <a class="navbar-brand" href="#"><%= user.firstName %> <%=
user.lastName %> Dashboard</a>
        </div>
    </div>
</nav>


<div class="container">

    <div ui-view></div>
</div>
<script src="/javascripts/controllers/dashMainController.js"></script>
<script src="/javascripts/controllers/giftappFormController.js"></script>
<script src="/javascripts/services/giftlistFactory.js"></script>
```

```
<script>      angular.module("csrfValue", [])
              .value("csrfToken","<%= csrfToken %>");</script>
</body>
</html>
```

We create a new Angular module inside our page and add a value to it. A value is basically an injectable name value pair we can use in our application. We do this in the dashboard template, because we need the server to provide the `csrfToken` to the UI.

We've also added a script tag to load a new controller script file that we will use to handle processing and submitting the form.

Connecting the form

Next, we need to connect the giftlist form to the controller and have the controller talk to the backend.

Creating the controller

Create a new file in your `javascripts/controllers` directory called `giftappFormController.js`:

```
angular.module('giftappControllers')
    .controller('GiftappFormController', ['$scope','List','csrfToken',
'$state', function($scope, List, csrfToken, $state) {
        $scope.formData = {};
        $scope.formData.items = [];
        $scope.formData._csrf = csrfToken;


        $scope.create = function() {
            console.log("create");
            var myList = new List($scope.formData);
            myList.$save(function(giftList){
                console.log(giftList);
                $state.go('dash');
            });


        }
    }]);
```

We add a new controller into our `giftappControllers` module. We inject a number of things into the controller, including our List resource, and $state. We're also injecting `csrfToken`. We don't have access to that quite yet, but we'll inject its module into our module in a bit.

Inside the controller, we set up an object on `$scope` called `formData`. This will hold the data entered by a user on our form. We also add a function to scope, called `create`, which will be invoked when a user submits the form. We create a new instance of our List resource, add our data to it, and save it to the backend. After saving, we trigger a state change to return to the dashboard.

Since our module is actually defined `insidedashMainController.js`, this is where we want to inject the module containing our `csrfToken` value:

```
angular.module('giftappControllers',['giftlistServices','csrfValue'])
    .controller('DashMainController', ['$scope','List',
function($scope,List) {
        $scope.lists = List.query();

    }]);
```

Simply by adding the name of the module to our module's dependencies, we get access to the value service inside our module.

Angularizing the form

The next thing we need to do is to add some AngularJS directives to our template at `public/templates/dash-add.tpl.html`:

```html
<div class="row">
    <div class="col-md-12">
        <h2>Add a new list</h2>
        <form class="form-horizontal" ng-submit="create()">
            <div class="form-group">
                <label for="listname" class="col-sm-2 control-label">List
                Name</label>
                <div class="col-sm-10">
                    <input type="text" class="form-control" id="listname"
                    placeholder="Name" ng-model="formData.name">
                </div>
            </div>
            <div class="form-group">
                <label class="col-sm-2 control-label">Item 1</label>
                <div class="col-sm-10">
                    <input type="text" class="form-control" ng-
```

```
                model="formData.items[0]">
            </div>
        </div>
        <div class="form-group">
            <label class="col-sm-2 control-label">Item 2</label>
            <div class="col-sm-10">
                <input type="text" class="form-control" ng-
                model="formData.items[1]">
            </div>
        </div>
        <div class="form-group">
            <label class="col-sm-2 control-label">Item 3</label>
            <div class="col-sm-10">
                <input type="text" class="form-control" ng-
                model="formData.items[2]">
            </div>
        </div>
        <div class="form-group">
            <div class="col-sm-offset-2 col-sm-10">
                <button type="submit" class="btn btn-default btn-lg
btn-
                block">
                    <span class="glyphicon glyphicon-flash"></span>
Create
                        List
                </button>
            </div>
        </div>
    </form>
    {{formData}}
    </div>

</div>
```

The first change is adding the ng-submit directive to the form. On submitting the form, the controller's $scope.create() function will be invoked.

We then connect the inputs to the $scope.formdata using ng-model directives. This creates two-way data binding. To demonstrate this, we add {{formData}} into the template. This will show you all the data held by $scope.formdata and is a great way to troubleshoot your form. Obviously it's not something you'd leave in the template in production.

Connecting to the backend controller

Now that our form is connected to our controller, we need to connect our controller to our backend to store and retrieve our data from the database. Open your `controllers/giftlist_controller.js` file:

```javascript
var Giftlist = require('../models/giftlist');

exports.index = function(req, res){

        Giftlist.find({'user_id':req.user._id}, {},
function(err,giftlists){
            if(err){
                res.send(err);
            }else if(giftlists){
                res.json(giftlists);

            };
        });


};


exports.create = function(req, res){
    var newGiftlist = new Giftlist();
    newGiftlist.name = req.body.name;
    newGiftlist.user_id = req.user._id;

    var gifts = [];
    req.body.items.forEach(function(item){
        gifts.push({name:item});
    });
    newGiftlist.gifts = gifts;

    newGiftlist.save(function(err){
        if(err){
            throw err
        } else {
            res.json(newGiftlist);
        }
    });

};

exports.show = function(req, res){
    Giftlist.findOne({_id:req.params.id}, function(err, list){
```

```
        if(req.params.format == "json" || req.isJSON){
            res.json(list);
        }else{
            res.render('giftlist/show',{giftlist:list});
        }
    });

};
```

We require in our `giftlist` model, and we've edited the index, show, and create routes to take advantage of the Mongoose database functions. Because we want to be able to share lists easily with people who aren't logged into our dashboard, non-JSON requests to show are going to render in a separate page.

Inside your views directory, create a new `giftlist` directory and create a template called `show.ejs`:

```
<!DOCTYPE html>
<html>
<head>
    <title>Show Users</title>
    <link rel='stylesheet' href='/stylesheets/style.css' />
</head>
<body>
<h1>User List: <%= appName %></h1>

<table>
    <thead>
        <tr>

            <th>First Name</th>
            <th>Last Name</th>
            <th>Email Address</th>
            <th>Dashboard</th>
        </tr>
    </thead>
    <tbody>
    <% users.forEach(function(user, index){ -%>
        <tr>
            <td><a href="show/<%= user._id%> "><%= user.firstName
%></a></td>
            <td><%= user.lastName %></td>
            <td><%= user.email %></td>
            <td><a href="/dash/<%= user._id %>">View</a></td>
        </tr>
    <% }); %>
    </tbody>
```

```
    </table>


  </body>
  </html>
```

This is a pretty straightforward template that renders the list name and the gifts on the list.

Adding the ability to share lists on social media

Next, we want to allow users to easily share their lists. We need to make a minor adjustment to the `dash-main` template:

```
<div class="row">
    <div class="col-xs-12 col-md-6">
        <h2>My Lists</h2>

        <a class="btn btn-primary" role="button" ui-sref="add"
href="#/add">
            <span class="glyphicon glyphicon-plus" aria-
hidden="true"></span>
            Add List</a>
        <ul class="list-unstyled">
            <li ng-repeat="list in lists"><a class="btn btn-link"
             href="/giftlist/{{list._id}}" role="button">{{ list.name
}}</a></li>


        </ul>
    </div>

    <div class="col-xs-12 col-md-6">
        <h2>Lists Shared With Me</h2>
    </div>
</div>
```

The URL we've added to the link will trigger the show route in our controller, passing it the ID of the list we want to show.

Next, we'll add sharing buttons to our `giftlist/show.ejs` template:

```
<!DOCTYPE html>
<html>
<head >
    <title>Giftlist: <%= giftlist.name %></title>
```

```
    <meta name="viewport" content="width=device-width, initial-scale=1">

    <link rel="stylesheet"
href="https://maxcdn.bootstrapcdn.com/bootstrap/3.3.6/css/bootstrap.min.css
">
    <link rel="stylesheet"
href="https://maxcdn.bootstrapcdn.com/bootstrap/3.3.6/css/bootstrap-theme.m
in.css">

    <!-- You can use open graph tags to customize link previews.
    Learn more: https://developers.facebook.com/docs/sharing/webmasters -->
    <meta property="og:url"
          content="http://localhost:3000/giftlist/<%= giftlist._id %>" />
    <meta property="og:type"
          content="website" />
    <meta property="og:title"
          content="Giftlist App" />
    <meta property="og:description"
          content="<%= giftlist.name %>" />

</head>
<body>
<div id="fb-root"></div><script>(function(d, s, id)
 {
        var js, fjs = d.getElementsByTagName(s)[0];
        if (d.getElementById(id)) return;
        js = d.createElement(s); js.id = id;
        js.src =
"//connect.facebook.net/en_US/sdk.js#xfbml=1&version=v2.5&appId=22888730384
5448";
        fjs.parentNode.insertBefore(js, fjs);
    }
(document, 'script', 'facebook-jssdk'));
</script><nav class="nav navbar-default">
    <div class="container-fluid">
        <div class="navbar-header">
            <a class="navbar-brand" href="#">Giftlist</a>
        </div>
    </div>
</nav>


<div class="container">
    <h1><%= giftlist.name %></h1>

    <div class="row">
        <div class="col-md-12">
            <ul>
```

```
            <% giftlist.gifts.forEach(function(gift, index){ -%>
            <li><%= gift.name %></li>
            <% }); -%>
        </ul>
        <a href="https://twitter.com/share" class="twitter-share-
button" data-via="JohnMooreNinja" data-size="large" data-
hashtags="giftapp">Tweet</a>              <script>!function(d,s,id){var
js,fjs=d.getElementsByTagName(s)[0],p=/^http:/.test(d.location)?'http':'htt
ps';if(!d.getElementById(id)){js=d.createElement(s);js.id=id;js.src=p+'://p
latform.twitter.com/widgets.js';fjs.parentNode.insertBefore(js,fjs);}}(docu
ment, 'script', 'twitter-wjs');
</script>
        <div class="fb-like"></div>

    </div>
  </div>


</div>


</body>
</html>
```

We add some open graph tags, and some code to enable Twitter and Facebook sharing.

Twitter has a neat form-based wizard to set up Twitter sharing buttons. You can find it at `https://about.twitter.com/resources/buttons#tweet`.
You'll want to configure the Facebook button specifically for your app ID. Facebook also has a form-based configuration tool, at
`https://developers.facebook.com/docs/plugins/like-button`.

Summary

We began this chapter by setting up Passport strategies for authenticating with Facebook and Twitter. Setting up developer accounts with each social media site is a straightforward, but necessary, step.

We then utilized our `Mongoose Giftlist` model, as well as our resourceful controller, to enable creating gift lists from within the SPA. We enabled the frontend code and AJAX functionality by building a new AngularJS controller. To be able to post data to the backend, we added an injectable value service to carry the CSRF token.

There are a few things we leave to you to round out the application. This includes a way to add more gift inputs dynamically, and share lists with other registered users.

13
Testing with Mocha, Karma, and More

Testing is an integral part of software development, especially when dealing with applications that interact with end-users and various clients, as is the case with JavaScript SPAs. The results of web application code can often be unpredictable due to the variety of clients potentially consuming the application, so all possible scenarios should be accounted for and tested appropriately.

In this chapter, we will cover the following topics:

- What is unit testing, integration testing, and **end-to-end** (**E2E**) testing?
- How to perform JavaScript unit testing with Mocha, Chai, and Sinon.js
- How to configure Karma with Jasmine to test AngularJS
- How to perform unit testing with AngularJS
- How to perform end-to-end testing with AngularJS

Types of testing

There are various types of testing known throughout the software industry, but there are three main types that are consistently used, especially in web application development. They are as follows:

- Unit testing
- Integration testing
- End-to-end testing, also known as *functional* testing

These three types of testing comprise what is known as the *software testing pyramid*. The pyramid can be broken down into more granular forms of testing, but this is how it looks from a high vantage point:

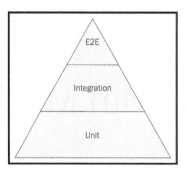

Unit testing

The bottom level of the software testing pyramid is *unit testing*. Unit testing targets the smallest pieces of an application, or units, in *isolation* from the remainder of the application. A unit is typically an individual method or object instance. When you test a unit in isolation, it means that the test should not interact with any application dependencies, such as network access, database access, user sessions, and any other dependencies that may be needed in the real-world application context. Instead, a unit test should only perform operations within local memory.

The goal of any unit test should be to test only a single feature of the application, and that feature should be encapsulated within the unit. If that unit does have any dependencies, they should be *mocked*, or simulated, instead of invoking the actual dependencies. We will discuss more about that later in the chapter.

Knowing that you will perform unit testing will help you write smaller and more focused methods in your application because they are easier to test. Many will argue that you should always write your tests first before writing any application code. This is not always practical, however, because you may have been pushed into a speedy development cycle that didn't allow time for the tedious process of writing unit tests. Writing unit tests against existing code may prove tedious as well, but it is quite acceptable, and better than having no unit tests at all.

Let's look at some well-known JavaScript unit testing frameworks that can quickly and easily be integrated into a new or existing application.

Mocha

Mocha is a popular JavaScript unit testing framework that is commonly used throughout the Node.js community. Let's revisit our Node.js sample project from the beginning of the book and install Mocha so we can try out a few unit testing examples:

```
$ npm install mocha -g
```

Install mocha globally so that you can access it easily from any directory.

Now, let's create a test directory at the root of our project to store testing related files:

```
$ mkdir test
```

Create a file in the test directory named test.js and open it for editing. Place the following code in the file and save it:

```
var assert = require('assert');
describe('String', function() {
    describe('#search()', function() {
        it('should return -1 when the value is not present', function() {
            assert.equal(-1, 'text'.search(/testing/));
        });
    });
});
```

To run the test, issue the following command from your console under the test directory:

```
$ mocha test.js
```

You should then see the following output in your console:

```
String
    #search()
        should return -1 when the value is not present
    1 passing (8ms)
```

Using the Mocha describe method, this unit test performs a simple **assertion** on the search method of the String constructor. An assertion in testing is simply an evaluation of whether something is true or not. In this example, we are testing the assertion that the search method returns −1 when its argument is not found within the search context.

Assertions with Chai

The previous example uses the Node.js `assert` module, but with Mocha, you will want to use a full-fledged assertion library for a substantive testing environment. Mocha is compatible with multiple JavaScript assertion libraries, including the following:

- Should.js
- Expect.js
- Chai
- Better-assert
- Unexpected

Chai is a popular and active open source assertion library, so we will use it for our Mocha assertion examples throughout this chapter. First, install `chai` in your local Node.js environment:

```
$ npm install chai --save-dev
```

Chai includes three styles of assertions,`should`, `expect`, and `assert`, allowing you to choose the flavor you like best.

Should-style assertions

Should-style assertions are accessible in Chai using `chai.should()`. This interface allows for a chainable method syntax that is familiar to many JavaScript developers, especially if you have worked with libraries such as jQuery. The chainable method names use natural language to make writing the tests more fluid. Additionally, Chai's `should` method extends `Object.prototype` so that you can chain it directly to the variables you are testing, as follows:

```
var should = require('chai').should(); // Execute the should function
var test = 'a string';
test.should.be.a('string');
```

This example will perform a simple assertion that the given variable is a string.

Expect-style assertions

Expect-style assertions are accessible in Chai using `chai.expect`. This interface is similar to `should`, in that, it uses method chaining, but it does not extend `Object.prototype`, so it is used in a more traditional fashion, as follows:

```
var expect = require('chai').expect;
var test = 'a string';
```

```
expect(test).to.be.a('string');
```

This example performs the same assertion as the previous example, but with Chai's `expect` method instead of `should`. Notice that the `require` call to the `expect` method does not execute it, as is the case with `should`.

Assert-style assertions

Assert-style assertions are accessible in Chai using`chai.assert`. This interface uses the more traditional style of assertions, much like the Node.js native `assert` module:

```
var assert = require('chai').assert;
var test = 'a string';
assert.typeOf(test, 'string');
```

This example performs the same assertion as the two previous examples but with Chai's `assert` method. Notice that this example calls upon the `assert.typeOf` method, which is akin to the native JavaScript `typeof` operator, rather than using natural language method names as `should` and `expect` do.

Testing with Mocha and Chai does not favor any particular style of assertion available in Chai, but it is best to choose one and stick with it so that a testing pattern is established. We will use the `should` style of assertion for the remaining examples in this chapter.

Using Mocha with Chai-and Should-style assertions

Now, let's go back to our original Mocha test example in `test.js` and add a similar test right under it, but use Chai's `should` assertion method instead:

```
var should = require('chai').should();
describe('String', function() {
    describe('#search()', function() {
        it('should return -1 when the value is not present', function() {
            'text'.search(/testing/).should.equal(-1);
        });
    });
});
```

This performs the same test as shown earlier using the native Node.js `assert` module, but with Chai's `should` method instead. The advantage of working with Chai in this scenario, however, is that it provides additional tests beyond what Node.js can provide out of the box, and the Chai tests are also browser compatible.

Back in the console, run the Mochas tests:

```
$ mocha test.js
```

This should yield the following output from your two tests:

```
String
  #search()
     should return -1 when the value is not present
String
  #search()
     should return -1 when the value is not present
2 passing (9ms)
```

Now, let's write a more interesting test that might be used in a real-world application context. A JavaScript SPA will often be dealing with the DOM, so we should test that interaction accordingly. Let's consider the following method as an example:

```
module.exports = {
    addClass: function(elem, newClass) {
        if (elem.className.indexOf(newClass) !== -1) {
            return;
        }
        if (elem.className !== '') {
            newClass = ' ' + newClass;
        }
        elem.className += newClass;
    }
};
```

The `addClass` method simply adds a `className` to a DOM element if it does not already have that `className`. We are defining it with `module.exports` so that it is consumable as a Node.js module. To test this code, save it in a new file named `addClass.js` under your `test` directory.

Now, back in the `test.js` file, add the following unit test code under the other two tests that we have written so far:

```
var addClass = require('./addClass').addClass;
describe('addClass', function() {
    it('should add a new className if it does not exist', function() {
        var elem = {
            className: 'existing-class'
        };
        addClass(elem, 'new-class');
        elem.className.split(' ')[1].should.equal('new-class');
    });
```

```
});
```

Due to the no-dependencies constraint of unit testing, we are faking, or **mocking**, a DOM element here by defining a simple JavaScript object called elem and giving it a className property, just as a real DOM object would have. This test is written strictly to assert that calling addClass on an element with a new, non-existent className will, in fact, add that className to the element.

Running the tests from the command line should now yield the following output:

```
String
  #search()
    should return -1 when the value is not present
String
  #search()
    should return -1 when the value is not present
addClass
  should add a new className if it does not exist
3 passing (10ms)
```

Running Mocha tests in the browser

Mocha is easy enough to run from a CLI, but it also comes bundled with assets that allow you to easily run your tests in a browser. As we are currently working with frontend JavaScript code, it is best to test it in the environment it will actually be run. To do this, let's first create a file named test.html at the root of the project and add the following markup to it:

```html
<!doctype html>
<html>
    <head>
        <title>Mocha Tests</title>
        <link rel="stylesheet" href="node_modules/mocha/mocha.css">
    </head>
    <body>
        <div id="mocha"></div>
        <script src="node_modules/mocha/mocha.js"></script>
        <script src="node_modules/chai/chai.js"></script>
        <script>mocha.setup('bdd');</script>
        <script src="test/addClass.js"></script>
        <script src="test/test.js"></script>
        <script>
            mocha.run();
        </script>
    </body>
</html>
```

Mocha provides CSS and JavaScript assets to view tests in a browser. All that is required of the DOM structure is to have a `<div>` defined with an ID of mocha. The styles should be included in `<head>`, and the JavaScript should be included under `<div id="mocha">`. Additionally, the call to `mocha.setup('bdd')` tells the Mocha framework to use its **Behavior-Driven Development(BDD)** interface for testing.

Now, remember that our JavaScript files are written as Node.js modules, so we will have to modify their syntax to work properly in a browser context. For our `addClass.js` file, let's modify the method to be defined in a global `window` object named DOM:

```
window.DOM = {
    addClass: function(elem, newClass) {
        if (elem.className.indexOf(newClass) !== -1) {
            return;
        }
        if (elem.className !== '') {
            newClass = ' ' + newClass;
        }
        elem.className += newClass;
    }
};
```

Next, modify `test.js` to load `chai.should` and `DOM.addClass` from the `window` context, instead of as Node.js modules, and let's go ahead and remove the original Node.js `assert` module test that we created:

```
// Chai.should assertion
var should = chai.should();
describe('String', function() {
    describe('#search()', function() {
        it('should return -1 when the value is not present', function() {
            'text'.search(/testing/).should.equal(-1);
        });
    });
});

// Test the addClass method
var addClass = DOM.addClass;
describe('addClass', function() {
    it('should add a new className if it does not exist', function() {
        var elem = {
            className: 'existing-class'
        };
        addClass(elem, 'new-class');
        elem.className.split(' ')[1].should.equal('new-class');
    });
```

```
});
```

You should now have two tests contained in `test.js`. Finally, run a local Node.js server from the root of the project so that you can view the `test.html` page in a browser:

```
$ http-server
```

Using the global `http-server` module, your local server will be accessible to your browser at `localhost:8080` and the test file at `localhost:8080/test.html`. Go to that page in a browser and you will see the tests run automatically. If everything is set up correctly, you should see the following output:

```
String
    #search()
        ✓ should return -1 when the value is not present

addClass
    ✓ should add a new className if it does not exist
```

Sinon.js

Due to the requirement of isolation in unit testing, dependencies must often be simulated by providing `spies`, `stubs`, and `mocks` or objects that imitate the behavior of real objects. *Sinon.js* is a popular JavaScript library that provides these tools for testing and it is compatible with any unit testing framework, including Mocha.

Spies

Test spies are functions that can be used in place of callback dependencies and also are used to *spy* or record arguments, return values, and any other related data to other functions that is used throughout an application. Spies are available in Sinon.js through the `sinon.spy()` API. It can be used to create an anonymous function that records data on itself every time it is called throughout a test sequence:

```
var spy = sinon.spy();
```

An example use case of this is testing that a callback function is invoked properly from another function in a `publish` and `subscribe` design pattern, as follows:

```
it('should invoke the callback on publish', function() {
    var spy = sinon.spy();
    Payload.subscribe('test-event', spy);
    Payload.publish('test-event');
    spy.called.should.equal(true);
});
```

In this example, a spy is used to act as a callback for a `Payload.js` custom event. The callback is registered through the `Payload.subscribe` method and expected to be invoked upon publishing the custom event `test-event`. The `sinon.spy()` function will return an object with several properties available on it that give you information about the returned function. In this case, we are testing for the `spy.called` property, which will be `true` if the function was called at least once.

The `sinon.spy()` function can also be used to wrap another function and spy on it, as follows:

```
var spy = sinon.spy(testFunc);
```

Additionally, `sinon.spy()` can be used to replace an existing method on an object and behave exactly like the original method, but with the added benefit of collecting data on that method through the API, as follows:

```
var spy = sinon.spy(object, 'method');
```

Stubs

Test `stubs` build on top of `spies`. They are functions that are spies themselves with access to the full test spy API, but with added methods to alter their behavior. Stubs are most often used when you want to force certain things to happen inside of functions when a test is being run on it, and also when you want to prevent certain things from happening.

For example, say that we have a `userRegister` function that registers a new user to a database. This function has a callback that is returned when a user is successfully registered, but if saving the user fails, it should return an error in that callback, as follows:

```
it('should pass the error into the callback if save fails', function() {
    var error = new Error('this is an error');
    var save = sinon.stub().throws(error);
    var spy = sinon.spy();

    registerUser({ name: 'Peebo' }, spy);
```

```
        save.restore();
        sinon.assert.calledWith(spy, error);
    });
```

First, we will create an `Error` object to pass to our callback. Then, we will create a stub for our actual `save` method that replaces it and throws an error, passing the `Error` object to the callback. This replaces any actual database functionality as we cannot rely on real dependencies for unit testing. Finally, we will define the `callback` function as a spy. When we call the `registerUser` method for our test, we will pass the spy to it as its callback. In a scenario where we have a real `save` method, `save.restore()` will change it back to its original state and remove the stubbed behavior.

Sinon.js also has its own assertion library built in for added functionality when working with spies and stubs. In this case, we will call `sinon.assert.calledWith()` to assert that the spy was called with the expected error.

Mocks

Mocks in Sinon.js build upon both spies and stubs. They are fake methods, like `spies`, with the ability to add additional behaviors, like `stubs`, but also give you the ability to define *expectations* for the test before it is actually run.

 Mocks should only be used once per unit test. If you find yourself using more than one mock in a unit test, you are probably not using them as intended.

To demonstrate the use of a mock, let's consider an example using the Payload.js `localStorage` API methods. We can define a method called `incrementDataByOne` that is used to increment a `localStorage` value from 0 to 1:

```
describe('incrementDataByOne', function() {
    it('should increment stored value by one', function() {
        var mock = sinon.mock(Payload.storage);
        mock.expects('get').withArgs('data').returns(0);
        mock.expects('set').once().withArgs('data', 1);

        incrementDataByOne();

        mock.restore();
        mock.verify();
    });
});
```

Notice that instead of defining a spy or a stub here, we will define a mock variable that takes the `Payload.storage` object API as its only argument. A mock is then created on the object to test its methods for expectations. In this case, we will set up our expectations that the initial value of data should return 0 from the `Payload.storage.get` API method, and then after calling `Payload.storage.set` with 1, it should be incremented by 1 from its original value.

Jasmine

Jasmine is another popular unit testing framework in the Node.js community, and it is also used for most AngularJS applications and referenced throughout the AngularJS core documentation. Jasmine is similar to Mocha in many ways, but it includes its own assertion library. Jasmine uses `expect` style assertions, much like the Chai `expect` style assertions, which were covered earlier:

```
describe('sorting the list of users', function() {
    it('sorts in ascending order by default', function() {
        var users = ['Kerri', 'Jeff', 'Brenda'];
        var sorted = sortUsers(users);
        expect(sorted).toEqual(['Brenda', 'Jeff', 'Kerri']);
    });
});
```

As you can see in this example, Jasmine uses `describe` and `it` method calls for its tests that are identical to those used in Mocha, so switching from one framework to the other is pretty straightforward. Having knowledge of both Mocha and Jasmine is quite useful as they are both used commonly throughout the JavaScript community.

Karma test runner

Karma is a JavaScript *test runner* that allows you to run your tests in browsers automatically. We have already demonstrated how to run Mocha unit tests in the browser manually, but when using a test runner such as `Karma`, this process is much easier to set up and work with.

Testing with Karma, Mocha, and Chai

Karma can be used with multiple unit testing frameworks, including Mocha. First, let's install the Node.js modules that we'll need to work with Karma, Mocha, and Chai:

```
$ npm install karma karma-mocha karma-chai --save-dev
```

This will install Karma and its Node.js plugins for Mocha and Chai to your local development environment and save them in your `package.json` file. Now, in order to have Karma launch tests in browsers on your system, we'll need to install plugins for those as well, which are as follows:

```
$ npm install karma-chrome-launcher karma-firefox-launcher --save-dev
```

This will install the `launcher` modules for the Chrome and Firefox browsers. If you do not have one or both of these browsers on your system, then install the launchers for one or two that you do have. There are Karma launcher plugins for all major browsers.

Next, we will need to create a config file for Karma to run our tests and launch the appropriate browsers. Create a file at the root of the project named `karma.conf.js` and add the following code to it:

```
module.exports = function(config) {
    'use strict';
    config.set({
        frameworks: ['mocha', 'chai'],
        files: ['test/*.js'],
        browsers: ['Chrome', 'Firefox'],
        singleRun: true
    });
};
```

This configuration simply tells Karma that we're using the Mocha and Chai testing frameworks, we want to load all JavaScript files under the test directory, and we want to launch the tests to run in the Chrome and Firefox browsers, or the browsers that you have chosen. The `singleRun` parameter tells Karma to run the tests and then exit, rather than continue to run.

Now, all we have to do is run Karma from the CLI to run our tests in the defined browsers. As Karma is installed locally, you will have to add the relative path from your project root to the module in order to run it, as follows:

```
$ ./node_modules/karma/bin/karma start karma.conf.js
```

You will notice that this command also specifies the configuration file you want to use for your Karma instance, but it will default to the `karma.conf.js` file that you created at the root directory if you exclude it in the command.

Alternatively, if you would like to run Karma from any directory globally, you can install the `karma-cli` module, just like you did with Grunt and `grunt-cli` in Chapter 1, *Getting Organized with NPM, Bower, and Grunt*:

```
$ npm install karma-cli -g
```

Make sure that you add the `-g` parameter so that `karma` is available as a global Node.js module.

Now, you can simply run the following command from the CLI:

```
$ karma start
```

Running this command will open the specified browsers automatically while yielding an output similar to the following command:

```
28 08 2016 18:02:34.147:INFO [karma]: Karma v1.2.0 server started at
http://localhost:9876/
28 08 2016 18:02:34.147:INFO [launcher]: Launching browsers Chrome,
Firefox
with unlimited concurrency
28 08 2016 18:02:34.157:INFO [launcher]: Starting browser Chrome
28 08 2016 18:02:34.163:INFO [launcher]: Starting browser Firefox
28 08 2016 18:02:35.301:INFO [Chrome 52.0.2743 (Mac OS X 10.11.6)]:
Connected on socket /#TJZjs4nvaN-kNp3QAAAA with id 18074196
28 08 2016 18:02:36.761:INFO [Firefox 48.0.0 (Mac OS X 10.11.0)]:
Connected on socket /#74pJ5Vl1sLPwySk4AAAB with id 24041937
Chrome 52.0.2743 (Mac OS X 10.11.6):
Executed 2 of 2 SUCCESS (0.008 secs / 0.001 secs)
Firefox 48.0.0 (Mac OS X 10.11.0):
Executed 2 of 2 SUCCESS (0.002 secs / 0.002 secs)
TOTAL: 4 SUCCESS
```

If you follow along from the beginning of this output, you can see that Karma launches its own server on `port 9876` and then launches the specified browsers once it is running. Your two tests are run in each browser with success, thus a total of 4 SUCCESS is noted in the final line of the output.

The reason for doing this type of testing is so that your unit tests can run in multiple browsers and you can ensure that they pass in all of them. With frontend JavaScript, there is always the possibility that one browser will work differently than another, so as many scenarios as possible should be tested so you can be sure that your app won't have bugs in some browsers that may be experienced by any end users with those browsers.

This is also a great way to help you define the browsers you want to support for your application and which browsers you may want to detect and notify the user that it is not supported. This is a common practice when you want to use modern JavaScript techniques and methods that may not be supported by older, outdated browsers.

Testing AngularJS with Karma and Jasmine

The AngularJS community has embraced Jasmine as its unit testing framework of choice, and it can also be used with Karma. Let's install our dependencies to work with Karma and Jasmine now:

```
$ npm install jasmine karma-jasmine --save-dev
```

This will install the Jasmine unit testing framework and its corresponding plugin for Karma, saving it to your `package.json` file.

Now, let's install AngularJS to our sample project, simply to test example code, so we can learn how to apply unit testing to our actual AngularJS app.

AngularJS is available on both NPM and Bower. We will use Bower for the following example, as this is for frontend code:

```
$ bower install angular --save
```

Save `angular` as a dependency. Next, install the `angular-mocks` library as a development dependency:

```
$ bower install angular-mocks --save-dev
```

The `angular-mocks` library gives you the `ngMock` module, which can be used in your AngularJS applications to mock services. Additionally, you can use it to extend other modules and make them behave synchronously, providing for more straightforward testing.

Now, let's change the `karma.conf.js` file to reflect the use of Jasmine instead of Mocha, and the addition of `angular-mocks`. Your configuration should look like the following code block:

```
module.exports = function(config) {
    'use strict';
    config.set({
        frameworks: ['jasmine'],
        files: [
            'bower_components/angular/angular.js',
            'bower_components/angular-mocks/angular-mocks.js',
```

```
            'test/angular-test.js'
        ],
        browsers: ['Chrome', 'Firefox'],
        singleRun: true
    });
};
```

Here, we have changed the `frameworks` parameter of the Karma configuration to use only Jasmine. Jasmine can be dropped in as a replacement for both Mocha and Chai because Jasmine includes its own assertion methods. Additionally, we have added `angular.js` and `angular-mocks.js` from the `bower_components` directory to our `files` array to test AngularJS code with `ngMock`. Under the test directory, we will load a new file named `angular-test.js`.

Now, let's use Jasmine and `ngMock` to write some tests for a simplified version of `DashMainController`, which we wrote for the gift app in Chapter 10, *Displaying Views*. Create a file under the test directory named `angular-test.js` and add the following code:

```
var giftappControllers = angular.module('giftappControllers', []);
angular.module('giftappControllers')
    .controller('DashMainController', ['$scope', function($scope, List) {
        $scope.lists = [
            {'name': 'Christmas List'},
            {'name': 'Birthday List'}
        ];
    }]);
```

This will load the `giftappControllers` module into memory and subsequently register `DashMainController`. We are excluding any other services and factories here to ensure the isolated testing of the controller. Next, let's write a simple Jasmine test to assert that the length of the `$scope.lists` array is 2:

```
describe('DashMainController', function() {
    var $controller;
    beforeEach(module('giftappControllers'));
    beforeEach(inject(function(_$controller_) {
        $controller = _$controller_;
    }));
    describe('$scope.lists', function() {
        it('has a length of 2', function() {
            var $scope = {};
            var testController = $controller('DashMainController', {
                $scope: $scope
            });
            expect($scope.lists.length).toEqual(2);
        });
```

```
    });
  });
```

In the initial `describe` call for `DashMainController`, we will initialize a `$controller` variable that will be used to represent the AngularJS `$controller` service. Additionally, we will make two calls to the Jasmine `beforeEach` method. This allows code to be run before each test is run and do any setup that is needed. In this case, we will need to initialize the `giftappControllers` module, done in the first call to `beforeEach`, and next we must assign the local `$controller` variable to the AngularJS `$controller` service.

In order to access the AngularJS `$controller` service, we will use the angular-mock `inject` method, which wraps a function into an injectable function, making use of Angular's dependency injector. This method also includes a convention in which you can place an underscore on each side of an argument name and it will get injected properly without conflicting with your local variable names. Here, we will do this with the `_$controller_` argument, which is interpreted by the `inject` method as Angular's `$controller` service. This allows us to use the local `$controller` variable to take its place and keep the naming convention consistent.

With this code in place, you are ready to run the test, as follows:

```
$ karma start
```

This will yield an output similar to the following command:

```
03 09 2016 01:42:58.563:INFO [karma]: Karma v1.2.0 server started at
http://localhost:9876/
03 09 2016 01:42:58.567:INFO [launcher]: Launching browsers Chrome,
Firefox
with unlimited concurrency
03 09 2016 01:42:58.574:INFO [launcher]: Starting browser Chrome
03 09 2016 01:42:58.580:INFO [launcher]: Starting browser Firefox
03 09 2016 01:42:59.657:INFO [Chrome 52.0.2743 (Mac OS X 10.11.6)]:
Connected on socket /#sXw8Utn7qjVLwiqKAAAA with id 15753343
Chrome 52.0.2743 (Mac OS X 10.11.6):
Executed 1 of 1 SUCCESS (0.038 secs / 0.03 secs)
Chrome 52.0.2743 (Mac OS X 10.11.6):
Executed 1 of 1 SUCCESS (0.038 secs / 0.03 secs)
Firefox 48.0.0 (Mac OS X 10.11.0):
Executed 1 of 1 SUCCESS (0.001 secs / 0.016 secs)
TOTAL: 2 SUCCESS
```

You should see that the test passed in all browsers because the length of the `$scope.lists` array is 2, as the Jasmine assertion tested for.

Integration testing

The second level of the software testing pyramid is *integration testing*. Integration testing involves testing at least two units of code that interact with each other, so in its simplest form, an integration test will test the outcome of two unit tests, such that they *integrate* with your application as expected.

The idea behind integration testing is to build upon your unit tests by testing larger pieces, or *components*, of your application. It is possible that all of your unit tests may pass because they are tested in isolation, but when you start testing the interaction of those units with each other, the outcome may not be what you expect. This is why unit testing alone is not sufficient to adequately test a SPA. Integration testing allows you to test key functionality in various components of your application before you move on to end-to-end testing.

End-to-end testing

The top level of the software testing pyramid is *end-to-end testing*, abbreviated as E2E, and also referred to as *functional testing*. The goal of end-to-end testing is to test the true functionality of your application's features in their entirety. For example, if you have a user registration feature in your app, an end-to-end test will ensure that the user is able to register properly through the UI, added to the database, a message to the user that they were successfully registered displayed, and, potentially, an e-mail sent to the user, or any other follow-up actions that may be required by your application.

The angular-seed project

In order to demonstrate a simple AngularJS application with examples of both unit and end-to-end testing, AngularJS created the `angular-seed` project. It is an open source project that is available on GitHub. Let's install it now so that we can run some simple unit and end-to-end testing with AngularJS.

Let's clone the angular-seed repository from GitHub into a new, clean project directory, as follows:

```
$ git clone https://github.com/angular/angular-seed.git
$ cd angular-seed
```

The angular-seed project has both NPM dependencies and Bower dependencies, but you only need to run the NPM install that will install the Bower dependencies for you:

```
$ npm install
```

This will install many tools and libraries, some of which you have seen already, including Jasmine, Karma, AngularJS, and angular-mocks. Next, all you have to do is start the NPM server using the following command line:

```
$ npm start
```

This will run a few tasks and then start up a Node.js server for you. You should see the following output:

```
> angular-seed@0.0.0 prestart /angular-seed
> npm install
> angular-seed@0.0.0 postinstall /angular-seed
> bower install
> angular-seed@0.0.0 start /angular-seed
> http-server -a localhost -p 8000 -c-1 ./app
Starting up http-server, serving ./app
Available on:
  http://localhost:8000
Hit CTRL-C to stop the server
```

Now, go to http://localhost:8000 in a web browser and you will see a simple layout displayed. It consists of two view labels, view1 and view2, with view1 being displayed by default after the page loads. Each view requests a partial template file to be loaded upon the first view, and then caches it for any subsequent view.

Let's first run the angular-seed unit tests so we can see how they are set up. Karma is used to launch Jasmine unit tests, just as we did with our example controller test earlier; however, by default, they are set with the singleRun property in karma.conf.js set to false, which is intended for continuous integration. This allows Karma to watch for changes to your code as you make them so that the unit tests are run each time you save a file. In this way, you will get immediate feedback from the test runner and know if any tests are failing, which will prevent you from coding too far down a broken path.

To run the angular-seed tests in continuous integration mode, simply run the following NPM test command from the CLI:

```
$ npm test
```

This will yield an output similar to the following:

```
> angular-seed@0.0.0 test /angular-seed
> karma start karma.conf.js
03 09 2016 13:02:57.418:WARN [karma]: No captured browser, open
http://localhost:9876/
03 09 2016 13:02:57.431:INFO [karma]: Karma v0.13.22 server started at
http://localhost:9876/
03 09 2016 13:02:57.447:INFO [launcher]: Starting browser Chrome
03 09 2016 13:02:58.549:INFO [Chrome 52.0.2743 (Mac OS X 10.11.6)]:
Connected on socket /#A2XSbQWChmjkstjNAAAA with id 65182476
Chrome 52.0.2743 (Mac OS X 10.11.6):
Executed 5 of 5 SUCCESS (0.078 secs / 0.069 secs)
```

This output shows that 5 of 5 unit tests were executed successfully. Notice that the command continues to run as it is in continuous integration mode. You will also have a Chrome browser window open that is awaiting file changes so that it can rerun the tests, the results of which will be immediately printed back to the CLI.

The project also includes a command to run Karma in singleRun mode, as we did with our previous Karma examples. To do this, hit Ctrl + C to close the currently running Karma instance. This will shut down the Chrome browser window as well.

Next, you will use the following NPM run command to launch Karma just once and shut back down:

```
$ npm run test-single-run
```

You will see the same output as you did earlier, but the browser window will open and close, the tests will run successfully, and the CLI will bring you back to the command prompt.

Now that we've done some simple unit testing with the angular-seed project, let's move on to end-to-end testing.

End-to-end testing with AngularJS and angular-seed

AngularJS emphasizes the importance of end-to-end testing and they have their own testing framework, **Protractor**, to do so. Protractor is an open source Node.js application that is built upon WebdriverJS, or just Webdriver, a component of the Selenium project.

Selenium has been around for a long time and is extremely well known throughout the web development community. It comprises multiple tools and libraries that allow for web browser automation. WebdriverJS is one of those libraries, and it is designed to test JavaScript applications.

Protractor is similar to Karma, in that, it is a test runner, but it designed to run end-to-end tests rather than unit tests. The end-to-end tests in the angular-seed project are written with Jasmine and Protractor is used to launch and run them.

First, we will need to install Webdriver as Protractor is built on top of it. The project comes with the following script to do this:

```
$ npm run update-webdriver
```

This will yield an output similar to the following, installing the latest version of Webdriver:

```
Updating selenium standalone to version 2.52.0
downloading
https://selenium-release.storage.googleapis.com/2.52/selenium-
    server-standalone-2.52.0.jar...
Updating chromedriver to version 2.21
downloading
https://chromedriver.storage.googleapis.com/2.21/chromedriver_mac32.zip...
    chromedriver_2.21mac32.zip downloaded to /angular-
    seed/node_modules/protractor/selenium/chromedriver_2.21mac32.zip
    selenium-server-standalone-2.52.0.jar downloaded to /angular-
    seed/node_modules/protractor/selenium/selenium-server-
standalone-2.52.0.jar
```

Once Webdriver is installed successfully, run the following NPM server again with Karma running so that Protractor can interact with the web application:

```
$ npm start
```

Next, as Protractor is set up to test with Chrome by default, we will need to bypass the Selenium server as it uses a Java NPAPI plugin that the newer versions of Chrome do not support. Fortunately, Protractor can test directly against both Chrome and Firefox, which circumvents this problem. To use a direct server connection with Chrome or Firefox, open the protractor.conf.js file in the E2E-tests directory, add a new configuration property named directConnect at the bottom, and set it to true. The Protractor config file should now look like the following block of code:

```
//jshint strict: false
exports.config = {

  allScriptsTimeout: 11000,

  specs: [
    '*.js'
  ],

  capabilities: {
```

```
    'browserName': 'chrome'
},

baseUrl: 'http://localhost:8000/',

framework: 'jasmine',

jasmineNodeOpts: {
  defaultTimeoutInterval: 30000
},

directConnect: true

};
```

Keep in mind that the directConnect setting is only intended to be used with Chrome and Firefox only. If you decide to run your tests in another browser, you will want to set it to false, or remove the property from the config, otherwise an error will be thrown. Using Chrome and Firefox to run your tests with directConnect also gives you a boost in speed when running your tests as the Selenium server is bypassed.

Now, with the server running, open another CLI session in the angular-seed root directory and run the following command for Protractor:

```
$ npm run protractor
```

The console output will indicate that ChromeDriver is being used directly and that one instance of WebDriver is running. You should see an output similar to the following command:

```
> angular-seed@0.0.0 protractor /angular-seed
> protractor e2e-tests/protractor.conf.js
[14:04:58] I/direct - Using ChromeDriver directly...
[14:04:58] I/launcher - Running 1 instances of WebDriver
Started
...
3 specs, 0 failures
Finished in 1.174 seconds
[14:05:00] I/launcher - 0 instance(s) of WebDriver still running
[14:05:00] I/launcher - chrome #01 passed
```

Notice that 3 specs is indicated in the output? This indicates that those three E2E tests were run. Let's take a closer look at these tests by opening the e2e-tests/scenarios.js file in an editor.

At the beginning of this file, you will see an opening `describe` method call used to describe the application you are testing:

```
describe('my app', function() {
    ...
});
```

This `describe` block is used to contain all E2E tests for the application. Now, let's examine the first test:

```
it('should automatically redirect to /view1 when location hash/fragment is
empty', function() {
    browser.get('index.html');
    expect(browser.getLocationAbsUrl()).toMatch("/view1");
});
```

This test asserts that the application will redirect the URL in the browser to `/#!/view1` when the `#!` route is empty. This is because the application is configured to auto-load the `view111` partial when it loads, so the URL should reflect the route to that partial when it is loaded. You will notice that this does indeed occur when you load the application at `http://localhost:8000` in your browser and it redirects to `http://localhost:8000/#!/view1`. This uses WebDriver's direct connection to Chrome to run the application and test the functionality through the `browser` API method, combined with an `expect` assertion that the URL matches the test path.

The second test in `scenarios.js` is a bit more verbose, as shown in the following block of code:

```
describe('view1', function() {

    beforeEach(function() {
        browser.get('index.html#!/view1');
    });

    it('should render view1 when user navigates to /view1', function() {
        expect(element.all(by.css('[ng-view]
        p')).first().getText()).toMatch(/partial for view 1/);
    });

});
```

This test asserts that the text shown in the view for the partial route /#!/view1 is in fact what it is expected to be. If you watch your developer console when you load the app in a browser, you will notice that it automatically makes an AJAX request to retrieve the local file, view1.html, which contains the partial for this view. The subsequent text that is displayed from this view is what this end-to-end test is looking for. This test uses the browser API method again, and additionally it uses the element API method to access DOM selectors, combined with an expect assertion that the text in the view matches the test string.

The third and final test in scenarios.js is much like the second test, but it is used to test the text shown in the view for the partial route rendered at /#!/view2. To view that text, first click on the **view2** link in the running angular-seed application in your browser. You will see the URL update to view2, the console will show that another AJAX request is made to retrieve the local file view2.html, and the rendered view is updated, displaying the text (**This is the partial for view 2**). Now, let's take a look at the test, which is as follows:

```
describe('view2', function() {

    beforeEach(function() {
        browser.get('index.html#!/view2');
    });

    it('should render view2 when user navigates to /view2', function() {
        expect(element.all(by.css('[ng-view]
        p')).first().getText()).toMatch(/partial for view 2/);
    });

});
```

For this test to work, the browser must first be directed to go to the /#!/view2 route so that the respective view will be displayed. This is accomplished by the beforeEach method that is run before the it method call. As discussed earlier, Jasmine provides the beforeEach method for any setup that needs to occur before each time a test is run. In this case, it runs code directing the browser API method to perform a get request to the /#!/view2 URL, which will subsequently update the view for the application to display the view2 partial. Only after this is complete will the test be run. This test also uses the element API method to access the DOM and find the text that it is looking to match against the expect assertion that the text (**This is the partial for view 2**) is found in the view.

End-to-end testing should certainly be more thorough for a real-world application, but the angular-seed project is a good place to start with experimenting on both unit testing and end-to-end testing for an AngularJS application. Once you have learned how it all works, gotten familiar with the Protractor and WebDriver APIs, and feel comfortable using Jasmine and Protractor together, you can begin writing custom tests for your own AngularJS applications with confidence.

Summary

In this chapter, you have learned the differences between unit testing, integration testing, and end-to-end testing and how they can, and should, all be combined together to provide full-fledged testing for a JavaScript SPA. You have learned about the Mocha and Jasmine unit testing frameworks, and how to write unit test with both of them, including how to write unit tests for AngularJS with Jasmine. You have also learned how to launch multiple browsers to test cross-browser compatibility of your unit tests with Karma, and about various other tools that can be added to your testing stack, including Chai and Sinon.js.

Now that you have all the tools you need to build and test a JavaScript SPA, we will bring you to the final chapter to learn about deployment and scaling.

14
Deploying and Scaling the SPA

Having built the core functionality of the application, now it's time to move the SPA into a production-like environment that is accessible from the Internet. For this, we will be using **Platform as a Service (PaaS)**.

PaaS is a type of a cloud-based service that allows developers to launch applications on managed infrastructure. Before PaaS, developers or operations engineers had to perform a lot of setup and maintenance tasks, such as provisioning hardware, installing operating software, and insuring uptime.

There are a number of PaaS providers, but I have chosen Heroku. One reason for this is that you can stand up an application for free on a sandbox, which will allow you to experiment on the app and scale up when you're ready. Deploying an app to Heroku is also quite easy, as, you'll see, Heroku uses Git to deploy.

We will also set up a production database in the cloud. We will use MongoLab, which also has a free sandbox tier with enough memory to get started.

We'll finish this chapter by briefly discussing the following concerns for scaling your application:

- Packaging the application with the Grunt task runner
- Setting up a production database online
- Moving the SPA into the cloud
- Considerations for scaling

Packaging for deployment

Our application is still quite small and not complicated, but we will begin by setting up an automated process for packaging our application up for deployment.

Setting up Grunt for deployment

We will use the Grunt JavaScript task runner to set up some automated tasks to package up our files for deployment. There's not a lot for us to do here, but you'll get a sense of what can be done and be able to explore the rich selection of Grunt plugins to further customize your automated tasks.

Installing Grunt

If you haven't already, install the grunt CLI using NPM:

```
$ npm install -g grunt-cli
grunt-cli@0.1.13 /usr/local/lib/node_modules/grunt-cli
|- resolve@0.3.1
|- nopt@1.0.10 (abbrev@1.0.7)
|_ findup-sync@0.1.3 (lodash@2.4.2, glob@3.2.11)
```

For Grunt to run correctly, you'll need two files in your project root directory. The first one is a `package.json` file to declare dependencies. You already have one in your root directory. The next file you need is `Gruntfile.js`, where you will load grunt modules and configure the tasks that Grunt can run. Go ahead and create this file in your root directory and add the following code to it:

```
module.exports = function(grunt) {

grunt.initConfig({
pkg: grunt.file.readJSON('package.json'),

    });

};
```

This is the framework for `Gruntfile`. We export a function that expects to receive a reference to the grunt object as its argument. Inside that function, we call the `grunt.initConfig()` function, passing it a configuration object. Currently, that configuration object has a single property, that is, a reference to the `package.json` file.

The power of Grunt comes from employing any number of the thousands of plugins made available by its active community. At the time of writing this book, there were over 5,000 Grunt plugins listed at `http://gruntjs.com/plugins`. If there's some automated task you want to run, chances are that somebody's already created a plugin to support it.

Grunt plugins, which are officially maintained, are always named `grunt-contrib-X`. You can generally trust the quality of these plugins, although there are many great unofficially maintained plugins.

Installing Grunt plugins

A nice feature of Grunt is that plugins are installed using NPM. Let's install a few useful plugins that we will use:

```
$ npm install grunt-contrib-clean--save-dev
grunt-contrib-clean@1.0.0node_modules/grunt-contrib-clean
|- async@1.5.2
|_ rimraf@2.5.2 (glob@7.0.0)
$ sudonpm install grunt-contrib-uglify--save-dev
grunt-contrib-uglify@0.11.1node_modules/grunt-contrib-uglify
|- uri-path@1.0.0
|- maxmin@2.1.0 (figures@1.4.0, pretty-bytes@3.0.1, gzip-size@3.0.0)
|- chalk@1.1.1 (escape-string-regexp@1.0.5, supports-color@2.0.0, has-
ansi@2.0.0, strip-ansi@3.0.1, ansi-styles@2.2.0)
|- uglify-js@2.6.2 (uglify-to-browserify@1.0.2, async@0.2.10, source-
map@0.5.3, yargs@3.10.0)
|_ lodash@4.5.1
$ sudonpm install grunt-contrib-htmlmin--save-dev
grunt-contrib-htmlmin@0.6.0node_modules/grunt-contrib-htmlmin
|- chalk@1.1.1 (escape-string-regexp@1.0.5, supports-color@2.0.0,
strip-ansi@3.0.1, has-ansi@2.0.0, ansi-styles@2.2.0)
|- pretty-bytes@2.0.1 (number-is-nan@1.0.0, get-stdin@4.0.1,
meow@3.7.0)
|_ html-minifier@1.2.0 (relateurl@0.2.6, change-case@2.3.1, concat-
stream@1.5.1, cli@0.11.1, clean-css@3.4.9, uglify-js@2.6.2)
$ sudonpm install grunt-contrib-copy--save-dev
grunt-contrib-copy@0.8.2node_modules/grunt-contrib-copy
|- file-sync-cmp@0.1.1
|_ chalk@1.1.1 (supports-color@2.0.0, escape-string-regexp@1.0.5, ansi-
styles@2.2.0, strip-ansi@3.0.1, has-ansi@2.0.0)
```

We installed Grunt plugins for `clean`, `uglify`, `htmlmin`, and `copy` tasks. Clean will clean files out of a directory. Uglify minimizes JavaScript files. `Htmlmin` minifies HTML files. The `Copy` task copies files. The `--save-dev` flag will add these modules to your `package.json` file as `devdependecies`. You need these packages only in your development environment, not in your production environment.

Before we go any further, let's create a `dist` folder in the root of our project. This is where our production-ready assets will be found.

Configuring the Gruntfile

Now, we need to modify our `Gruntfile` to load the plugins:

```
module.exports = function(grunt) {

grunt.initConfig({
pkg: grunt.file.readJSON('package.json'),

    });

    //load the task pluginsgrunt.loadNpmTasks('grunt-contrib-
uglify');grunt.loadNpmTasks('grunt-contrib-
copy');grunt.loadNpmTasks('grunt-contrib-
htmlmin');grunt.loadNpmTasks('grunt-contrib-clean');

};
```

Here, we use a call to `grunt.loadNPMTasks()` for each Grunt plugin we want to load, passing it the name of the module to be loaded.

Next, we need to configure each of our tasks inside our `Gruntfile`. Note that every plugin will have its own configuration properties. Consult the documentation for each plugin you use to see how it is configured. Open up your `Gruntfile.js` and make the following edits:

```
module.exports = function(grunt) {

grunt.initConfig({
pkg: grunt.file.readJSON('package.json'),
        clean: ['dist/**'],
        copy: {
            main: {
                files: [
                    {expand: true, src: ['*'], dest: 'dist/',
                     filter: 'isFile'},
                    {expand: true, src: ['bin/**'], dest:
```

```
                                'dist/', filter:
                                 'isFile'},
                                {expand: true, src: ['config/**'], dest:
                                'dist/', filter:
                                 'isFile'},
                                {expand: true, src: ['models/**'], dest:
                                'dist/', filter:
                                 'isFile'},
                                {expand: true, src: ['passport/**'], dest:
                                'dist/', filter:'isFile'},
                                {expand: true, src: ['public/**'], dest:
                               'dist/', filter:'isFile'},
                                {expand: true, src: ['routes/**'], dest:
                                'dist/', filter: 'isFile'},
                                {expand: true, src: ['scripts/**'], dest:
                                'dist/', filter: 'isFile'},
                                {expand: true, src: ['utils/**'], dest:
                                'dist/', filter:'isFile'},
                                {expand: true, src: ['views/**'], dest:
                                 'dist/', filter:
                                 'isFile'}


                    ]
                }
            },
uglify: {
                options: {
                    mangle: false
                },
my_target: {
                    files: {
'dist/public/javascripts/giftapp.js':
['dist/public/javascripts/giftapp.js'],
'dist/public/javascripts/controllers/dashMainController.js':
['dist/public/javascripts/controllers/dashMainController.js'],
'dist/public/javascripts/controllers/giftappFormController.js':
['dist/public/javascripts/controllers/giftappFormController.js'],
'dist/public/javascripts/services/giftlistFactory.js':
['dist/public/javascripts/services/giftlistFactory.js']
                }
            }
        },
htmlmin:{
                options: {
removeComments: true,
colapseWhitespace: true
                },
dist: {
```

```
          files: {
'dist/public/templates/dash-add.tpl.html': 'dist/public/templates/dash-
add.tpl.html',
'dist/public/templates/dash-main.tpl.html': 'dist/public/templates/dash-
main.tpl.html'
                    }
              }
        }
   });

   //load the task plugins
grunt.loadNpmTasks('grunt-contrib-uglify');
grunt.loadNpmTasks('grunt-contrib-copy');
grunt.loadNpmTasks('grunt-contrib-htmlmin');
grunt.loadNpmTasks('grunt-contrib-clean');
   //register the default task
grunt.registerTask('default', ['clean','copy','uglify','htmlmin']);

};
```

The first change we made was adding a number of task configuration properties inside the `grunt.InitConfig()` function. Each of these properties decorates the grunt object when grunt is run and tells the various tasks how to execute.

The first task configuration is for clean. This task is configured to delete all the files and folders in the `dist` folder. The clean configuration takes an array of paths; the syntax of the path definition is pretty standard for the `grunt-contrib` plugins. For more information on Grunt's URL globbing, refer to `http://gruntjs.com/configuring-tasks#globbing-patt erns`.

The other task configurations are similar, but take objects, and can include some options, a target, and lists of files to operate on. For configuration options for grunt plugins, find the plugin you're interested in at `http://gruntjs.com/plugins` and click on the name of the plugin to get the documentation.

The next section after the configuration is where we load each plugin that will be used by this `Gruntfile`. We do this by passing the name of the plugin as an argument to the `grunt.loadNPMTasks()` function. Grunt will look for these plugins in our `node_modules` folder. If we were to use custom tasks, such as the one we wrote ourselves, we could load them using calls to `grunt.loadTasks()`, passing in a path.

The last thing we did was to register a task. We did this by calling
`grunt.registerTask()`. This took two arguments. The first is a string, the name of the
task. In our case, this is the default task. Grunt requires that all `Gruntfiles` register a
default task. The next argument is an array of strings containing the name of any tasks and
targets required to run as part of this task.

Right now, we are just running tasks without listing any individual targets. If we had
targets we wished to run on the tasks, the syntax would be `task:target`. For example, if
we defined a test target for our `uglify` task, we would register it in our array as
`['uglify:test']`.

Running Grunt

Running grunt couldn't be simpler.

First, ensure that the grunt CLI is installed, as shown in the following:

```
$ npm install -g grunt-cli
Password:
/usr/local/bin/grunt -> /usr/local/lib/node_modules/grunt-cli/bin/grunt
grunt-cli@1.2.0 /usr/local/lib/node_modules/grunt-cli
|- grunt-known-options@1.1.0
|- nopt@3.0.6 (abbrev@1.0.9)
|- resolve@1.1.7
|_ findup-sync@0.3.0 (glob@5.0.15)
```

From the directory where your `Gruntfile` lives, simply run grunt followed by the name of
the task you wish to run. To run the default task, you can omit the `taskname`. Now, let's try
running grunt:

```
$ grunt
Running "clean:0" (clean) task
>> 53 paths cleaned.
Running "copy:main" (copy) task
Copied 35 files
Running "uglify:my_target" (uglify) task
>> 4 files created.
Running "htmlmin:dist" (htmlmin) task
Minified 2 files
```

If you look in your `dist` folder now, you'll notice it's no longer empty. Grunt has cleaned it,
moved a bunch of files in, and minified some things. Note that the first time you run this
with an empty `dist` folder, the clean task will report 0 paths cleaned. When you run this
subsequently, you should see the number of files in the `dist` folder actually being cleaned.

Another thing you might notice is that each task is running a target. Copy is running main, uglify is running my_target. By default, if no target is specified, Grunt will run the first-defined target.

If you open up your dist/public/javascripts/giftapp.js file, you should see that it has been minified:

```
angular.module("giftapp",["ui.router","giftappControllers"]).config(["$stat
eProvider","$urlRouterProvider",function($stateProvider,$urlRouterProvider)
{$urlRouterProvider.otherwise("/dash"),$stateProvider.state("dash",{url:"/d
ash",templateUrl:"/templates/dash-
main.tpl.html",controller:"DashMainController"}).state("add",{url:"/add",te
mplateUrl:"/templates/dash-
add.tpl.html",controller:"GiftappFormController"})}]);
```

Code minification makes our files smaller and somewhat harder to read. It can improve the files' performance on the web significantly. For a more significant performance improvement, we might have to look into concatenating script files and use tools such as the Closure compiler to make them even more efficient.

> There is no need to minify server-side JavaScript code. The main reason for minification is reduced data transfer with a client.

Setting up our config for production

One issue we're going to run into when moving our application into a production environment is that there will be a difference between our development and our production environment. Right now, all our database references point to our local MongoDB database.

We're going to use Git to push our files to production later on, and we also don't want to store configuration variables in Git repositories. We also don't want to store node_modules in Git or push them to production environment since they can be fetched on the fly using our package.json file.

Create a .gitignore file

In the root of your project, create a file called .gitignore. This file contains a list of files and paths that we don't want Git to store or track:

```
node_modules
config
.idea
dist/config
```

Line by line we just list the files and folders we want Git to ignore. The first is node_modules. Again, there's no reason to store these. I then want to ignore anything in my config folder, which contains sensitive information.

In here, I ignore .idea. You may or may not have this folder. This is a folder created by my development environment to store project information. I'm using JetBrains IDE for JavaScript called Webstorm. Whatever you're using, you'll want to exclude your IDE files, if any. Finally, I explicitly exclude dist/config, which will be a copy of config.

Create an environment-based configuration module

What we want is for the configuration to be handled dynamically. If you're in the development environment, use our configuration for your local machine. If you're in the production environment, you would want to use appropriate configuration variables for that environment.

The safest way to do that in the production environment setting up environment variables that can be read in the application. We will set them up when we set up our deployment environment, but we can set the stage now.

In your root giftapp folder, create a new file called appconfig.js, using the following code:

```
module.exports = function(){
    if(process.env.NODE_ENV&&process.env.NODE_ENV === 'production'){
        return{
db: process.env.DB,
facebookAuth : {
clientID: process.env.facebookClientID,
clientSecret: process.env.facebookClientSecret,
callbackURL: process.env.facebookCallbackURL,
            },

twitterAuth : {
```

```
'consumerKey': process.env.twitterConsumerKey,
'consumerSecret': process.env.twitterConsumerSecret,
'callbackURL': process.env.twitterCallbackURL
              }
          }
    } else {
varauth = require('./config/authorization');
        return {
db: 'localhost:27017/giftapp',
facebookAuth : {
clientID: auth.facebookAuth.clientID,
clientSecret: auth.facebookAuth.clientSecret,
callbackURL: auth.facebookAuth.callbackURL
              },

twitterAuth : {
'consumerKey': auth.twitterAuth.consumerKey,
'consumerSecret': auth.twitterAuth.consumerSecret,
'callbackURL': auth.twitterAuth.callbackURL
              }
          }
      }

};
```

We first check to see whether there is a NODE_ENV environment variable and whether it is set to *production*. If it is, we will have to grab our database and our Facebook and Twitter authorization information from environment variables. We will set up our environment variables later on when we set up our deployment environment.

If our test fails, we assume we're in our development environment and then manually set our database. We grab our authorization.js file out of the config directory and use that to set up our Twitter and Facebook authorization variables.

Using the new config file

Now, we need to employ our configuration file. Open up your main app.js file and make a couple of edits:

```
var express = require('express');
var path = require('path');
var favicon = require('serve-favicon');
var logger = require('morgan');
varcookieParser = require('cookie-parser');
varbodyParser = require('body-parser');
varisJSON = require('./utils/json');
```

```
var routing = require('resource-routing');
var controllers = path.resolve('./controllers');
var helmet = require('helmet');
varcsrf = require('csurf');
varappconfig = require('./appconfig');varconfig = appconfig();

//Database stuff
varmongodb = require('mongodb');
var monk = require('monk');
vardb = monk(config.db);

var mongoose = require('mongoose');
mongoose.connect(config.db);

var routes = require('./routes/index');
var users = require('./routes/users');
var dashboard = require('./routes/dashboard');
varauth = require('./routes/auth')

var app = express();

// view engine setup
app.set('views', path.join(__dirname, 'views'));
app.set('view engine', 'ejs');

app.set('x-powered-by', false);

app.locals.appName = "My Gift App";

// uncomment after placing your favicon in /public
//app.use(favicon(path.join(__dirname, 'public', 'favicon.ico')));
app.use(logger('dev'));
app.use(bodyParser.json());
app.use(bodyParser.urlencoded({ extended: false }));
app.use(cookieParser());
app.use(express.static(path.join(__dirname, 'public')));
app.use(isJSON);

var flash = require('connect-flash');
app.use(flash());

var passport = require('passport');
varexpressSession = require('express-session');
app.use(expressSession({secret: 'mySecretKey'}));
app.use(passport.initialize());
app.use(passport.session());

varinitializePassport = require('./passport/init');
```

```
initializePassport(passport);

//Database middleware
app.use(function(req,res,next){
req.db = db;
    next();
});

app.use(helmet());
app.use(csrf());

app.use('/', routes);
app.use('/users', users);
app.use('/dash', dashboard);
app.use('/auth', auth);


var login = require('./routes/login')(passport);
app.use('/login', login);

routing.resources(app, controllers, "giftlist");
routing.expose_routing_table(app, { at: "/my-routes" });

// catch 404 and forward to error handler
app.use(function(req, res, next) {
var err = new Error('Not Found');
err.status = 404;
  next(err);
});

// error handlers

// development error handler
// will print stacktrace
if (app.get('env') === 'development') {
app.use(function(err, req, res, next) {
res.status(err.status || 500);
res.render('error', {
    message: err.message,
    error: err
  });
  });
}

// production error handler
// no stacktraces leaked to user
app.use(function(err, req, res, next) {
res.status(err.status || 500);
```

```
res.render('error', {
    message: err.message,
    error: {}
  });
});


module.exports = app;
```

First, we load our `appconfig.js` file and assign it to the variable `appconfig`. Remember, our `appconfig` module exports a function. We need to invoke that function to run the code and get access to the dynamically set properties. So, we invoke `appconnfig()` and assign the returned object to the variable `config`.

Finally, we use `config.db` in the call to `monk()` to create the database object. You should now be able to start up your database and server, and there should be no difference in the functionalities.

Next, we need to use the `appconfig` in our passport `OAuth` strategies. Let's start with `passport/facebook.js`:

```
varFacebookStrategy = require('passport-facebook').Strategy;
var User = require('../models/user');
varappconfig = require('../appconfig')varauth = appconfig();

module.exports = function(passport){

passport.use('facebook', new FacebookStrategy({
clientID: auth.facebookAuth.clientID,
clientSecret: auth.facebookAuth.clientSecret,
callbackURL: auth.facebookAuth.callbackURL,
profileFields: ['id', 'displayName', 'email']
        },
        function(accessToken, refreshToken, profile, cb) {
User.findOne({ 'facebook.id': profile.id }, function (err, user) {
                if(err){
                    return cb(err)
                } else if (user) {
                    return cb(null, user);
                } else {
                    for(key in profile){
                        if(profile.hasOwnProperty(key)){
console.log(key + " ->" + profile[key]);
                        }
                    }
var newUser = new User();
newUser.facebook.id = profile.id;
```

```
newUser.facebook.token = accessToken;
newUser.facebook.name = profile.displayName;
                    if(profile.emails){
newUser.email = profile.emails[0].value;
                    }

newUser.save(function(err){
                    if(err){
                        throw err;
                    }else{
                        return cb(null, newUser);
                    }
                });
            }
        });
    }
));
}
```

Once again, we require `appconfig.js` from the root of our application. We then invoke the returned function and assign it to the variable `auth`. We should require no additional changes, and restarting our server should show that our changes have worked.

Finally, let's do the same thing to our `passport/twitter.js` file:

```
varTwitterStrategy = require('passport-twitter').Strategy;
var User = require('../models/user');
varappconfig = require('../appconfig')varauth = appconfig();

module.exports = function(passport){

passport.use('twitter', new TwitterStrategy({
consumerKey     : auth.twitterAuth.consumerKey,
consumerSecret  : auth.twitterAuth.consumerSecret,
callbackURL     : auth.twitterAuth.callbackURL
        },
        function(token, tokenSecret, profile, cb) {
User.findOne({ 'twitter.id': profile.id }, function (err, user) {
                if(err){
                    return cb(err)
                } else if (user) {
                    return cb(null, user);
                } else {
                    // if there is no user, create them
var newUser             = new User();

                    // set all of the user data that we need
newUser.twitter.id      = profile.id;
```

```
newUser.twitter.token      = token;
newUser.twitter.username   = profile.username;
newUser.twitter.displayName = profile.displayName;

newUser.save(function(err){
                if(err){
                    throw err;
                }else{
                    return cb(null, newUser);
                }
            });
        }
    });
    }
));
}
```

As you can see, we've made exactly the same change to the Twitter authorization strategy file. Once again, give it a test and it should work exactly the same way.

Setting up a cloud database

Our SPA will soon live in the cloud, and it needs to be connected to a database. Moving our application to the cloud requires our database also to be accessible from the Web. Having a database running on your local machine isn't going to cut it.

There are a number of cloud-based database services, but I have found that MongoLab is one of the easiest to set up, use, and maintain. They offer a free sandbox database, which is perfect for development and experimentation. For production-level applications, you'd want to look into a higher subscription rate.

The PaaS we will use to deploy our application, Heroku, plays really well with MongoLab, and even offers Mongolab as a one-click add-on. We will set things up manually for now so you can learn how things work a little better.

Creating a MongoLab account

The first thing you need to do is to set up your account on MongoLab. This couldn't be simpler. Go to `https://mongolab.com/signup/` and fill in the form. After you've signed up, you'll be taken to a dashboard that looks like this:

Currently, I have two databases provisioned in my account. If you've just signed up, you won't see anything here. It's from this dashboard that you can set up and manage databases and your account.

Creating a database

Right now, you have an account on MongoLab, but you don't have a database. We need to create a new database. Fortunately, MongoLab makes this super easy for us. On your dashboard, click on the button that says **Create New**:

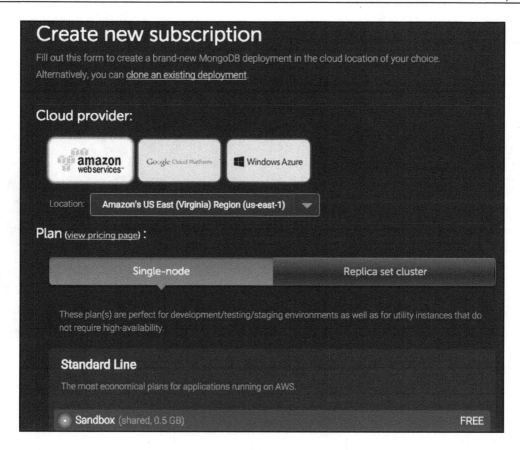

On the Create a new subscription page, there are a lot of different choices for setting up a new deployment. We want to set up a sandbox deployment, which is free and will give you 500 MB of storage. I chose Amazon Web Services for storage in the US East region, and **Single-node | Sandbox**.

Scroll down to the bottom of the page, name your database and click on the button marked Create new MongoDB deployment. I named mine `giftapp`. Voila! You are now the proud owner of a shiny and new cloud-based MongoDB deployment.

Setting up a user to access the database

We can't connect to the database from our application yet. To do so, you'll need to set up a username and password for the database access. From your dashboard, click on the name of your new database, and on the next screen, click on the **Users** tab:

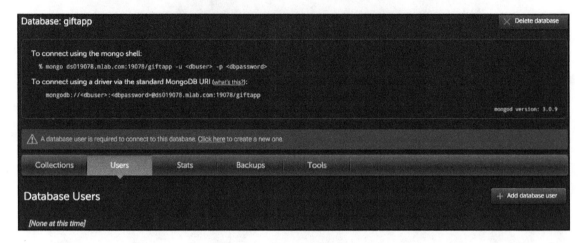

From here, make note of the standard MongoDB URI, which will include the username and password you're about to set up. Click on **Add database user**:

You'll get the preceding pop-up window. Fill it out; do not check read-only. Now, you have a database and a user who can access the data. Make a note of the URI; you will have to use this to access this database. If you want to test it out, you can plug it into your `appconfig` file in place of your local database.

Deploying the application to Heroku

Now, we have most of the pieces in place for web deployment. We will deploy our app to Heroku, a PaaS that supports Node.

Getting ready to use Heroku

There are just a few steps that are required to deploy your application to Heroku. You'll have to install Git, set up a Heroku account, create a new project on Heroku, and then it will be ready for deploying.

Setting up Git

Deployment to Heroku is done using Git, so you will need to have it installed. If you don't already have Git installed, go to `https://git-scm.com/book/en/v2/Getting-Started-Installing-Git` and follow the instructions for your operating system.

After you have Git installed, you need to initialize a Gitrepository in your `giftapp` folder. From the root, in your command line, type the following command:

```
$ gitinit
```

After you have initialized Git, you'll want to add all your files and commit them to your repo:

```
$ git add .
$ git commit -m "initil commit"
```

That's it for now.

Signing up for a Heroku account

The next thing you need to do is to sign up for a Heroku account, if you don't already have one. Like MongoLab, this is simple. Go to `https://signup.heroku.com/login` and fill out the form shown in the following screenshot:

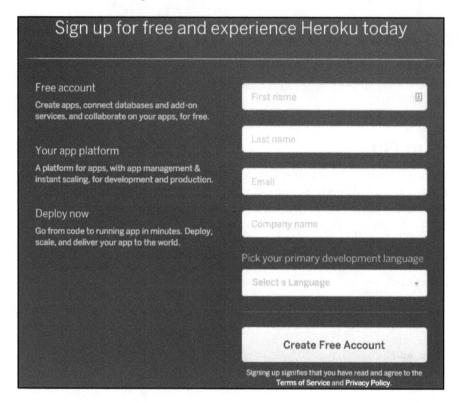

Now you're all set with a free Heroku account.

Installing the HerokuToolbelt

Heroku provides a CLI app for managing apps called HerokuToolbelt. You'll need to install this to deploy your application to Heroku. To install for your operating system, go to `https://toolbelt.heroku.com/` and follow the instructions for your operating system.

Once installed, you can log in to Heroku from your command line:

```
$ heroku login
Enter your Heroku credentials.
Email: john@notreallymyemail.com
Password (typing will be hidden):
Authentication successful.
```

Now, you're good to go.

Setting up the Heroku project

Now we need to actually set up your `giftapp` project to be deployed to Heroku. In your terminal, make sure you are in the root directory of your `giftapp` project:

```
$ heroku create
Creating app... done, stack is cedar-14
https://guarded-lake-23534.herokuapp.com/
https://git.heroku.com/guarded-lake-23534.git
```

The create command has created a Heroku app for us. In this case, the app will be accessed at `https://guarded-lake-23534.herokuapp.com/`. Navigating to that URL now won't be very exciting, since we haven't actually deployed anything yet.

Heroku generates a random app name for you. You can pass an app name you would like as part of the call to create, and, as long as it's unique, your app will live there. You can also point a custom domain to your Heroku app, but only if you have a paid account-refer to the Heroku documentation for more information.

The second thing the create command has done is to create a remote Git repository for us. This is how we will get our files deployed. There are a couple more steps we need to perform in order to deploy our app.

Deploying to Heroku

Now that most of the setup work is done, it's time to take the final steps to move our application online.

Defining a Procfile

We need a **Procfile** to tell Heroku what to run when we deploy. A Procfile is a file that tells the dynos at Heroku which commands to run. For Heroku to read this file, you must name the file Procfile (without any extension) and include it in the top-level directory of your project.

Create a file called `Procfile` in the root of your `giftapp` project and add the following line to it:

```
web: node ./dist/bin/www
```

This tells Heroku to run the www script out of our `dist` directory.

App environment variables

If you remember, our application is expected to use a number of environment variables to operate correctly. To set these up, log into your Heroku account and navigate to your dashboard at https://dashboard.heroku.com/login.

Click on the name of your app to access its dashboard. Click on the settings tab, which will then reveal the `config` variables. This is where we will add all of the environment variables we need, as shown in the following screenshot:

You can see I've added variables for **NODE_ENV**, **PORT**, and **facebookClientID**. You'll do the same and add one for each of the environment variables used in your `appconfig.js` file, including DB.

Make sure to adjust your Facebook and Twitter callback IDs to use your new Heroku domain. If you're confused about what it is, scroll down to the bottom of the settings page and it will be revealed.

Another step I'll leave you to do is to authorize your Heroku domain for your Facebook and Twitter apps. Just go into your app settings and add the new domain.

Deploying

Deploying is very easy, now that everything is completely ready. We will use a simple Gitpush. First let's make sure that our `dist` files are ready to go and everything is committed to `git` properly by running the following code:

```
$ grunt
Running "clean:0" (clean) task
>> 53 paths cleaned.
Running "copy:main" (copy) task
Copied 39 files
Running "uglify:my_target" (uglify) task
>> 4 files created.
Running "htmlmin:dist" (htmlmin) task
Minified 2 files
Done, without errors.
$ git add .
$ git commit -m "heroku commit"
[master 42e6f79] heroku commit
 17 files changed, 451 insertions(+), 207 deletions(-)
 create mode 100644 Procfile
 create mode 100644 appconfig.js
 create mode 100644 dist/Procfile
 create mode 100644 dist/appconfig.js
 create mode 100644 dist/bin/www
```

Great, everything is checked in. If you want a sanity check, you can always try `git status`.

Now let's push everything we just committed to Heroku:

```
$ git push heroku master
Counting objects: 234, done.
Delta compression using up to 4 threads.
Compressing objects: 100% (207/207), done.
Writing objects: 100% (234/234), 46.90 KiB | 0 bytes/s, done.
Total 234 (delta 95), reused 0 (delta 0)
remote: Compressing source files... done.
remote: Building source:
remote:
remote: -----> Node.js app detected
remote:
remote: -----> Creating runtime environment
remote:
remote:        NPM_CONFIG_LOGLEVEL=error
remote:        NPM_CONFIG_PRODUCTION=true
remote:        NODE_ENV=production
remote:        NODE_MODULES_CACHE=true
remote:
remote: -----> Installing binaries
remote:        engines.node (package.json):  unspecified
remote:        engines.npm (package.json):   unspecified (use default)
remote:
remote:        Resolving node version (latest stable) via semver.io...
remote:        Downloading and installing node 5.6.0...
remote:        Using default npm version: 3.6.0
remote:
remote: -----> Restoring cache
remote:        Skipping cache restore (new runtime signature)
remote:
remote: -----> Building dependencies
remote:        Pruning any extraneous modules
remote:        Installing node modules (package.json)
remote:        giftapp@0.0.0
/tmp/build_4e2a4d5757c9fb2834a0950c5e35235f
remote:
remote: -----> Discovering process types
remote:        Procfile declares types -> web
remote:
remote: -----> Compressing...
remote:        Done: 14.2M
remote: -----> Launching...
remote:        Released v11
remote:        https://guarded-lake-23534.herokuapp.com/ deployed to
Heroku
remote:
remote: Verifying deploy.... done.
```

```
To https://git.heroku.com/guarded-lake-23534.git
 * [new branch]      master -> master
```

And we're live! I omitted a significant portion of the output of the push. It's a very long output. If you go through what's here, you can see what **HerokuToolbelt** will do when we push it. You can see our application starting. You can see that the deployment was a success.

Scaling the SPA

I want to conclude with a few ideas about scaling the application. Scaling an application is a bit of a black art, but you do want to be prepared should you build out an application and it gets very popular very fast.

One of the really nice things about using PaaS tools is that they simplify scaling significantly.

Scaling the database

There are a number of options and considerations for scaling the database. You can see this just by looking at the different packages offered by MongoLab. MongoDB itself supports sharding and replication, as it was built for scaling.

Concerns about scaling include the size of the database – how much storage, and performance – usually a factor of RAM or using dedicated clusters.

MongoLab and other providers offer numerous combinations of high-storage and high-performance plans along with several steps, allowing you to incrementally increase your scaling without missing a beat, or installing or configuring a new hardware.

It's important to understand its usage, which only comes over time with an application, and how that's going to affect the storage. If your application is growing and making many hits on your database, you'll want to think about its performance. As your database fills up, you'll want to manage its storage.

Scaling the server

Heroku makes it extremely easy to scale your app to exactly the right size that you need; it's one of the things they built their business around. On Heroku, apps are run inside dynos. Think of a dyno as a lightweight container that runs your app.

Heroku has a number of different dynos running at different performance levels, and you can add and remove them, even at different levels of performance, from the command line or from your dashboard.

Heroku also offers a number of add-ons, for a fee of course, for doing things such as performance monitoring.

Not to be a sales pitch for Heroku, other PaaS providers offer similar options. Amazon Web Services is a popular choice for Node.js. There are others, such as Modulus and Digital Ocean. If you're deploying a real-world commercial app, it pays to shop around to find the right solution for you.

Summary

We began this chapter by using Grunt to package up our app into a dist folder. We used Grunt plugins, installed using NPM, to do things such as minify our code. We spent a little time exploring the Grunt plugin ecosystem, which is quite vast and well supported.

We then prepared to deploy our app to the web by setting up a cloud-based database. We created an account on MongoLab, and then created a new database. We then added a user to the database so that we could access it from our application.

We then set up an account on Heroku, and prepared our application for deployment. We installed the HerokuToolbelt, which allowed us to create a new Heroku application deployment. We accessed our application through the Heroku dashboard and added our environment variables. Finally, we pushed our project to Heroku using Git.

We wrapped up by briefly touching on topics such as scaling the database and the server. Using PaaS and a web-based database management system, we are well set up for when our application becomes as popular as Facebook.

Thanks for reading all the way through the book. If you have followed all of the instructions, you have a cloud-deployed, tested, SPA written in JavaScript. You now have all the skills to build an application front-to-back, database-to-presentation tier, in modern JavaScript. You should have a firm grasp of SPA architecture, modular code, and separation of concerns, and should have worked with every aspect of the MEAN stack. Congratulations, and good work!

Index

CPSIA information can be obtained
at www.ICGtesting.com
Printed in the USA
FFHW020835190819
54326366-60011FF